P9-CJL-946

N. L. Terteling Library

Swisher
Memorial Collection

Albertson
College of Idaho

WILLIAM FAULKNER: FIRST ENCOUNTERS

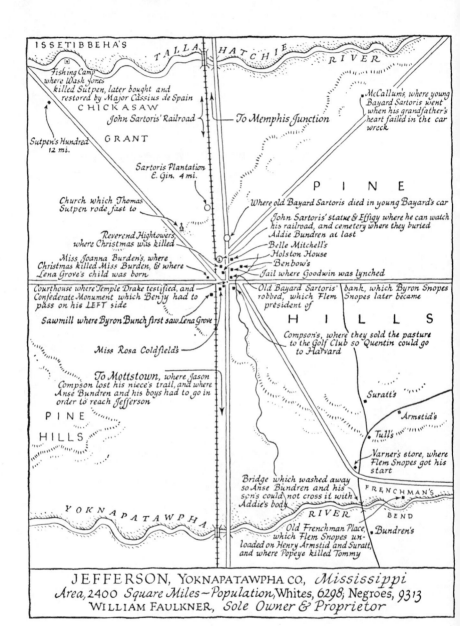

ISSETIBBEHA'S — TALLA — HATCHIE — RIVER

Fishing Camp
where Wash Jones
killed Sutpen, later bought and
restored by Major Cassius de Spain

CHICKASAW

John Sartoris' Railroad

McCallums, where young
Bayard Sartoris went
when his grandfather's
heart failed in the car
wreck

GRANT

To Memphis Junction

Sutpen's Hundred
12 mi.

Sartoris Plantation
E. Gin. 4 mi.

PINE

Church which Thomas
Sutpen rode fast to

Where old Bayard Sartoris died in young Bayard's car

John Sartoris' statue & Effigy where he can watch
his railroad, and cemetery where they buried
Addie Bundren at last

Reverend Hightowers,
where Christmas was killed

Belle Mitchell's

Holston House

Miss Joanna Burden's, where
Christmas killed Miss Burden, & where
Lena Grove's child was born

Benbow's

Jail where Goodwin was lynched

Courthouse where Temple Drake testified, and
Confederate Monument which Benjy had to
pass on his LEFT side

Old Bayard Sartoris'   bank, which Byron Snopes
robbed, which Flem   Snopes later became
president of

HILLS

Sawmill where Byron Bunch first saw Lena Grove

Compson's, where they sold the pasture
to the Golf Club so Quentin could go
to Harvard

Miss Rosa Coldfield's

To Mottstown, where Jason
Compson lost his niece's trail, and where
Anse Bundren and his boys had to go in
order to reach Jefferson

Suratt's

Armstid's

PINE

Tull's

HILLS

Varner's store, where
Flem Snopes got his
start

Bridge which washed away
so Anse Bundren and his
sons could not cross it with
Addie's body

FRENCHMAN'S

YOKNAPATAWPHA

RIVER   BEND

Old Frenchman Place,
which Flem Snopes un-
loaded on Henry Armstid and Suratt,
and where Popeye killed Tommy

Bundren's

JEFFERSON, YOKNAPATAWPHA CO., *Mississippi*
Area, 2400 *Square Miles~Population,* Whites, 6298; Negroes, 9313
WILLIAM FAULKNER, *Sole Owner & Proprietor*

WILLIAM FAULKNER
FIRST ENCOUNTERS

CLEANTH BROOKS

YALE UNIVERSITY PRESS
NEW HAVEN AND LONDON

N. L. TERTELING LIBRARY
ALBERTSON COLLEGE 83605

Published with assistance from the
Louis Effingham deForest Memorial Fund.

Copyright © 1983 by Yale University.
All rights reserved.
This book may not be reproduced, in whole
or in part, in any form (beyond that
copying permitted by Sections 107 and 108
of the U.S. Copyright Law and except by
reviewers for the public press), without
written permission from the publishers.

Designed by Sally Harris
and set in Palatino type by Brevis Press.
Printed in the United States of America by
Vail-Ballou Press, Binghamton, New York.

The chapters of this book (with the exception
of the chapter on *As I Lay Dying*) were
originally prepared as lectures, which are
available on tape from Everett/Edwards, Inc.,
P. O. Box 1060, De Land, Florida 32720.

The frontispiece "Jefferson, Yoknapatawpha
County, Mississippi" is reprinted from *Absalom,
Absalom!* (New York: Random House, Modern
Library, 1951) by permission of the publisher.

Library of Congress Cataloging in Publication Data

Brooks, Cleanth, 1906–
  William Faulkner: first encounters.

  Bibliography: p
  Includes index.
  1. Faulkner, William, 1897–1962—Criticism and
interpretation.   I. Title.
PS3511.A86Z639   1983   813'.52   83-3634
ISBN 0–300–02995–0

OCLC
9324546

10 9 8 7 6 5 4 3 2

To Louis D. Rubin, Jr., and Lewis P. Simpson

CONTENTS

PREFACE

This book is not intended for the Faulkner specialist. It has been written for the general reader and for the student coming to Faulkner for the first time.

Any sensible advice would insist that a reader start by encountering the fiction at first hand, undistracted by too much critical apparatus such as discussion of influences and sources or analysis of fictional techniques. Such matters have their importance, but they properly ought to come later on. In fact, for the reader who has become interested in Faulkner, there awaits a very considerable library of books and articles, a body of critical work that is growing by large increments every year that passes. A short, highly selective list of these will be found on pages 225–26, below.

This little book limits itself to such considerations as theme, character, and plot, with some attention to the historical and fictional world in which the actions narrated take place. I cannot stress too much the importance of reading the commentaries in close conjunction with a reading of the stories and novels themselves.

All six of the novels dealt with in this volume are available in paperback editions in the Vintage Books series published by Random House of New York; I have used these editions in citing page numbers. The original dates of publication are as follows: *The Sound and the Fury*, 1929; *As I Lay Dying*, 1930;

Light in August, 1932; *Absalom, Absalom!*, 1936; *The Hamlet*, 1940; *Go Down, Moses*, 1942.

"An Odor of Verbena," discussed in chapter 2, has been excerpted from *The Unvanquished* (Random House, 1938). "Old Man," also discussed in chapter 2, has been excerpted from *The Wild Palms* (Random House, 1939). Both may be found in the *Portable Faulkner*, ed. Malcolm Cowley (Viking/ Penguin). *Go Down, Moses* provides the text for "Pantaloon in Black," which I have treated as a short story. The six remaining stories, "A Rose for Emily," "A Justice," "Red Leaves," "That Evening Sun," "Barn Burning," and "There Was a Queen," can be found in *Collected Stories of William Faulkner* (Random House/Vintage Books). Page number citations for the stories are to these editions.

1 · INTRODUCTION

Most of us identify Faulkner with the South, and it is natural that we should do so, for his fiction is filled with references to its history, its geography, its customs; and his prose often employs its special idiom. Though there are exceptions, most of his great fiction has a Southern setting. Yet Faulkner's identification with the South can be misleading, for his value as a writer is not at all limited to what he can tell us about a particular regional culture. He was not a mere provincial in either time or space.

Thus, Faulkner differs radically from the typical Southern local colorists who preceded him by a generation. The local colorist in his crassest form is engaged in exploiting the local scene for the amused curiosity of the outsider. He stresses the differences between the "locals" and the national norm, his tacit assumption, of course, being that his reader represents the norm.

Even when the local colorist cherishes his region's differences and does not mean to hold them up to scorn, he is usually very much aware of his typical reader's assumption that the customs and attitudes depicted are different and even quaint. George Washington Cable, perhaps the best of the Southern local colorists, will serve to illustrate. His first great success, *Old Creole Days,* the book that established his reputation, makes the point. Though the setting for these stories is New Orleans, Cable's own home city, Cable himself was of Anglo-Saxon stock. To him, the Creoles, with their Latin culture and their Roman Catholic religion, were exotics. Cable felt keenly, and thus could not help emphasizing, the Creoles' differences from the Anglo-Saxon American culture which he knew and which his readers in New York and Boston also knew.

How, then, does a writer like Faulkner, whose fiction is suffused with references to Southern history, folk ways, and attitudes, and whose characters' natural speech is the Southern idiom, whether in its cultivated or illiterate forms—how does Faulkner differ from the local colorist? The difference can be put simply: Faulkner's use of the local material is never allowed to become an end in itself. His ultimate aim, as he often tells us in his various interviews, is to talk about people—and he evidently meant by *people*, men and women in their universal humanity.

In 1958 he told the students at the University of Virginia that an author "is writing about people in the terms that he is most familiar with. That is [though his writing] could have sociological implications, . . . he's not too interested in that. He's writing about people." Faulkner's stories and novels bear out such a conception of fiction. Using one's own environment ("what he knows," as Faulkner put it) in order to get at universal problems and relationships is very different from using the environment that one knows for its own sake or because it differs, interestingly or shockingly, from his reader's environment. For fiction, that difference is crucial.

True, the difference is sometimes blurred, and even when distinct it can be overlooked. A hasty or an insensitive reader will be likely to miss it altogether. Nevertheless, the ability to discern that difference will have everything to do with a reader's ability to appreciate fully a given piece of fiction and to take an accurate measure of its literary worth. It will have a great deal to do with the reader's enjoyment of Faulkner's work and it will make plain why so many critics at home and abroad regard him as one of the great novelists of our century.

Even so, it may seem odd that an introductory essay on Faulkner's work should begin by insisting on a principle that obviously applies to all fiction of genuine worth. The explanation lies in Faulkner's preoccupation with a region that is still not apprehended by the rest of the country as fully "American." Thus, the South's differences—real and imagined—from the rest of the country can prove to be a distraction.

An analogy may be useful here. Though Melville's masterpiece is entitled *Moby-Dick, or the Whale,* we do not read Melville primarily to learn about whales. Though Hawthorne's greatest novels are set in the Puritan New England of earlier centuries, we do not read *The Scarlet Letter* to learn about New England Puritanism. We read Hawthorne's novels because they set forth the human predicament in its most dramatic phases, or because, as Faulkner himself once put it with regard to his own basic aims, they show the human "heart in conflict with itself." It is true that in order to experience Melville's presentation of the human drama we may have to learn something about whaling; or with Hawthorne, to learn about the Puritan mind, but we do so in order to reach a more important goal. So also with Faulkner.

In short, Faulkner's world is worth the reader's possessing because his themes are finally universal human issues and his characters have a relevance to basic humanity. Nevertheless, Faulkner's world does have its own fascination, as even European readers have testified. Among other things, it points back to an earlier America. If Faulkner's world has lagged behind industrialized America, that very fact gives it a special interest. The family is still important, whether as a sustaining or a suffocating force. (In his novels, Faulkner does full justice to the family's blessed and its baleful aspects.)

In addition, the community is still in being. There is an almost instinctive consensus about basic issues. If the community also has its darker aspect in its tendency to suppress the rebel, it provides real resistance to the rebel who means business and is not merely posturing. His attempt to assert his individuality becomes no play-act, no mere pillow fight.

Faulkner's world is furthermore a world suffused with history. In it, history is not a series of far-off events. Battles were fought on Southern soil. Evidence of rifle fire and even cannon fire remains in the walls of public buildings. In Faulkner's boyhood and youth there were still plenty of Confederate veterans about, of whom a boy might ask questions and to whom he might listen as they described their campaigns.

Moreover, for the world depicted in Faulkner's fiction, evil is real and tragedy is close at hand. The South was the one part of America that had suffered defeat, and smashing defeat at that. In the South the typical American optimism had for decades been in short supply. In this regard, Faulkner's world is close to the world of Thomas Hardy's imagination or that of William Butler Yeats.

Faulkner writes, and often very sympathetically, of the older order of the antebellum plantation society. It was a society that valued honor, was capable of heroic action, and believed in courtesy and good manners. It had all the virtues and also many of the faults to which such a society was prone, and Faulkner, as the reader of this discussion of his fiction will discover, does justice to both. "An Odor of Verbena," for example, provides a striking example.

Yet some of Faulkner's finest examples of heroism come from the ranks of his yeoman whites, most of whom neither owned slaves nor came from former slave-owning families. These yeomen are, by the way, as jealous of their honor as any of Faulkner's aristocrats, and some of them—V. K. Ratliff of The Hamlet, for instance—are as interesting and attractive as any characters that Faulkner ever created.

The blacks, on whose labor the older plantation system rested, are also very important in Faulkner's work. In some novels, to be sure, the Negro hardly appears, as in As I Lay Dying, or he remains largely in the background, as in The Hamlet. But in others, he or she becomes a very important character, as does Dilsey in The Sound and the Fury or Lucas Beauchamp in Go Down, Moses.

Faulkner was properly cautious in trying not to impose his own ideas and sentiments on his black characters. He rarely, if ever, forgot that in describing such characters he was looking at them from the outside. But he treats them sympathetically, and fully accords them their human dignity.

Much the same might be said with regard to Faulkner's female characters. This point is worth making in view of the fact that the notion has got about that Faulkner was something of a misogynist and was really comfortable only with gray-haired matriarchs. A review of the whole of his fiction ought to dispel this illusion, and even the relatively limited selection presented in this volume will indicate that Faulkner admired such young women as Eula Varner in *The Hamlet*, Lena Grove in *Light in August*, Caddy Compson in *The Sound and the Fury*, and Judith Sutpen in *Absalom, Absalom!*.

Was there no period of development in Faulkner? Did this young man from a small north Mississippi town begin his career as an accomplished novelist? How did he learn his craft? Or did it come to him instinctively?

Faulkner possessed a great natural gift. The record shows that. His *Soldiers' Pay* (1926) is a remarkable first novel, and his first published short story, "A Rose for Emily" (1930), displays a brilliant fictional technique. But he definitely went through a period of growth and development which shows, among other things, a movement from a rather decadent Swinburnian romanticism to a robust acceptance of reality and a tough-minded appraisal of it. It also shows a shift from poetry, his acknowledged first love, to prose, albeit a rich and at times an even highly rhetorical prose, as his proper instrument. More than once, Faulkner called himself a "failed poet."

Yet a book which presumes to be no more than a brief introduction does not offer the possibility of providing a really useful account of Faulkner's development as a literary artist. Besides, most of us are not interested in the story of preparation and development unless we already have a lively sense of what that preparation and development came to.

Hence I have limited my selections to the great achievements —what most people would regard as clearly his masterpieces. My only conscious concessions to other interests are to be found in my choice of a few of the stories, some of which I included for the sake of providing further aspects of Faulkner's world.

In limiting myself to the great works, I have been unfair to Faulkner's later career, for his career did not end in 1942 with the publication of *Go Down, Moses*. Novels were yet to come, novels such as *The Wild Palms* or *The Mansion* that contain some of Faulkner's most daring fictional experiments and some of his most accomplished writing. But if this book achieves its purpose in bringing new readers to Faulkner, such readers can explore for themselves both his later and his earlier fiction.

One further point ought to be made: is the reader to prepare himself to experience tragedy or comedy? He should not, of course, "prepare" himself for either. He should open his mind and imagination to what Faulkner is capable of providing him. He must not block out possibilities for either a tragic or a comic response by assuming in advance what response will be appropriate. Actually, the sensitive, open-minded reader will find both comedy and tragedy, and often both in the same novel. For Faulkner's vision of reality is broad enough to encompass both, and the presence of both is a testimony to the artist's honesty and integrity in presenting his characters. What the reader will not find is mawkish sentimentality or mere farce, nor will he find special pleading for a thesis or cause.

There is tragedy to be found in Faulkner, and his *Absalom, Absalom!* seems to me to approach more nearly to great tragedy than does any other twentieth-century American work. But Faulkner is also one of our great masters of comedy. The novice reader must not assume that all is somber and melancholy in Faulkner's Yoknapatawpha County. There is gusto and laughter in which he is expected to join.

2 · SHORT STORIES

Perhaps the best way to begin a study of William Faulkner's writing is to start with his first published story, "A Rose for Emily," which appeared in *The Forum* for April 1930. (By then he had already published three novels, but he had not published a single short story.) "A Rose for Emily" is a shocking story, for it tells that a woman about to be deserted by her lover poisons him and keeps his body in an upstairs bedroom. The body is not discovered until forty years later, after Miss Emily Grierson's death. This story has been widely misunderstood. It is more than a horror story, more than an attempt to outdo Edgar Allan Poe, more than the prime example of what has come to be called modern Southern Gothic. I propose to treat it as an excellent example of Faulkner's skillful craftsmanship, and as a useful port of entry into the special world that Faulkner created.

When a student at the University of Virginia asked Faulkner why so many of "the best Southern writers write about the degeneration of the old aristocracy,"* Faulkner's answer indicated that he was not having any of that. He agreed that what a Southern writer puts into his fiction could have sociological implications, but he made it plain that he was

*F. L. Gwynn and Joseph Blotner, *Faulkner in the University* (Charlottesville, 1959), p. 57.

himself interested in "writing about people." And when another questioner asked him why he sometimes severely satirized the South, Faulkner answered: "It's my country, my native land and I love it. I'm not trying to satirize it." He conceded that the South had "its faults and [said that he would] try to correct them," but he also said—and this is most important—"I will not try to correct them when I am writing a story, because I'm talking about people then."*

Faulkner's comment provides a sound way in which to approach this story. Let's begin by asking: What kind of person was Miss Emily Grierson? What does her story mean? The Griersons had been looked up to by everybody in the little town of Jefferson, Mississippi. They had held their heads high—some of the townspeople felt, too high. But Miss Emily has fallen upon evil days. She lives in a neighborhood that has gone down, and her house, Faulkner tells us, now lifts "its stubborn and coquettish decay above the cotton wagons and the gasoline pumps. . . ."

In the opening sentence of the story, the narrator mentions Miss Emily's death and tells us that the "whole town went to her funeral." Though she has lived all her later years in relative isolation, her funeral becomes a public event. As we shall find, Miss Emily's relation to the small community is of great significance. The narrator can be regarded as a kind of spokesman for the community. He never says, "I did not say she was crazy then," but "We did not," "We believed," "We knew," and so forth.

Who is this narrator? We are not told, and it does not matter that we never learn his name. But clearly he knows Miss Emily's history, has a sympathetic understanding of her basic aberration, and can mediate to the reader the meaning of her story—if only the reader will let him. Moreover, he is a born storyteller. Thus he moves from the mention of her funeral to the day in 1894 when she became not only a "tradition, a duty, and a care," but a sort of "hereditary

*Ibid., p. 83.

obligation" on the town. For in that year the mayor had used a flimsy subterfuge to remit her taxes, taxes that he was aware Miss Emily could no longer afford to pay.

Later on, a new generation decides that Miss Emily ought to pay taxes like everybody else and sends a delegation to explain the situation to her. This occasion provides the narrator with the first of a series of scenes in which crucial events of Miss Emily's story are depicted. This first scene is in Miss Emily's dusty parlor. She refuses to admit that she owes any taxes; she denies the authority of the tax notice that has been sent to her; and she tells the delegation to see Colonel Sartoris. "I have no taxes in Jefferson." Colonel Sartoris has been dead for nearly ten years. Has Miss Emily lived alone for so long that she has not heard that he is dead? Or are the dead for her more alive than the living?

At any rate, as the narrator tells us, "she vanquished them, horse and foot, just as she had vanquished their fathers thirty years before about the smell." So we go back thirty years and learn of the awful smell that complaining neighbors claimed emanated from Miss Emily's house. One cannot tell a lady to her face that she smells bad, and Miss Emily is a lady; besides, Judge Stevens, the mayor at the time, is a gentleman of the old school. So the cleanup of Miss Emily's premises that he arranges is private and done at night, with men strewing lime at the cellar openings of her house.

"After a week or two the smell died away." But the smell gives the narrator an opportunity to tell us that it was about this time that "people had begun to feel sorry for her"; and, to explain why, the narrator tells us a bit more of Miss Emily's past. The Grierson family had a streak of general insanity along with their insane pride. Miss Emily's father thought that none of the young men who came courting her were good enough. So he discouraged them—really drove them away—and when he finally died, his daughter was still unmarried and with little more left to her than the house itself. In a way, the narrator says, the "people were glad. At last they could pity Miss Emily. Being alone, and a pauper, she had become humanized." Now she would know, like other people, what it felt like to have to count pennies.

But when Mr. Grierson died, a strange thing happened. Miss Emily refused to admit that he was dead. After three days, and a lot of persuasion, she finally allowed the body to be taken out of the house and buried. Readers who already know this story will see that the narrator has provided here two bits of evidence which, as prosecuting attorneys like to say, will be connected later—the smell and Miss Emily's insistence that the dead body of her father should not leave the house.

The narrator, however, does not connect them at this point. He leaves that to the reader. Instead, he tells us how Miss Emily, now that her father was no longer alive to prevent her, allowed herself to receive the attentions of Homer Barron, a construction boss from the North, who had arrived in Jefferson with a crew to pave the sidewalks. So we have the occasion for two more brilliant scenes. The first shows Miss Emily driving about on Sunday afternoons with Homer Barron "in the yellow-wheeled buggy and the matched pair of bays from the livery stable." Naturally, the Jefferson ladies are aghast that a Grierson should condescend in such shameless fashion to "a Northerner, a day laborer." But Miss Emily contrives to carry "her head high enough," the narrator tells us, even when "we believed that she was fallen." It is as if she demanded "more than ever the recognition of her dignity as the last Grierson."

She stands on her dignity most of all when she appears at a local drugstore to buy some arsenic, a truly electrifying scene, too good to paraphrase. I will present it as Faulkner presents it in the story:

> "I want some poison," she said to the druggist. She was over thirty then, still a slight woman, though thinner than usual, with cold, haughty black eyes in a face the flesh of which was strained across the temples and about the eye-sockets as you imagine a lighthouse-

keeper's face ought to look. "I want some poison," she said.

"Yes, Miss Emily. What kind? For rats and such? I'd recom—"

"I want the best you have. I don't care what kind."

The druggist named several. "They'll kill anything up to an elephant. But what you want is—"

"Arsenic," Miss Emily said. "Is that a good one?"

"Is . . . arsenic? Yes, ma'am. But what you want—"

"I want arsenic."

The druggist looked down at her. She looked back at him, erect, her face like a strained flag. "Why, of course," the druggist said. "If that's what you want. But the law requires you to tell what you are going to use it for."

Miss Emily just stared at him, her head tilted back in order to look him eye for eye, until he looked away and went and got the arsenic and wrapped it up. The Negro delivery boy brought her the package; the druggist didn't come back. When she opened the package at home there was written on the box, under the skull and bones: "For rats." (Pp. 125–26)

Naturally the news about the arsenic spreads rapidly through the town. The townsfolk believe that she means to kill herself, for an aristocratic lady would prefer death to dishonor. But she does not kill herself, though clearly Homer Barron has not married her, and seems to have left town for good.

He does appear in town once more. A neighbor sees Miss Emily's servant admit him at the kitchen door at dusk one evening. But that was all, and, as the years pass, less and less is seen of Miss Emily herself. For a time she gives china-painting lessons to the daughters and granddaughters of Colonel Sartoris's contemporaries. But six or seven years later, no one ever enters the house except her aging Negro servant to bring in necessary food or supplies. Yet sometimes one might catch a glimpse of Miss Emily "in one [of her] downstairs windows . . . like the carven torso of an idol in a niche, looking or not looking at us. . . ." The narrator sums it all up in a fine sentence which is well worth pondering: "Thus she passed from generation to generation—dear, inescapable, impervious, tranquil, perverse."

If some of these terms seem inconsistent with one another, nevertheless they all do significantly pertain to the woman. She has become part of the history of the town. She is a kind of monument, a landmark. But the narrator does not further spell out what her significance to Jefferson is. Instead he provides us with a powerful culminating scene.

At Miss Emily's funeral, the past is in some sense recovered. The older people talk about what Miss Emily was like as a girl and some of the old Confederate veterans tell about having danced with her. It is only after the funeral is over that an exploration of the upper rooms of the house is undertaken, for the narrator is careful to note that they "waited until Miss Emily was decently in the ground before they opened" the locked room. It is as if the town recognized that she had earned a right to this extension of her hard-won and bitterly maintained privacy.

When the door of one of the bedrooms is forced, it is revealed to be a macabre bridal chamber. The groom's body, clad in a nightshirt, lies—what is left of it, that is—on the bed, and about the room is evidence of the man's last disrobing, just as if it had been the night before. On the bed, there is a second pillow, and in it "the indentation of a head." From this pillow "one of us lifted," the narrator tells us, a "long strand of iron-gray hair."

The scene is one of horror and is meant to be. But the horror has not been worked up for its own sake. It would be wrong to push the theme of necrophilia further than makes fictional sense. Thus, it is reasonable from the text to suppose that Miss Emily held Barron in her arms after he had died—perhaps while he died. And the reference to the iron-gray hair and its length would suggest that perhaps Miss Emily had lain in that bed at least some months after his death. For her hair had been cut short about the time Barron came to town, and mention of its having turned "iron-gray" is not made until some time after his disappearance. But the dust that covers everything in that room, including the dust on the second pillow, would indicate that Miss Emily had not entered the room for many years before her own death.

A far more important problem about this story has to do with whether it has a meaning for humanity in general. Does this account of Emily Grierson amount to anything more than a clinical case history? Or, to put it in another way, since a person who is insane cannot be held accountable for her actions, can her actions have any significance for all of us?

Miss Emily's mania is a manifestation—warped though it be—of her pride, her independence, her iron will. She has not crumpled up under the pressures exerted upon her. She has not given in. She has insisted on choosing a lover in spite of the criticism of the town. She has refused to be jilted. She will not be either held up to scorn or pitied. She demands that the situation be settled on her own terms.

What she does in order to get her own way is, of course, terrible. But there is an element of the heroic about it too, and the town evidently recognizes it as such. Can an act be both monstrous and heroic? For a person who can hold two contradictory notions in his head at the same time, the answer will be yes. We can give Miss Emily her due without condoning her crime and, in an age in which social conformity and respectability are the order of the day, her willingness to flout public opinion may even seem exhilarating. Faulkner, by the way, never shows any regard for respectability: in his fiction respectability is the first temptation to which every cowardly soul succumbs. Miss Emily is crazy, but she is no coward. She is the true aristocrat: let others strive to keep up with the Joneses, if they will. She will not. She is the "Jones" with whom others will do well to keep up.

I have said that the narrator never spells out what Miss Emily's story meant to him or to the town, but he has provided a very illuminating simile. He tells us that Miss

Emily with her "cold, haughty black eyes" and her flesh "strained across the temples" looked "as you imagine a lighthouse-keeper's face ought to look."

A lighthouse provides a beacon for other people, not for the keeper of the light. He looks out into darkness. He serves others but lives in sheer isolation himself. His job is to warn others from being wrecked on the dangerous rocks on which his lighthouse is built. The simile really answers to Miss Emily's condition very well. For readers who demand a moral, this will have to serve. Miss Emily's story constitutes a warning against the sin of pride: heroic isolation pushed too far ends in homicidal madness.

Another fine story, "There Was a Queen" (published in January 1933), has to do with a woman who is also a descendant of one of the old established families of Jefferson. Her name is Narcissa Benbow, and she marries, though with some misgivings, young Bayard Sartoris, the scion of another aristocratic family. He has been a fighter pilot in World War I and returns home disturbed, restless, and utterly unfitted to resume life in an old-fashioned, traditional society. In fact, he soon leaves Jefferson and gets himself killed while flying a highly experimental plane as a test pilot.

Narcissa in due time bears his son, the last Sartoris male. Indeed, he is the last of all Sartorises except Virginia Du Pre (always referred to as Miss Jenny) who is the sister of Bayard Sartoris's great-grandfather.

In the big Sartoris house, then, there live the child and the two women, who represent entirely different generations. Miss Jenny, born in 1840, lived through the Civil War. Narcissa, born in 1897, is still a comparatively young woman at the time of the story.

Miss Jenny is one of Faulkner's finest and most interesting female characters. She represents the aristocratic virtues in their best sense, though she can be tart and vinegary, and has wit and a sharp tongue. We shall have occasion to see her at her very best when we later discuss "An Odor of Verbena." In "There Was a Queen" she provides a foil for Narcissa, who is a woman too wrapped up in herself. (Her very name suggests her quality of self-absorption.) Whereas Miss Jenny knows who *she* is, is confident of her role in life, and inherits a set of moral principles and a code of conduct, Narcissa is uncertain, confused, and even a bit neurotic.

Before her marriage to Bayard, someone had begun to send Narcissa obscene, anonymous letters. She had at once told Miss Jenny about them. The letters worried her and made her feel unclean. Miss Jenny's counsel was forthright: if Narcissa had done nothing to encourage such letters (and she had not), then there was not the slightest reason for her to feel soiled. In such circumstances, Miss Jenny certainly would not feel soiled. She would throw the letters in the fire unread just as fast as they arrived. An alternative action would be to turn them over to a male family member who might be able, from an examination of them, to identify the culprit and so put a stop to this nuisance.

Narcissa does neither, however. From some obscure motive—perhaps the letters provide her with a vague, erotic excitement—she preserves them. Later on the writer of the letters breaks into her room, finds the packet of letters where she has hidden it, and takes it away with him. But this was not the last that Narcissa heard of the letters; for, many years later, a Federal agent gets in touch with her to say that he has the letters. They have turned up among the papers of a man who has been indicted for a Federal offense, whose whereabouts he wants to trace.

Naturally, Narcissa cannot help the agent locate the man, but it makes her almost frantic to think that anyone else might read the letters. As she later confesses to Miss Jenny, "I thought of people, men, reading them, seeing not only my name on them, but the marks of my eyes where I had read them again and again."

So Narcissa persuades the Federal agent to give her the letters in return for two nights spent with him in a hotel. Narcissa's capitulation to her notion of respectability is complete. It is better to give her body to a stranger than to risk having others believe that she has been the object of erotic fantasies.

When Miss Jenny hears this confession, she is ready to depart the ancestral house. She calls for her hat, as if she were going to leave, but she is, after all, ninety years old and in a wheelchair. She cannot depart from the house except by dying. And die she does. When Elnora, the servant, comes to see about her, she finds the old woman sitting erect by the window, but quite motionless.

If, in Faulkner's work, one seeks evidence of degeneration in the old plantation class of the South, Narcissa's complacent acceptance of the *fact* in order to safeguard the *appearance* presents pertinent evidence. Miss Emily Grierson's disregard for appearances or what people would say is, by contrast, a maintenance of the aristocratic ethos, though carried to an insane extreme. But one does not have to appeal to mad Miss Emily. Miss Jenny is utterly sane and her condemnation of Narcissa is absolute.

When we come to a discussion of "An Odor of Verbena," we shall have an opportunity to see Miss Jenny's sanity as positive action when her nephew has to make a heroic decision.

The characters of Faulkner's stories and novels, however, are not all confined to the so-called aristocracy. Some of his noblest characters are poorer whites and one of his finest treatments of honor occurs in a story entitled "Barn Burning." The story involves a sharecropper's son who rejoices in the name of Colonel Sartoris. The boy is Colonel Sartoris Snopes, or "Sarty," and his father, Ab Snopes, is a hard-bitten sharecropper who has become soured on the world. After Ab had named his son, his relations with the gentry wore pretty thin.

Being landless, Ab arranges with a landowner to occupy a cabin or tenant's house and is furnished with food and perhaps other supplies through the winter, in return for planting and raising a crop on certain specified acres of land. At harvest time, Ab shares with the landowner half or perhaps two-thirds of what has been gathered, and out of his share pays his bill for supplies. It was not a good system for the tenant, often not for the landowner either, and certainly not for the land. For a sharecropper had little incentive to try to improve the land. Too often, the temporary tenant fell out with the landowner because he had been defrauded, or thought he had been defrauded, of his fair share, and, after living a year or two at one place, moved on.

Ab Snopes became so embittered that he retaliated against the last landowner by setting fire to his barn. But it was hard to prove that Ab committed arson, and so he was not jailed but allowed to move on to another part of the country where, late in the season, he took up a tenancy on land belonging to Major de Spain.

Ab arrives with a chip on his shoulder, practically picks a disagreement with De Spain, and almost before his family has settled in the paintless two-room house, prepares to burn De Spain's barn. It is a desperate act as well as criminal, and little Sarty Snopes finds himself caught between loyalty to his father, with whose rage and despair he sympathizes, and his own sense of honor and decency.

He is thoroughly aware that Major de Spain is not at fault and that it is wrong wantonly to destroy his property. This knowledge would prove a considerable burden for an adult to bear, but the Snopes boy has an additional burden: as Faulkner describes it, "the terrible handicap of being young." Sarty has been impressed by the "peace and dignity" of the De Spain mansion. He is not envious of it. He simply recognizes in it a desirable orderliness that casts a spell over him. He thinks that perhaps it will cast such a spell over his father. As he walks beside him he thinks: *Maybe he will feel it too. Maybe it will even change him now from what maybe he couldn't help but be.*

What enchants the boy, though, stirs the embittered man to jealous rage. That evening Sarty hears his mother's voice expostulating with his father: "Abner! No! No! Oh, God. Oh, God. Abner!" and he sees his father emptying the reservoir of the kerosene lamp into the five-gallon kerosene can.

Sarty tries to get away to warn Major de Spain, but Abner anticipates his dash out of the house and orders the boy's mother and aunt to hold him. Sarty manages to break free and rushes to the De Spain house to give the alarm. Though the Major tries to stop the boy, Sarty eludes him too and rushes back to his father's house, presumably to warn his father that De Spain is coming. Maybe he will be in time to prevent Ab's striking the match, and with the knowledge that De Spain is on the way, maybe Ab will desist. But a rider on his galloping horse passes the boy on the road and he hears a shot followed an instant later by two more. The author tells us that Sarty pauses "without knowing he had ceased to run, crying 'Pap! Pap!', running again before he knew he had begun to run, stumbling, tripping over something . . . looking backward over his shoulder at the glare as he got up, running on among the invisible trees, panting, sobbing, 'Father! Father!'"

The boy does not try to go back. Later, as he sits on the crest of a hill, there is "no glare behind him now." He walks,

> shaking steadily in the chill darkness, hugging himself into the remainder of his thin, rotten shirt, the grief and despair now no longer terror and fear but just grief and despair. *Father. My father*, he thought. "He was brave!" he cried suddenly, aloud but not loud, no more than a whisper: "He was! He was in the war! He was in Colonel Sartoris' cav'ry!" not knowing that his father had gone to that war, . . . admitting the authority of and giving fidelity to no man or army or flag . . . [going] for booty—for loot whether it came from the enemy or from his own. (Pp. 24–25)

Yet the boy has to believe in his father. A man must believe in something if he is to make a life-and-death choice—and such a choice is Sarty's. He loves his father though he believes that in trying to do the honorable thing he has himself caused his father's death. But did he cause his father's death? No, because if we read *The Hamlet*, of which "Barn Burning" was originally meant to be the opening chapter, we shall find that Ab Snopes evidently escaped and lived on like Falstaff, if not to burn another barn, at least to threaten another barn. And Sarty? What of him? Again, we simply do not know. Perhaps he lived to a ripe old age, perhaps not, but he apparently never came home.

Faulkner's great theme, as he was to describe it in his Nobel Prize acceptance speech, was the human heart in conflict with itself. "Barn Burning," first published in 1939, is a fine instance of this. It should be read in full and savored. In this chapter I have abridged it heavily and used it simply to make three important points.

First, Faulkner's heroes may come from any station of society. Though the name Snopes has become a byword for a sharp-trading scoundrel, one may find honor and self-sacrifice among the Snopeses. Second, for Faulkner, as for so many authors, the important conflicts are internal conflicts. Third, Faulkner knows when to end a story. "Barn Burning" shows his customary economy. The story that Faulkner wanted to tell really ends when Sarty makes his commitment and sticks to it.

The poor white's sense of honor is the great theme of "Old Man," Faulkner's story of the adventures of the Tall Convict in the great flood of 1927 that inundated so much of the lower Mississippi Valley. "Old Man," though it has been published as a tale or a long story under that title, was originally part of a novel entitled *The Wild Palms* (1939) of which the two parts are, confusingly enough, entitled "The Wild Palms" and "Old Man." None of the characters in "The Wild Palms" ever meet any of the characters in "Old Man," and yet Faulkner conceived of the stories as contrapuntally related. That issue, important as it is, does not concern us here. Instead, we shall simply treat the story of the Tall Convict (for he is never given a name in the story) as a long story in its own right. Whatever its contribution to the novel, it can stand on its own as a story of man's endurance under the most trying of circumstances.

The Tall Convict is sufficiently naive to believe the advertisements that are printed in the cheap magazines that he reads. He orders certain articles—robbers' equipment—from the *Detective Gazette* and attempts to hold up a railroad train. His bungling attempt is foiled and he is sent to Parchman, the Mississippi State Penal Farm, convicted of armed robbery. When the levees on the Mississippi River begin to break, he and the other convicts are summoned to help with various kinds of work, and some of the convicts are put into boats to go out and rescue men and women who have taken refuge on the tops of barns or in trees from the rising waters. The Tall Convict is sent with one of his fellows (the Short Convict) to rescue a woman in a tree and a man who is standing on the roof of a cotton house. Navigation is difficult. The Short Convict is speedily lost from the boat. (He is later rescued.) Meanwhile, the Tall Convict does manage to find the woman, who turns out to be pregnant and very close to her time of delivery.

Thenceforward, the Tall Convict experiences a nightmare of dangers and difficulties. Some of the tributaries of the river are actually running backward, the great river forcing its swollen waters back into them; all sorts of misadventures happen, and they culminate when the Convict and the woman are finally swept out onto the raging Mississippi River itself.

The space at hand does not allow me to treat in detail the various episodes in the Convict's weeks away from the penal farm. The chronology that Thomas McHaney has worked out in his admirable book entitled *William Faulkner's "The Wild Palms": A Study* (Jackson: Mississippi University Press, 1975), has the Convict leave the penal farm for service on the levees on May 4 and not get back until June 23. In these weeks he is driven down almost to the mouth of the great river, tries to find a landing place, but where wind and flood do not operate against him, human beings do. For example, guards along the river, who note his convict's uniform, will not allow him to land. He is picked up at one point by a steamboat loaded with flood refugees, but he will not go aboard unless they will also take aboard the skiff in which he and the woman have been voyaging. His care to preserve it comes not from sentimental affection for a sturdy little craft that has for days kept him from drowning. Quite the contrary: it is simply that the Convict regards the little boat as government property committed to his care and for which he will be held accountable, and he means to return it. Return it he does, for he insists on making the slow trip upstream in the little craft except for a stretch in which he is able to pay a man with a motorboat to tow him as far as Baton Rouge.

By far the greatest problem for the Tall Convict, however, is the problem posed by the pregnant woman who is his cargo, his ward, and his responsibility. Even more than most other men, the Tall Convict is uncomfortable with the whole idea of childbirth. He tries desperately to get the woman ashore, somewhere, anywhere, to get help and assistance for her in her hour of travail. But the workings of nature cannot be forbidden or manipulated or even postponed. In fact, nature insisting on pushing the child out of the woman's womb is, for the Convict, even more awesome and formidable than nature outside and all around the little skiff hurtling it along over the fierce waters.

Yet the Convict does find a hummock of sodden land on which to beach the boat and there on this desolate spot, partially occupied by snakes, themselves refugees from the waters, the birth takes place. Since the Convict does not even possess a knife to sever the umbilical cord, he has to use the jagged edge of an open metal can that he finds in the boat. Yet the child survives. The woman does happen to find a waterproof matchbox in her jacket pocket. The Convict is able at last to make a fire, and the woman—for Faulkner, women are the resourceful and practical human beings—actually manages to bathe the newborn child.

If for the Convict it is a point of honor to return the skiff undamaged, it is even more a point of honor to return the woman and her child unharmed. Of course, the Convict has not the slightest romantic interest in the woman. He treats her kindly and protects her as best he can through the whole dangerous odyssey, but she holds no sexual interest for him. On his return journey, he gets into trouble with a man over the man's wife—but he makes no attempt on his passenger. She is for him inviolate.

Thus far I have touched on only a few episodes of the Tall Convict's adventure. It is important for me to speak now, if only briefly, about the basic themes of "Old Man" and about the spirit in which this epic adventure is narrated. Yet I cannot forbear to say that for brilliant description and convincing narration of violent action, "Old Man" can scarcely be surpassed elsewhere in Faulkner. The writing is superb and the obvious course is for one to read it for oneself.

As for the themes, the theme of honor has already been implied. Faulkner's true aristocrats pride themselves on being men of honor, but in this matter they do not necessarily surpass the poorer whites, some of whom possess nothing except their honor. They cling to it: to give it up means giving up their humanity.

The theme of endurance needs only to be mentioned. Few of Faulkner's characters have harder tests set for them than the test the great flood sets for the Tall Convict. He measures up to it and so does his companion, the heroic woman. Faulkner's characters are often surprised at what they are asked to endure, and often just as surprised that they are able to endure it after all. The Convict expresses this surprise again and again as he narrates his adventures to his fellows back at the penal farm. Man's ability to endure is an important general theme in Faulkner's work. When he wanted to pay his highest compliment to Dilsey (of *The Sound and the Fury*) and the black people whom she represented, he put it very simply: "They endured."

Lastly there is the theme of innocence. Faulkner has a fondness for the simple and unsophisticated character. The Tall Convict is at once pathetic and comic in the way in which he is taken in by men and events. Only a very innocent man could have believed literally the stories that he had read in paperback novels, or would have secured from the *Detective Gazette* a toy pistol and a black handkerchief wherewith to mask his face, not as a child's play toy, but as proper equipment for a serious attempt at robbery. But the Tall Convict's innocence is also winning: he is no braggart. He does not in the least realize that some of the things that he accomplishes in his flood adventure are truly heroic.

As for Faulkner's mode of storytelling: the Convict's adventures become a sort of tall tale. Here I use the term technically. In the mid-nineteenth century, what we call the tall tale of the Old Southwest flourished in the region below the Ohio River and west of the Appalachians. Exaggeration became a device for comic effect. Things were made larger than life: hyperbole was part of the fun.

Now, I do not mean to imply that Faulkner turns the Tall Convict into a grandiose liar in recounting his adventures. The Convict does not boast; we are to believe that he really did the things that he quietly says he did.

Nor do I mean that Faulkner himself is telling a tall tale. The 1927 flood was awesome in its power and destruction. Yet Faulkner has pushed credibility about as far as one can push it without inflating it into absurdity. The story of the Tall Convict constantly hovers at the very edge of the impossible, and so something of the spirit of the tall tale does inform Faulkner's narrative. If the story is not impossible, parts of it are, to say the least, extraordinary—as the way in which the Tall Convict goes into the alligator hide business in the marsh country below New Orleans with a Cajun trapper who speaks no English, just as the Convict speaks no French. Yet the two men manage to work out a proper division of their profits and the Tall Convict reduces his Cajun partner to almost speechless admiration by the way in which, armed only with a knife, he will jump astraddle an alligator as it cruises along in the water. No wonder his startled partner shouts: "'Magnifique!'"

What the reader must finally come to understand is that the spirit of "Old Man" is generally comic. Faulkner's humor appears in many ways. There is understatement, for example, such as when the woman perilously perched in the tree tells the Convict, "I thought for a minute you wasn't aiming to come back." The Convict, caught in the swirling currents, is indeed not sure whether he is coming or going—his previous departure from the tree had not been in the least purposed, and his unplanned return had been at the whim of the stream. Still, he is glad he has located the woman he was sent to rescue.

In addition, there is a great deal of the Convict's conscious folk humor, and of the unconscious humor connected with the speech of an innocent, a simple country boy. Noting his nosebleed, a doctor asks the Convict whether anyone has ever suggested that he is a hemophiliac? (As a matter of fact, he is.) But the Convict is puzzled. For him a hemophiliac is a calf that is a bull and a cow at the same time.

There is even an element of black humor, as when the Convict's reward for his heroic adventure and his dogged resolve to get back to the penal farm with the boat and the woman intact is to have ten more years added to his sentence. The Convict, like the stoic that he is, accepts this without protest. A fellow convict, a sort of Job's comforter, commiserates with him. "Ten more years to do without a woman, no woman a tall a fellow wants—" But the Tall Convict has had enough of the society of women for a lifetime. "Women—! the tall convict said," and this is the end of the tale. But the humor does not cancel out the stoic endurance that is the substance of this story, nor does it smudge the quality of heroism. Indeed, the most attractive hero of all is the hero who is not only without heroic pretensions, but is not even aware that he is a hero.

Earlier, I have tried to deal with two of the social strata of Yoknapatawpha County, the whites of plantation stock and the poorer whites. But north Mississippi was mainly frontier country until the second quarter of the nineteenth century, and another important stratum in the early days of the county were the Indians, the oldest inhabitants of all. Those Indians belonged to the Chickasaw tribe, though a related tribe, the Choctaws, occupied central Mississippi, a bit to the south of Yoknapatawpha County. Actually, Faulkner began by calling his Indians Choctaws, though he soon shifted them over to the other nation.

In the story entitled "A Justice," Sam Fathers, part black, part Indian, tells how he came by his name, which in its full form is Had-Two-Fathers. The Indian known as Doom (a corruption of the French *d'homme*, "the man"), who became a chieftain, has lived for a while among the whites. When he comes home to his tribe, he brings with him six black people, one of whom is a woman. Did the Indians ever own black slaves? Yes, they did, and that circumstance is very important in this story and in another of Faulkner's Indian stories, "Red Leaves."

Doom is an ambitious man and something of a rogue. He brings back from New Orleans not only the six slaves, but a little gold box filled with what turns out to be poison. In fact, it is by means of the poison that Doom quickly makes his way to head of the tribe. But this story, as one of Doom's cousins, Herman Basket, told it to Sam Fathers years later, does not emphasize Doom's cold-blooded cruelty. In fact, Doom turns out to be a man with a sense of humor and with a commitment to a sort of rough justice among his people.

He *is* ambitious. When a steamboat goes aground in one of the nearby tributaries of the Mississippi River, Doom marshals his people and, by using logs as rollers and having his men haul on ropes to supply power, Doom brings the boat overland to his village, where it becomes his palace.

In the meantime, Craw-ford (short for Crawfish-ford), one of Doom's court followers, has taken a fancy to the black female slave. He plans to take the woman home with him, but one of the male slaves points out that the woman is *his* wife and that he has no intention of letting her go. But Craw-ford will not give up.

Pretending that he has hurt his back, he stays in the Indian village while all the men are away hauling the boat overland. Doom notices his absence and learns that although Craw-ford is sitting with his feet in the hot spring all day as treatment for his back, he evidently has access to the woman at night, for Doom keeps all the men, including the woman's husband, shut up each night in the boat. Doom summons Craw-ford and suggests that since his sickness is persistent, perhaps he should sit in the spring all night too.

Craw-ford protests that the night air will make it worse. Doom counters:

> "Not with a fire there. . . . I will send one of the black people with you to keep the fire burning."
> "Which one of the black people?" [Craw-ford] said.
> "The husband of the woman which I won on the steamboat," Doom said.
> "I think my back is better," [Craw-ford] said.
> "Let us try it," Doom said.
> "I know my back is better," [Craw-ford] said. (P. 353)

After five months the steamboat arrives at last at the plantation, but Craw-ford does not stop his attempts to get the woman. The husband comes to Doom once more, and Doom tells him: "I have done what I could for you. Why don't you go to Craw-ford and adjust this matter yourself?" The husband says that he has done so; that Craw-ford has suggested a cockfight to settle the matter, but the black man points out that he does not own a fighting cock, and that Craw-ford has now taken the woman, claiming to have won her by default.

Doom, as chieftain, owns the best fighting cock in the tribe and offers to lend it to the black man. Craw-ford is for the moment foiled. But the damage has apparently already been done. When the black woman's child is born, its appearance clearly shows that something is wrong. When Doom asks "What is wrong with this [new] man?" the aggrieved black man says, "Look at the color of him." He then puts it to

Doom: "Do I get justice? . . . You are the Man." That is, the chief, the man in charge.

Doom responds to this appeal. He makes Craw-ford work all that winter and all the next summer to build a fence of a measured height around the black man's cabin. The lithe black man can sail over the fence like a bird, but the wretched Craw-ford cannot, and in time the black man proudly shows a new infant to Herman Basket with the question: "What do you think about this for color?" The firstborn child was, of course, Sam Fathers, and this was how he came by his name, Had-Two-Fathers.

Another of Faulkner's Indian stories is entitled "Red Leaves." In this story the chieftain Issetibbeha has died rather mysteriously; there are hints that his son, Moketubbe, has poisoned him. At any rate, dead the chief is, and his horse, his favorite hound, and his black bodyservant are to be killed and buried with him so that he may have their services in the next world.

"Red Leaves" is only incidentally about Moketubbe; it centers on the black bodyservant, who knows very well what his fate is to be and who watches with quiet apprehension for the proof that the chieftain is actually dead. He accepts his fate and his death—indeed, he feels that he has already departed from the land of the living. And yet, when at last he hears Issetibbeha's hound begin to howl, he starts to run. "He ran on into full darkness, mouth closed, fists doubled, his broad nostrils bellowing steadily." Later we shall discover, as he himself will discover, that his body still wills to live—quite irrationally, since he already counts himself to be as good as dead. But the urge to live relentlessly pushes him on—almost, one might think, against his conscious will.

The bodyservant is completely alone. For when he returns to the slave quarters, he gets no protection or comfort from his fellows. He hears the drums beating and follows the sound until he stands among the other slaves. The black headman receives him but tells him to go, and when the bodyservant repeats the word *go* questioningly, the headman tells him: "Eat, and go. The dead may not consort with the living; thou knowest that." And the bodyservant agrees: "Yao. I know that." After he accepts some cooked meat, he makes for the swamp.

The Indians dutifully pursue him, but it is the most half-hearted and desultory pursuit imaginable. They need not hurry; there is nowhere for the wretched man to go. He cannot escape. Besides, they are not bloodthirsty or vindictive. It is a ritual pursuit. Therefore, they let the poor man take his time.

So the Indians do not press him too hard. Actually, at one point the bodyservant and an Indian come face-to-face on a log that crosses a stream—"the Negro gaunt, lean, hard, tireless, and desperate; the Indian thick, soft-looking, the apparent embodiment of the ultimate and the supreme reluctance and inertia. The Indian made no move, no sound; he stood on the log and watched the Negro plunge into the slough and swim ashore and crash away into the undergrowth." This, then, is the so-called pursuit by the Indians.

In the course of his wanderings the bodyservant is bitten by a large cottonmouth moccasin. He salutes the snake: "'Olé, grandfather,'" he says, and touches its head and watches it strike his arm again and again. For he is not trying to avoid death, and yet his body in its revulsion from death will not let him go and give himself up for the inevitable execution. He says to himself: "'It's that I do not wish to die'—in a quiet tone, of slow and low amaze, as though it were something that, until the words had said themselves, he found that he had not known, or had not known the depth and extent of his desire."

The Indians grumble that the chase has gone on too long, but when they finally reach the bodyservant and find him no longer trying to flee, but sitting still and beginning to sing, they stop and wait for him to finish his song. "He was chanting," we are told, "something in his own language, his face lifted to the rising sun. His voice was clear, full, with a quality wild and sad. 'Let him have time,' the Indians said."

Let me repeat: the reader must realize that the Indians hold no antagonism toward this man, that they understand that he finds it hard to accept his death, and that they are carrying out their mission simply as part of a necessary ritual. The bodyservant has had an easy life for twenty-three years. It is only just and proper that he follow his master into the grave. But he has run a good race. He has—according to their code—behaved well. They mean it when they say to him: "You ran well. Do not be ashamed." That the black man has acted, not in terms of their code, but under an irrational compulsion, does not impugn their intended compliment; but it does heighten the irony of the situation that the victim, soon to be sacrificed, is being commended, and even comforted, by his captors.

The words "You ran well. Do not be ashamed" make a magnificent ending for this story, and a merely good writer would end the story here. But Faulkner is more than a good writer. He is a great writer, and so he adds the brief but wonderfully moving final section. The black man, in the grip of an overwhelming impulse to gain even a few more minutes of life, asks for food. It is given him, but he cannot swallow it. Then he begs for water, but cannot drink it, though he tries, and the Indians watch the "unswallowed water sheathing broken and myriad down his chin, channeling his [mud] caked chest. They waited, patient, grave, decorous, implacable. . . . Then the water ceased, though still the empty gourd tilted higher and higher, and still his black throat aped the vain motion of his frustrated swallowing. . . . 'Come,' Basket said, taking the gourd from the Negro and hanging it back in the well."

Ordinarily, such a desperate clinging to the final moments of life would appear demeaning. It would suggest that the victim was a cringing coward, but not so here. The black man is not facing sudden death, death striking from behind and out of the shadows, but death calculated, foreordained, deliberate; and the very calm of his executioner heightens the horror. In any case, his mind has from the beginning been resigned to his death: it is that dark, deeper self that, to his own astonishment, will not give up.

In this story about the Yoknapatawpha Indians we have already encountered the fourth element of the society about which Faulkner writes, the black man. Some of Faulkner's most moving stories are about black people. One of them is entitled "That Evening Sun." It is about a black woman named Nancy. The title of the story comes from the opening line of the "St. Louis Blues": "I hates to see that evening sun go down." Nancy hates to see it go down because she is afraid of the dark—or, more specifically, she is afraid that she will be killed in the dark. Nancy is in trouble with her husband, Jesus. She has been unfaithful to him, has prostituted herself to a white man, Mr. Stovall, a deacon in the Baptist church, and Jesus knows that she is now carrying Mr. Stovall's child. Jesus has left town, perhaps for good, but Nancy is convinced that he is going to come back some night and cut her throat.

Nancy's story is told by Quentin Compson, who is, at the time Nancy's affairs have come to a crisis, a boy of nine. Dilsey, the Compson family's regular servant, is sick and Nancy is filling in for her. Quentin's little sister, Caddy, is seven and his younger brother, Jason, is five. The children do not understand what is going on. Quentin is, however, old enough to have some comprehension of Nancy's terror and despair. But whether or not the nine-year-old boy can fully understand, he does provide the reader with all the clues that the reader needs to understand the story.

Early in the story we learn that Nancy is desperately and even irrationally afraid of her husband; that Mr. Compson is essentially a kindly man and sympathizes with Nancy's fears, though he believes they are baseless; and that Mrs. Compson is a cold, selfish, neurotic woman who has no sympathy with Nancy and who would not lift a finger to help her even if she thought that Nancy was really about to be murdered. Furthermore, we come to see that Caddy is a bright little girl with an eye for particulars and a lively curiosity about all these adult mysteries, and that Jason is truly his mother's child, nasty, spoiled, utterly selfish. Yet these matters are incidental to Nancy's story. Faulkner keeps his focus unswervingly on her.

Nancy is so afraid of being alone in the dark that she wants to sleep in the Compson house. Mr. Compson humors this notion, but Mrs. Compson eventually puts a stop to it and even resents Mr. Compson's walking Nancy home to her little cabin some distance away.

The climax of the story comes when Nancy one evening entices the children to slip off to her cabin. Misery loves company; Nancy's unreasoning terror welcomes any company, even that of mere children. Perhaps she believes that Jesus will not kill her if the children are present. So Nancy tries to hold their interest by telling them stories and popping corn in her fireplace. But Mr. Compson discovers that the children are missing, guesses where they are, and appears at the cabin. He tries to reason with Nancy. How does she know that Jesus is lying out in the ditch, watching? Why will she not lock up her house and go over to Aunt Rachel's to spend the night? (Aunt Rachel has invited her to do so.) Mr. Compson had earlier tried to get Nancy's consent for him to notify the authorities. But Nancy refuses: "'Twont do no good,'" she says. "'Putting it off wont do no good.'" When Mr. Compson asks: "'Then what do you want to do?'" Nancy says, "'I don't know. . . . I reckon it belong to me. I reckon what I going to get ain't no more than mine.'"

Well, if Nancy will not leave the house, Mr. Compson urges her to "'Lock the door and put out the lamp and go to bed.'" But Nancy answers: "'I scared of the dark. . . . I scared for it to happen in the dark.'" And as Mr. Compson and the children leave, Nancy sits there with her lamp still turned up so high that it is smoking and with the door of the cabin wide open, waiting for Jesus. But after Mr. Compson and the children are out of sight they can still hear her keening, "the sound that was not singing and not unsinging." The younger children cannot take in the situation but the nine-year-old Quentin does. He asks his father: "Who will do our washing now?"

It is a beautifully told story and it has to be judged so even if Jesus did not come that night or on any subsequent night to cut Nancy's throat. For the story is really concerned with rendering vividly the helpless terror of a human being who feels that she is to die. It is essentially the same situation as that dramatized in "Red Leaves," though these two brilliant stories differ otherwise in nearly every respect.

Well, what did happen? Did Jesus come that night and cut Nancy's throat? We do not know. The story that Faulkner meant to tell quite properly ends just where he elected to end it. Actually, a woman named Nancy Mannigoe, who in several very significant ways closely resembles the Nancy of "That Evening Sun," reappears in Faulkner's novel *Requiem for a Nun*; and in *Faulkner in the University* he acknowledged to the University of Virginia students that the two characters were indeed the same woman. Perhaps Mr. Compson and Dilsey and Aunt Rachel were right after all in believing that Nancy's fear was unfounded. The real point is that this would make absolutely no difference to the meaning and the power of the story.

Another of Faulkner's finest stories has as its hero a black character. It is entitled "Pantaloon in Black." It is actually one of the episodes in Faulkner's novel *Go Down, Moses,* but it can readily be detached from the larger work and can stand apart as a short story in its own right.

Rider, the hero, is a man of enormous strength and energy, a man capable of great passion though he is almost inarticulate. His young wife, Mannie, dies after a brief illness a few months after their marriage. The story opens with her burial. Rider is so stunned and so psychologically disoriented that he shocks the other mourners by seizing a shovel and filling the grave himself. He simply cannot stay still.

After the grave has been filled and mounded up, his old aunt tries to prevent his going home, telling him that he must come with her and eat. He refuses. A male friend tries to lure him away by telling him "'We gots a jug in de bushes.'" And when Rider insists that he is going right home, the friend warns him: "'You dont wants ter go back dar. She be wawkin yit.'" But Rider brushes this aside: "'Lemme lone. . . . Doan mess wid me now.'"

The truth is that Rider hopes that Mannie is "walking," so great is his yearning to see her. Striding on alone, then, he reaches and enters his cabin; when his dog refuses to follow him, he rebukes it: "'Whut you skeered of? She lacked you too, same as me.'" But the dog does not heed him. It refuses to enter the cabin.

> Then the dog left him. The light pressure went off his flank; he heard the click and hiss of its claws on the wooden floor as it surged away and he thought at first that it was fleeing. But it stopped just outside the front door, where he could see it now, and the upfling of its head as the howl began, and then he saw her too. She was standing in the kitchen door, looking at him. He didn't move. He didn't breathe nor speak until he knew his voice would be all right, his face fixed too not to alarm her. "Mannie," he said. "Hit's awright. Ah aint afraid." Then he took a step toward her, slow, not even raising his hand yet, and stopped. Then he took another step. But this time as soon as he moved she began to fade. He stopped at once, not breathing again, motionless, willing his eyes to see that she had stopped too. But she had not stopped. She was fading, going. "Wait," he said, talking as sweet as he had ever heard his voice speak to a woman: "Den lemme go wid you, honey." But she was going. She was going fast now, he could actually feel between them the insuperable barrier. . . . (*Go Down, Moses*, pp. 140–41)

But Rider still will not give up. He sets the table for eating, not with one plate but with two, and ladled "onto the plates the food which his aunt had brought yesterday . . . and carried the plates to the scrubbed bare table . . . and drew two chairs up and sat down, waiting again until he knew his voice would be what he wanted it to be. 'Come on hyar, now,' he said roughly. 'Come on hyar and eat yo supper. Ah aint gonter have no—' "

Some readers will be puzzled by Rider's harsh tone. Why does he not beseech his wife's shade to sit down and eat her supper? But there is no real puzzle. Rider simply cannot accept that his wife is dead. After all, he has just seen her with his own eyes. If "talking as sweet as he had ever heard his voice speak to a woman" cannot make her stay, then he will command her to do so. He will say, in effect, "No more coy nonsense now. I mean it. Sit down and eat your supper." But the rough tone is simply a measure of his desperation and his agony. The peremptory order avails no more than his coaxing. The magic does not work, for having uttered the command, and having "held himself motionless for perhaps a half minute," he raises "a spoonful of the cold and gluti- nous peas to his mouth. The congealed and lifeless mass seemed to bounce on contact with his lips. Not even warmed from mouth-heat, peas and spoon spattered and rang upon the plate; his chair crashed backward and he was standing, feeling the muscles of his jaw beginning to drag his mouth open, tugging upward the top half of his head."

This is masterly writing. The food which was to become a means to a renewed communion with the dead loved one becomes "a congealed and *lifeless* mass." The vision cannot be recovered.

One is reminded of the Greek legend of Orpheus and Eurydice. Surely Orpheus, when he looked backward into the corridor leading down into Hades and saw Eurydice begin to fade away, slipping back into the infernal darkness, felt the agony of loss no more poignantly than does Rider. I find this scene one of the most moving in all American literature.

Now that Rider knows that Mannie is really dead, he can find no solace. Superhuman work or phenomenal amounts of whiskey do nothing to appease his spirit. His aunt proposes the consolation of religion, but that does not serve either. Finally, Rider gets into a dice game run by a white man who uses crooked dice. He detects the white man's cheating and when the white man reaches for his gun, Rider is quicker with his razor and cuts the man's throat.

Rider does not run. Instead, the deputy sheriff finds him at his own house sound asleep. Rider is brought to the jail and locked up. All goes well until a chain gang is brought back to the jail to be locked up for the night. Suddenly there is a great commotion and the deputy finds that Rider has gone berserk. As the deputy tells it, "'that nigger had done tore that iron cot clean out of the floor it was bolted to and was standing in the middle of the cell, holding the cot over his head like it was a baby's cradle.'" He throws the cot against the wall and "'comes and grabs holt of that steel barred door and rips it out of the wall, bricks hinges and all, and walks out of the cell toting the door over his head like it was a gauze window-screen, hollering, "'It's awright. It's awright. Ah aint trying to git away.'"

It takes the help of the whole chain gang to subdue Rider, and when they have finally pinned him to the floor, he lies there "laughing, with tears big as glass marbles running across his face, . . . laughing and saying, 'Hit look lack Ah just cant quit thinking.'" Indeed, it takes a lynching mob of the crooked white man's relatives to put an end to his thinking—something that they do later that day.

We have now looked at a number of Faulkner's finest tales and short stories. At his best, he is one of the great masters of short fiction. But our review of the eight stories thus far considered can also be regarded as a sort of introduction to Faulkner's celebrated mythical county. We have a glimpse of the elder plantation gentry and what had become of them after the Civil War. We have seen something of their relations with the poorer whites and with the blacks, their former slaves or the descendants of their former slaves. But even the few stories we have examined show that the world of the poorer whites and the world of the blacks have their own complexities and their own interests and concerns. One must be careful, by the way, not to lump all the poorer whites together in one indiscriminate mass, just as one cannot lump all the blacks together. Actually, the poorer whites range from sturdy yeomen to poverty-stricken sharecroppers and on down to white trash.

There is a further point to be kept in mind. Faulkner strives to enter sympathetically into the minds of the poorer whites and the blacks and, for that matter, into the minds of the Indians who had been in the land long before the whites and the blacks arrived. We make a great mistake if we think that Faulkner chooses his heroes from only one class or that he limits the code of honor to, say, his plantation gentry.

Yoknapatawpha is a rich and complicated world. Though it is characterized by a caste system based on color, the class system within the white community is not nearly so rigid as most readers have been led to believe. Even the relations between whites and blacks, in the plantation society at least, allowed more room for the expression of mutual respect and even affection than one might have supposed. Most important, the human relations within this world were highly personal and concrete. Yoknapatawpha constituted something approximating a true community.

This last point is well illustrated in one of Faulkner's finest long stories, "An Odor of Verbena." This story is in fact the concluding section of a novel, *The Unvanquished*. Although it gains from the larger fictional context, it also yields a great deal when read in isolation. It is a story told by Bayard Sartoris when he was a young man of twenty-four, and when his Aunt Jenny (the old woman of ninety in "There Was a Queen") was a young widow of about thirty-three.

The time of "An Odor of Verbena" is apparently 1874. The wounds of the Civil War have not healed. The white community is just emerging from the Reconstruction period and Bayard's father, Colonel John Sartoris, having built his railroad, has now quarreled with his business partner, Ben

Redmond. The Colonel is a hard-driving man who has had to make his way up from poverty to power and position. After the War he married as his second wife Drusilla Hawk, a much younger woman, who in fact is only eight years older than her stepson Bayard.

As the story opens, Bayard is staying with Professor Wilkins and his wife at the University and reading law. Ringo, a young black man who is Bayard's own age and who was Bayard's constant boyhood companion, rides up to tell Bayard that Redmond has shot down Colonel Sartoris on the street in Jefferson. Bayard prepares at once to ride home.

Professor Wilkins offers Bayard a fresh horse and, significantly, he also offers him a pistol. Professor Wilkins is not a bloodthirsty person. He is gentle by nature and he instructs in the law, but he fully expects that Bayard will need a weapon. The times are still unsettled. Moreover, there is an unwritten law that one is bound to retaliate for such an attack on a close kinsman. The Jefferson community expects that Bayard will personally call to account his father's assassin. Ringo expects it, as his conversation with Bayard shows. Drusilla expects it. Even Professor Wilkins obviously expects it. Bayard can almost hear the professor saying: "'Ah, this unhappy land, not ten years recovered from the fever yet still men must kill one another, still we must pay Cain's price in his own coin.'" Bayard adds that he did not actually say it; but then he had not needed to.

This matter of revenging an attack on the family is, then, not for Bayard an academic matter, a remote eventuality. At the close of the War, Bayard's grandmother had been murdered by a bushwhacker, and Bayard and Ringo, both teenaged boys, had tracked him down and killed him. Bayard knows through personal experience what it is to demand an eye for an eye and a tooth for a tooth.

When Bayard gets home, George Wyatt and other members of the Colonel's old cavalry troop are waiting outside the house and George, after informing Bayard that Redmond had not shot the Colonel in the back—"'It was all right. It was in front. Redmond ain't no coward,'" are his words—offers to take over the responsibility for dealing with Redmond. But Bayard refuses: "'I reckon I can attend to it.'"

Finally, there is Bayard's meeting with Drusilla, his young stepmother. She greets him not in widow's weeds but dressed in a yellow ball gown. She is in a mood of fierce exultation and she addresses him "in a voice like a bell: clear, unsentient, on a single pitch, silvery and triumphant."

Drusilla's fiancé had been killed early in the War. Later, after her father's plantation had been burned by the Yankees, she had begged her cousin John Sartoris to let her join his cavalry troop and ride with his cavalrymen. After the War, her mother, outraged that she should have so compromised herself, insists that she and Colonel Sartoris get married. They do, but it is obviously a loveless marriage. The Colonel, an older man, preoccupied with his own enterprises, lives in a world of his own schemes and projects. An incident occurs two months before the Colonel's death, which indicates that Drusilla is more than half in love with her young stepson.

At that time, Drusilla asked Bayard to kiss her. They were walking in the garden together at dusk. Bayard said: "'No. You are Father's wife,'" but she insisted. He kissed her, and then said—for Bayard is a man of honor—"'Now I must tell father.'" Drusilla agreed. She said, "'Tell John. Tell him tonight.'"

But when Bayard tries to tell his father, the Colonel is so preoccupied with his own projects and plans that he apparently fails to take in what Bayard is saying. Then he immediately shifts the talk to his own concerns. He says to the younger man: "'Yes, I have accomplished my aim, and now I shall do a little moral house-cleaning. I am tired of killing men.'" The Colonel had killed several more men after the war, including two carpetbaggers in a Reconstruction election context and later a white man who he mistakenly thought was trying to attack him.

"'I am tired of killing men, no matter what the necessity nor the end.'" He expects Bayard, who will soon be trained in the law, to fight any future battles where they should be fought, in the civil courts.

All of this is important background material for the scene in which Drusilla receives Bayard after the Colonel's death and presents him with the dueling pistols. Whether or not she is half in love with her stepson, she is completely in love with the masculine code of honor. Most of Faulkner's female characters see the code as an absurdity and tolerate it, if at all, only because they observe that the male ethos seems to require it. The real proof, then, of Drusilla's having unsexed herself is her passionate commitment to a code that demands that Bayard either kill Redmond or be killed by him. Bayard describes her as the "priestess of a succinct and formal violence," and so she is. With "feverish eyes brilliant and voracious," she says to Bayard:

> "How beautiful you are: do you know it? How beautiful: young, to be permitted to kill, to be permitted vengeance, to take into your bare hands the fire of heaven that cast down Lucifer. No; I. I gave it to you; I put it into your hands; Oh you will thank me, you will remember me when I am dead and you are an old man saying to himself, 'I have tasted all things.'—It will be the right hand, won't it?" (*The Portable Faulkner*, p. 130)

And she kisses his right hand.

Then something happens. Somehow she realizes that Bayard does not mean to kill Redmond and she goes into hysterics, screaming in horror, "*'I kissed his hand!'*"

After Drusilla has been packed off to bed, Aunt Jenny indicates that it is all right that he has decided not to kill Redmond, and when Bayard questions the phrase *all right*, Miss Jenny reaffirms it, adding "'Don't let it be Drusilla, a poor hysterical young woman. And don't let it be him, Bayard, because he's dead now. And don't let it be George Wyatt and those others . . . I know you are not afraid.'"

Yet as Bayard tells her, "'I must live with myself, you see.'" So off to Jefferson he rides the next morning. George Wyatt meets him, but like Drusilla he divines that Bayard does not mean to kill, and exclaims, "'Is your name Sartoris? By God, if you don't kill him, I'm going to.'" But at Bayard's quiet word that he is attending to this, George relaxes, and Bayard mounts the stairs to Redmond's law office.

Redmond is there waiting for him, wearing fresh linen, neatly shaved, and with a pistol lying flat on the desk in front of him. He raises the pistol and fires two shots, which Bayard sees are deliberately aimed away from him. Then Redmond descends the stairs, and such is his quiet presence and his deliberate demeanor that George Wyatt and his companions actually allow him to walk past them and down to the railroad station just in time to catch the south-bound train.

Wyatt and the rest run up the stairs where Bayard is now sitting behind the desk. George first thinks that Bayard had taken Redmond's pistol away from him and then missed him twice. But then he catches on: "'No . . . You walked in here without even a pocket knife and let him miss you twice. My God in heaven. . . . You, White, ride out to Sartoris and tell his folks it's all over and he's all right.'"

Though Wyatt is committed to the old ways, he accepts what Bayard has done. "'You ain't done anything to be ashamed of. I wouldn't have done it that way, myself. . . . But that's your way or you wouldn't have done it.'" Even Drusilla has silently approved his courage. Verbena, for her, is the odor of courage. She says that you can smell it even above the smell of horses. When Bayard finally gets home that evening, Drusilla has gone—gone back to her people in Alabama—and will never return. But when Bayard enters his own room, he finds that Drusilla has left on his pillow a single sprig of verbena, the smell of which fills the room.

It is a mistake to say that Bayard has rejected the old code and the traditional ways. The word *rejected* is not accurate. Bayard has *transcended* the old code. That is to say, he does all that the code demands: he risks his very life unflinchingly. He shows even more courage than does the man who goes to the encounter armed and may hope to get in the first accurate shot. Bayard has resolved from the beginning not to kill a second time. Grumby, his grandmother's murderer, was one thing; this affair is another. He loves his father, but he is aware that his father had pressed Redmond too hard. He may even be said to honor his father's resolve that he intended some moral house-cleaning. Too many men were killed in the Sartoris interest or defending their honor, real or supposed. Bayard's motives are not simple but complex, and they unite in forbidding him to fire at his father's assassin. And yet Bayard manages to honor the claims of his community too.

He disagrees with the community; but, as he tells his Aunt Jenny, he wants to be well thought of. It's all very well that she would still think him brave even if he " 'hid all day in the stable,' " but George and Ringo and the rest would not think him brave. The pressure of the community's values is strong, and Bayard feels he cannot disregard them. Maybe Bayard has indulged in a quixotic folly in choosing the course of unarmed confrontation. But Faulkner was interested in the men who maintained their honor to a quixotic degree.

Bayard is a brave young man, but he is also a very lucky young man. Though he could not have counted on it, Redmond proved to be a brave man too—and, according to his own lights, a man of honor. He had killed the father and doubtless he felt he had justification for doing so; but he was not going to kill the son simply because the son had felt honor-bound to take up the quarrel and avenge his father's death. On the morning of their encounter, Redmond had quite clearly prepared himself for death. He had planned to direct his shots into the woodwork of the office and to take the bullets that would be aimed at him. That is the meaning of his neat appearance, fresh linen, and careful shaving.

Faulkner did not worship the past and was properly scornful of those cowardly enough to try to live in the past. He interprets poor Miss Emily Grierson's attempt to live in the past as madness. But this is not to say that he did not regard the earlier decades of Yoknapatawpha as a heroic age. Miss Jenny—wise, stable, courageous, and womanly—is one of his most attractive female characters. And Bayard Sartoris, "Old Bayard" as he came to be called in the later novels and by then a rather crusty small-town banker, well set in his ways and utterly unheroic, was not always so. He has his hour of heroism too as "An Odor of Verbena" reveals.

In their actions both Miss Emily and Bayard Sartoris testify to the power of the community. Faulkner does not press the thesis that the community judgment is always right. Sometimes it is woefully wrong. But in the world that Faulkner depicts the community is an important aspect of social reality, and Faulkner's characters are forced to reckon with it. Emily Grierson defies it and, in a sense, so does Bayard, though Bayard honors its claims in the very process of denying its injunction that he shall demand blood for blood. The novels to be discussed will manifest, though in different degrees, the same basic state of affairs.

3 • THE SOUND AND THE FURY

I made mention of the Compson family in discussing the short story "That Evening Sun" in the previous chapter. Benjy, the idiot, does not appear in that story, although, since he was some five years younger than Quentin, who was nine years old, Benjy had already been born. The members of the Compson family as presented in "That Evening Sun" cast revealing shadows forward. Mrs. Compson is already the weak, whining, self-pitying woman who is seen in *The Sound and the Fury*. Quentin is already the rather sensitive, thoughtful boy, though it would be impossible from what we see of him in the short story to predict his suicide in 1910. The Caddy of the early novel is recognizably the seven-year-old child of "That Evening Sun"—bright, perceptive, warmly human, and sympathetic. Jason, alas, does not improve as he grows older. Wordsworth's line "The child is father to the man" applies to him with devastating force. The mean-spirited, selfish little brat of "That Evening Sun," who is always going to "tell" on the other children and who keeps rejoicing aloud in the fact that he is not a nigger, has grown into a cold, selfish, inhuman man. It is that man who appears in 1928 in *The Sound and the Fury*.

Benjy, though thirty-three years old and physically mature in 1928, is an infant in mentality. The first section of the book is Benjy's unspoken monologue, for he utters very little articulate speech. As for Caddy, long before 1928 she departed from Jefferson; as for Quentin, he took his life eighteen years before. Section two of the novel is a long interior monologue by Quentin and an extended flashback to an earlier time, the day of Quentin's death, June 2, 1910. The other three sections of the novel cover three days in April 1928: April 6, 7, and 8, which in the Christian calendar for that year were Good Friday, Holy Saturday, and Easter Sunday.

What happens to the Compson family during these days happens just at the time when the Church moves from a mournful commemoration of the Crucifixion to a high feast of joy at the Resurrection of Christ. But let symbolmongers beware. Attempts to find specific significances between, say, Benjy's monologue on Saturday and the body of Christ reposing in the tomb are, in my considered opinion, doomed to failure. They may even—to adopt the language of our modern industrial world—turn out to be counterproductive. The *general* symbolism of the novel is, of course, clear enough and becomes clearer as we come to the final paragraphs.

The structure of *The Sound and the Fury* is complex. To begin with a small but obvious matter, the novel does not open with Friday, April 6, and go on in chronological sequence with the flashback to 1910 coming somewhere within the sequence. Instead, we move from Holy Saturday, 1928, back to June 1910, then on to Good Friday, 1928, and end with Easter Sunday, 1928.

Greater confusion yet is to come. I have said that the novel opens with the monologue of Benjy the idiot. As we begin the novel, its title is immediately pertinent. We are reading what is literally a tale told by an idiot, for Faulkner is borrowing from Macbeth's great speech in which the Scottish king cries out that life itself is a "tale / Told by an idiot, full of sound and fury, / Signifying nothing." In accord with his own purposes, Faulkner seems to have deliberately begun his novel with the most incoherent of the four sequences, presenting his reader with a puzzle to unravel rather than a narrative exposition of the general situation out of which the narrative of the novel is to develop. The reader may well believe that Faulkner is ordering his sequences in the worst possible way.

Yet the testimony of thousands of readers amounts to an endorsement of Faulkner's method. Certainly the reader is confused as he works through the first section of the novel. Since he is compelled to experience the world as Benjy has to experience it, he finds himself in a topsy-turvy world in which the past and the present intermingle, and in which the principle of cause and effect simply does not exist. Faulkner evidently wanted his reader to participate in Benjy's experience of time and reality which means that the reader participates in Benjy's confusion. Yet—and here is where the testimony of thousands of readers becomes relevant—curiously enough most readers, even on a first reading, discover that they learn a great deal about the Compson family. They have been immersed in the family situation, they know what it feels like to live in this household.

Many of the particular references and events in Benjy's monologue are bound to be puzzling to the reader. But some of these will become clear as one reads on into the other sections and finds them mentioned again. Besides, there is nothing to prevent the interested reader's returning to Benjy's section after completing the book—we usually have to reread any intricate poem several times—and there may be a real pleasure in the recognitions that come from these rereadings.

Faulkner was quite aware of the burden he was imposing upon his reader. Though he saw no alternative to his general strategy, he suggested to his publisher certain special devices. Because Benjy makes no distinction between a past and a present event, and because, in addition to references to the present (that is, April 7, 1928), there are references to some dozen time strata in which past events occurred, Faulkner urged that Benjy's section be printed in different color inks, a particular hue to indicate a different segment of time to which Benjy was referring.

Since this matter may be confusing, let me illustrate. Open a copy of the Vintage Book edition, mark the passage beginning with the first line of page 1, "present." Then on page 3, mark the passage printed in italic, "A–3"; mark the passage in roman type that follows on page 3, "A–1"; mark the small block in italic on page 5, "present"; and mark the passage in roman type beginning with the last two lines on page 5 and ending with the block in italic on page 8, "A–2." The "A" passages refer to an especially cold day, December 23, 1909.

If we want to straighten the time sequence out, we might read passage A–1 (p. 3), and go right on to A–2 (pp. 5–8), and then back to A–3 (p. 3). Read consecutively, the sequence of events is thoroughly coherent. Benjy wants to go outdoors. In spite of the cold, he is finally allowed to do so. Caddy then returns from school and greets her little brother. But Uncle Maury calls Caddy aside and entrusts her with a letter she is to deliver to a neighbor. Having dismissed Versh (who ordinarily looks after Benjy), Caddy takes Benjy along with her on her walk to the neighbor's house. They have to get there by crawling through a barbed wire fence on which Benjy promptly snags his coat and so has to be freed by Caddy.

But why did Benjy's mind jump from April 7, 1928 (where the novel starts on page 1) to December 23, 1909? Because Luster, who is now looking after him, takes him through a gap in a fence and Benjy catches his clothing on a nail and Luster has to free him. The connection is " 'Cant you never crawl through here without snagging on that nail' " (ll. 2–3, p. 3) and *Caddy uncaught me*," and so forth (l. 4, p. 3).

Benjy's mind is now very much on Caddy, and his memories of the cold day before Christmas Eve. When Luster—we are once more back to April 7, 1928—complains *What are you moaning about*," the answer is Caddy. In fact, in a moment Benjy's mind (if you can call it a mind) is back with Caddy again, as we move to A–2 at the bottom of page 5.

Before the notion of printing in different color inks had been broached, Faulkner had already made use of the switch of typefaces in his manuscript to signal to the reader a shift in the time level, and this device was retained and so presented in the published text. Just how Faulkner meant to use his colored inks, we do not know. Perhaps he meant to print the A section (December 23, 1909) in red; the time of Mr. Compson's death (April, 1912) in blue; the time of Benjy's grandmother's death (in 1898) in green; the present in black; and so on. But since there may be a number of references to the same time level—there are twenty to the date (November 1900) on which Benjy's name was changed from Maury—and since Benjy does not necessarily get all the references to a time level in their proper sequential order—remember that the three A references we used in our illustration went A–3, A–1, and A–2—he might still have had to use some changes in typeface besides the colored-ink differentiation. Presumably, this was what Faulkner planned to do, but the publisher was not willing to use the dozen or more different colors required by Faulkner's proposal, and so Faulkner wrote to his friend Ben Wasson: "I'll just have to save the idea until publishing grows up to it."*

Yet I must not make Benjy's section seem more difficult than it is. Upon opening the book for the first time, the reader should not treat Benjy's monologue as a puzzle to be worked out rather than as a piece of fiction to be savored and enjoyed. If the reader later should want to contemplate the detail of a piece of brilliant literary engineering, help is at hand. Let him or her look at Edmund Volpe's careful dissection in *A Reader's Guide to William Faulkner* or read the article by George R. Stewart and Joseph M. Backus in *American Literature.*

For most readers, and especially for first readers of this novel, it is better to be content with experiencing the general quality of Benjy's world, the confusions in it that cause his sense of baffled helplessness, and the poignance for him of the loss of the one person who genuinely loved him and tried to comfort him, his sister Caddy.

*Michael Millgate, *The Achievement of William Faulkner* (New York, 1966), p. 94.

Though Benjy is almost subhuman in so many respects, he retains certain aspects of his humanity. He retains a dim awareness of the lost Caddy, whom he has not seen for many years now. When he hears golfers call out "caddie" as they play on the course that adjoins the Compson property, the word recalls Caddy to him. He has his own fetishes and talismans: one of Caddy's discarded slippers, bits of glass with which he plays, flowers to hold in his fist, the flicker of flames in the fireplace.

Yet I would misrepresent matters if I suggested that Faulkner's interest in Benjy was a coldly clinical interest in his primitive psychology. Faulkner is interested in Benjy because he tells us something about humanity at large and because he represents the human being reduced to its ultimate dimensions and essentials. In short, Faulkner uses Benjy not to debunk humanity, but to affirm its distinctive quality and value. Benjy calls forth love, and in his own manner he is able to return love.

One fruitful way in which to consider Benjy is to see how he is related to the realm of time. As we have already remarked, events of thirty years past have for him the same immediacy as events of thirty seconds past. In fact, Benjy may be said to live in what is a virtual present. He has no real past and no real future. Benjy's experiences on this plane are very much like an animal's or at least like what we suppose an animal's to be: his life is in effect timeless. He has associations, patternings, habitual couplings of experience just as a dog or a horse has them: the sight of flames somehow soothes him; the sound of Caddy's name stirs him to a vague but aching disquiet. But he has no ordered past to which he can consciously turn. This is what one means by saying that Benjy lives in a virtual present.

There is another and related way of regarding Benjy. He lives in a world of primitive poetry. Everything is concrete. Abstractions are beyond him and so is conceptual language in general. He responds to events in their immediacy. He does not sort them out and reorganize them as most of us do, albeit unconsciously. In this matter, then, Benjy is not so much a mere animal as a very primitive savage.

To repeat: he exists in a world of primitive poetry, whereas the rest of us distinguish between the prosaic, routine aspects of our lives and the poignant and significant moments. Let me illustrate: when Benjy says to himself, as he does continually, "Caddy smelled like trees," he is not trying to be poetic, though his comparison will seem poetic to most of us. Benjy does not even know what he means by saying this beyond the fact that in some wonderful way Caddy does smell to him like a tree. *We* can analyze his metaphorical language if we like. We can say that to Benjy, Caddy smells like a natural, organic plant that has its own dignity and unforced beauty. No wonder that Benjy becomes frantic when Caddy first puts on perfume; the new odor somehow seems to violate her integrity and inner nature since it is artificial, synthetic, unnatural. This is the way in which we might undertake to explain Benjy's violent reaction. But such words would be ours. Benjy is incapable of such articulation, but that is not to say that his inarticulate response is at odds with our interpretation.

I have been insisting on Benjy's limitations, deficiencies, and confusions. In addition, an attentive reading of Benjy's monologue can also give us some sense of the quality of the Compson household: a father, defeated and cynical, who drinks too much; a mother who lacks maternal feeling; a chronic unhappiness between the mother and father; a worthless uncle, Mrs. Compson's brother, who is a sponge, an encumbrance, and a disgusting caricature of the cultivated gentleman; and the four children. And how different the children are: Quentin, the eldest, hypersensitive, ineffectual, unsure of himself; Caddy, the daughter, sweet, natural, loving, brave, and desperate to break out of this hopeless gloom; and Jason, crass, hard, contemptuous of his father and his elder brother. Jason regards his sister as a plain bitch and his idiot brother as simply a nuisance, a family disgrace, a probable obstacle to the worldly success that he craves. If poor Benjy's helplessness in this hopeless situation and his inability even to understand it come home to us, then section one of the book has already done the most important part of its work even if many particular details remain obscure.

Quentin's monologue (section two of the novel) is very different from Benjy's. The thoughts he expresses are those of a highly literate, intelligent, and sensitive young man. Yet Quentin's monologue, like Benjy's, has its own difficulties. In the first place, he is talking to himself—or simply meditating, if you prefer—and he is not taking time to explain his meditations to any outsider. (For him, there are no outsiders: the reader simply overhears his thoughts.)

Benjy cannot explain and, of course, feels no need to explain. Quentin does not need to explain to himself. Thus, there are cryptic allusions to some of his experiences about the exact nature of which we can only guess: to an accident in which Quentin's leg was broken; to a fight that Quentin had with a schoolmate over something that the schoolmate had said about their young woman schoolteacher; and so on. But certain matters of importance to which Quentin's mind keeps returning are clear enough, especially his concern for virginity—for his own, but far more importantly, for Caddy's loss of her virginity and her pregnancy and hurried marriage to provide a name for her expected child. Also important are his feeling that his mother is no mother at all and his several conversations with his cynical father who evidently had heavily influenced Quentin's thinking, but who was able to offer him no consolation and no real guidance. Most of all, we shall find, Quentin is obsessed with a certain code of honor which he feels he must not violate, and with death, as a refuge, a way out of a hopeless situation, and an offering of peace to his tormented spirit.

But before we go further into Quentin's monologue, it may be helpful to compare him with his brother, Benjy, in the matter of their relation to time and in relation to the kind of language they use. Let us begin with the matter of time. Benjy lives in a virtual present and knows neither past nor future; Quentin lives in the past. It is the past which obsesses him and from which he sees no way to extricate himself. The Quentin who is talking to himself in section two is living the last day of his life. He has resolved to drown himself. His life has essentially ended. During these last hours, he is simply killing time until it is time to kill himself.

In a very real sense, Quentin has long been obsessed by the past. He has, for example, refused to accept the fact that his relation to Caddy is bound to change as she becomes a young woman and seeks a mate and a life of her own. He has an impossible wish, nothing less than to arrest the movement of time. Many years ago, Jean-Paul Sartre compared Quentin's situation to that of a man sitting in a speeding convertible automobile and looking backward. Such an observer cannot see where the car is going, nor can he see clearly what is immediately before his eyes as he looks backward. Objects near at hand are too blurred for him to see. The only things that achieve real form and perspective for him are things far down the road in the receding distance.*

Sartre's comparison is excellent. About all that Quentin can see clearly are certain things in the past. Unfortunately Sartre ascribed this situation to Faulkner's characters generally—which is absurd. But it does fit Quentin's perspective perfectly.

As to language: if Benjy's internal monologue has the virtues of a simple, primitive, barbaric poetry, Quentin's reminds one of the decadent poets of the 1890s. In the first place, Quentin's poetry is very "literary." It is mannered and quite consciously "poetic," but it is also languid, tired, and world-weary.

The fact is that Faulkner as a very young man came under the spell of English poets like Swinburne and Wilde and of French poets like Verlaine. He was, in time, to shake off the

*See *Three Decades of Faulkner Criticism*, ed. F. C. Hoffman and Olga Vickery (Ann Arbor: University of Michigan Press, 1960) for an English translation of Sartre's "A Propos de *Le Bruit et la Furor*," *La Nouvelle Revue Française* (52).

world-weary cadences and find his true poetry in his own energetic and muscled prose; but his fictional character, Quentin, has not shaken himself free of such poetry and why should he? The date of his death is 1910. The real point is that Quentin *is* world-weary. His language thoroughly suits his attitudes and psychic condition.

This last observation brings us to the reason for Quentin's suicide. Why has he decided to put an end to his life? I shall propose no simplistic answer, for Quentin is a complex character and the reader needs to respect his complexity. It is not enough, for example, to find Quentin's motive in the fact that he is disconsolate because the Compson family, a family of aristocratic pretensions, has gone to seed, and that his native land is a defeated, poverty-stricken part of the country. It is perfectly true that the family as we see it in *The Sound and the Fury* is in poor estate, and Quentin is fully conscious of its desuetude, but I find little evidence in his long monologue that he is much concerned about the loss of his family's past glories. I can recall only one reference to such glories and even that one merely glances at them. The reference (on p. 125) has to do with something else: Mrs. Compson's insecurity and her hostility toward her husband's family. The fragment in question reads: "do you think so because one of our forefathers was a governor and three were generals and Mother's weren't."

Quentin does come of decayed gentry and he is deeply Southern, but he does not commit suicide for either of these reasons, or for the combination of the two. At least two of Quentin's friends at Harvard are from the South. Gerald Bland is the wealthy Kentuckian who takes—or at least his vapid mother takes—his Southern heritage very seriously. His other friend, Spoade, is from South Carolina, and so Mrs. Bland approves of him, but she cannot forgive him for "having five names, including that of a great English ducal house."

But neither of these young men shows any suicidal tendencies. They are not melancholy at the defeat of the South and in fact are happy-go-lucky. Bland has done so well that Quentin has come to believe that God is not only "a gentleman and a sport; He is a Kentuckian." Even in Jefferson, Mississippi, where the gentry are not as wealthy as Bland or as noble in blood as Spoade, they seem able to bear their fate without too much repining. Within his own family, Quentin is the only one who ever thinks of taking his life.

We shall come closer to Quentin's basic motive for taking his life if we pay attention to his mother. She has somehow withheld her love from her children, all except the loathsome Jason, whom she regards as lacking the selfishness and "false pride" of the Compsons and who is more like her own people.

In his meditations on this last day of his life, Quentin touches on this matter very specifically. Quentin, thinking of his mother, says of his family, "Finished. Finished. Then we were all poisoned." Again, he says to himself, "If I could say Mother. Mother." He is conscious of the fact that he has no mother. Most pointed of all is his memory of an illustration in a book that he and Caddy used to look at (p. 215), a picture of a "dark place into which a single weak ray of light came slanting upon two faces lifted out of the shadow." The picture used to enrage Caddy as a child. She would say, "if I were King . . . I'd break that place open and drag them out and I'd whip them good." The sentiment is characteristic of Caddy. But Quentin's reaction is just as characteristic of him. He broods on the picture, turning back to look at it "until the dungeon was Mother herself she and Father upward into weak light holding hands and us lost somewhere below even them without even a ray of light." It is a measured indictment, uttered to himself, not in heat or in anger, but simply in weary, utter hopelessness.

The impact of the family situation on Caddy is just as drastic, but she reacts in a different way. Looking for warmth, joy, life itself, Caddy loses her virginity to a handsome young man, a stranger in town named Dalton Ames. Later she becomes promiscuous. There is something morbid not take proper care of his own sister and who gets falsely arrested on a charge of molesting another man's sister. Quentin is perceptive, alert, and even shows a certain wisdom. Consider, for example, his definition of the word *nigger*: "a nigger is not a person so much as a form of behaviour; a sort of obverse reflection of the white people he lives among." Or consider his remark on the name of his sister's seducer: "Dalton Ames. It just missed gentility. Theatrical fixture. Just papier-maché. . . ." Or note the quiet relish he takes in his black friend Deacon's answer to the question "Did any Southerner ever play a joke on you?" In his answer Deacon shows himself a diplomat and yet at the same time a realist: "They're fine folks. But you cant live with them." (Deacon was then living in Cambridge, Massachusetts.)

What I take to be the fatal wound inflicted on Quentin's spirit is relived by him in full detail on this last day of his life. During the past summer Quentin had tried to assume the role of the protective brother. When he found that Dalton Ames had seduced Caddy, he approached Dalton with the words: "I've been looking for you two or three days," and proposed that they meet at the bridge over the creek at one o'clock.

Caddy heard Quentin asking T. P. to saddle his horse for one o'clock, and when Caddy asked Quentin what it was that he planned to do, he replied: "None of your business whore whore" and told T. P. he had changed his mind and would walk.

Dalton is waiting at the bridge and Quentin then gives him his ultimatum: he is to leave town. When Dalton says nothing responsive to this, Quentin specifies that he has "until sundown to leave town." And when asked what he will do if Dalton does not, Quentin says, "Ill kill you dont think that just because I look like a kid to you . . ." But Dalton simply asks him how old he is and finally gives him a piece of advice: "listen no good taking it so hard its not your fault kid it would have been some other fellow." When Quentin asks Ames whether he ever had a sister, the reply is *no but theyre all bitches.*

any case, neither in his eyes nor in Caddy's has Quentin provided any real interference. Had Dalton wanted to marry her, he could have taken her off with him at any time. Quentin did not break up a true-love affair and, as we have seen, could not have done so had he wished.

What about Mr. Compson? What responsibility does he have for what happened to Caddy and to Quentin? A great deal, for Quentin, it becomes clear from his monologue, confided much of his anguish to his father and took with real seriousness his father's counsel. Mr. Compson is a kindly man. He loves his children, including Benjy. But he has probably never been a very effectual man, and by the time we meet him in *The Sound and the Fury*, two years before his death, he has failed his children and obviously lost control of the family situation. He is now a beaten man, worn down, and all too ready to take refuge in his decanter of bourbon.

He is not without wit. His brother-in-law, that outrageous fake Southern gentleman, is for him a constant source of merriment—if scarcely innocent merriment. The skepticism and cynicism that he affects is probably genuine enough. But in spite of his show of cynicism about Caddy, he is deeply hurt by her promiscuity. For this, there is plenty of proof. Caddy tells Quentin: "Father will be dead in a year they say if he doesn't stop drinking and he wont stop he cant stop since I since last summer." She is, of course, alluding to her affair with Dalton Ames. What Mr. Compson believes and what he has tried to instill in Quentin is a version of stoicism. One is not to whimper, not to bemoan his fate, but to endure it like a man.

Quentin's father once tells him that "we must just stay awake and see evil done for a little while its not always." Mr. Compson, by the way, did not get this sentiment out of his well-thumbed copy of Horace or even out of the bourbon bottle, but via Faulkner who took it from poem 48 of A. E. Housman's *A Shropshire Lad*. (In the mid-1920s Housman had become Faulkner's favorite poet, and one of the traits in Housman that Faulkner admired was what Faulkner called "the splendor of fortitude.") Lines 11–12 of poem 48 read as follows:

> Be still, be still my soul; it is but for a season:
> Let us endure an hour and see injustice done.

Mr. Compson is obviously paraphrasing these lines when he tells Quentin that we are asked just to "stay awake and see evil done for a little while[.] its not always," but Quentin replies that it does not even have to be a little while "for a man of courage."

When Mr. Compson asks whether he considers that expedient (in other words, suicide) a manifestation of courage, Quentin answers, "yes sir dont you." Mr. Compson refuses to take a stand on the matter, observing that "every man is the arbiter of his own virtues." But Quentin suspects that his father does not believe that he is serious about taking his own life and his father admits that he does not take Quentin's threat seriously.

Mr. Compson turns out to be a really shrewd psychologist. He tells his son "you cannot bear to think that someday it will no longer hurt you like this now" and he goes on to predict that Quentin will not take his life "until [he comes] to believe that even she [Caddy] was not quite worth despair."

Does Quentin finally drown himself because he has come to believe that Caddy was not worth despair? or is it because he fears that if he waits long enough his present despair will indeed die into apathy? We are not told, but his memory of this conversation with his father takes us down to the last page of Quentin's monologue. All that remains—one long paragraph—has to do with such mundane matters as Quentin's need to leave a letter for Shreve in their room, and his washing his teeth and brushing his hat, for Quentin is as meticulous about his final appearance as any Japanese warrior preparing to commit hari-kari. Quentin means at least to die like a gentleman and man of honor.

I have spent perhaps too much time discussing Quentin's character and the motives that expressed themselves in his life, and more importantly in his death. I have suggested that though Quentin is a thoroughly Southern type, his death is not really occasioned by the breakup of the Old South so much as by the breakup of an American family wrecked by parental strife and lack of love. Moreover, I have suggested that Quentin is a very special case—hypersensitive, idealistic, lonely, and almost absurdly romantic—even though in the novel Faulkner has been careful not to make him absurd.

Yet in stressing matters of this sort, I have not spoken in any detail of the power of the writing, sentence by sentence, or the dramatic force of some of the great scenes such as that in which Quentin proposes that he and Caddy commit suicide together and actually holds a knife to her throat. Most of all, I have failed to deal adequately with the atmosphere of the whole monologue, its deeply resonant and sustained quality of anguished suffering as Quentin gets through his last day, literally killing time, for he is quite contemptuous of time. Quentin has already abandoned his watch, having broken it and thrown it in a convenient garbage can. Alive in his head on this final day are the passionate memories of events, situations, confrontations, physical objects, and even sounds and odors of the past such as the smell of honeysuckle which from time to time gets mixed up with everything. Quentin's disastrous past surges and resurges through his head.

He cannot purge his mind of it. Since he can see no future for himself, there is no way out of the past, no way to redeem it; any Christian solution is meaningless to this intense, sad, and terribly honest young man. Having no future, he is indeed condemned to live with his past. He believes the only way out is death.

Oscar Wilde tells us that life imitates art. Maybe so, maybe not. But sometimes there *is* an uncanny resemblance between reality and fiction. A few years ago I read a very moving account of a young man of our time who, because he felt he had nothing to live for, though his body was healthy and though he had a good job and—whether or not he realized it sufficiently—loving parents and friends, resolved to kill himself. He went about it as quietly and methodically as Quentin did. The young man in question, however, had never read *The Sound and the Fury*.

One further note on life's imitating art. On one of the bridges spanning the Charles River in Cambridge, there is a small plaque commemorating Quentin's death on June 2, 1910. It was placed there several years ago by three admirers of *The Sound and the Fury* for whom Quentin's death in the river had become a real happening.

I pointed out above that Benjy lived in a virtual present since his many references to the past are for him indistinguishable from present experiences, and that Quentin is so completely committed to the past that for him even present events have no forward reference, being as dead and as finished as events that are already past. The third brother, Jason, has repudiated the past, and nearly everything that he thinks and does has a reference to the future. He yearns to make money and become a rich man. One means to that goal is to invest in the stock market. He speculates, for example, in futures, gambling on the price that cotton will bring in the months to come. Jason is not, however, a very successful business man. He cannot outguess the future. But his success or failure in dealing with the future is not my point here. I want simply to stress Jason's fixation on the future. He has a contempt for the past nor does he like to savor a present experience. He is not a sensualist or even an epicurean. He is always complaining about his present life.

One might sum up by saying that none of the three Compson brothers has a proper concept of time: Benjy (though through no fault of his own) is locked into a timeless present; Quentin is imprisoned in the past; Jason is fixated on an illusory future. But full humanity needs all three dimensions. I once met Jason in the flesh, though of course that was not his name. It was long ago in a New Orleans boardinghouse where I sojourned for a few weeks. It was my first experience in what seemed to me a charming, almost old-world city, mellow and gracious, and so I was shocked to hear my Jason remark one evening at the dinner table that he wished the whole of the French Quarter would burn down or be demolished. He believed the quaint old city was an obstacle to progress and good business. This outburst was typical of what I heard from my Jason in the weeks that followed. So when, years later, I read *The Sound and the Fury*, I knew that Faulkner had not really exaggerated. The type did exist.

In the matter of language, I have already suggested that Benjy's was a very simple language which, in some of his expressions, amounted to a primitive poetry, very concrete, very close to a world of immediate sensation. I suggested further that Quentin's language was also highly personal, but filled with literary allusions and reminiscent of late Victorian poets and the poets of the nineties.

What about the style of Jason's monologue? One's first impulse is to describe it as the antithesis of poetry, and in so far as we associate poetry with what is high-hearted and ardent and generous, Jason's language is certainly antipoetic. It is meant to cut and wound, and it does that. But Jason's monologue does possess verve and rhetorical power. It is a language bursting with intensity. Indeed, if we adopt Ezra Pound's definition of poetry as language fully charged with meaning, Jason's outburst does rise quite often to a kind of demonic poetry.

Listen to his opening paragraph. We are now back to April 6, 1928, Good Friday morning. Jason is speaking to his mother, and the subject of his diatribe is his niece, Caddy's daughter, whom Caddy had named Quentin in memory of her dead brother. The young Quentin had been brought as an infant to the Compson household to be reared. She is now seventeen, has been cutting her high school classes, and is beginning to get a reputation as one of the easy-to-get girls in town. But listen to Jason on the subject of Quentin:

Once a bitch always a bitch, what I say. I says you're

lucky if her playing out of school is all that worries you. I says she ought to be down there in that kitchen right now, instead of up there in her room, gobbing paint on her face and waiting for six niggers that cant even stand up out of a chair unless they've got a pan full of bread and meat to balance them, to fix breakfast for her. (P. 223)

Jason's indictment of Quentin is partly true, but as we shall find, his treatment of the girl is largely responsible for what she has become. His indictment of the black servants is not true at all. It is Dilsey, the cook and general servant, who actually holds together what is left of the Compson family. She is as much a mother as the forlorn and twisted Quentin will ever know. She looks after the chronically whining Mrs. Compson, who certainly does not control her delinquent niece. Dilsey is the only person who occasionally overawes Jason himself. And, of course, it is Dilsey who does what little can be done for the unfortunate Benjy, who is now a lumbering man of thirty-three, but who still possesses an infantile mind.

Further comment on Dilsey, however, can be postponed until later in this chapter. After all, the third section of the novel is Jason's. He deserves his day in court, and though his testimony will for any sensible jury amount to hanging evidence against him, Faulkner wants us to hear him out as a witness in his own defense.

One of the things that we learn early in Jason's section is the damage that he, primarily, and his mother, secondarily, have done to the girl Quentin. Caddy, her mother, was badly warped by having to grow up in the Compson household. Mrs. Compson, for example, had put on mourning when she learned that Caddy had allowed a boy to kiss her. Certainly that is neurotic behavior! But Caddy did get some nurture from her association with her father and her brother, Quentin. Now the household is limited to a neurotic grandmother, an idiot uncle, and the cruel and even sadistic uncle Jason. What has happened as a result to Quentin's psyche comes out early in this section of the novel.

Quentin has become so callous and so embittered that she has no real feeling of kindness even for the one person who tries to give her something of a mother's love. Witness what happens when Dilsey puts her hand on the girl. Jason has threatened to strike Quentin with his belt. Dilsey tries to shame him out of this action. But Quentin is afraid that Jason means business, and appeals to Dilsey. Dilsey reassures her: "I aint gwine let him. Dont you worry, honey." Dilsey grasps Jason by the arm, only to be flung off. Mrs. Compson comes down the stairs when she hears voices raised. At that point Jason finally says: "We'll just put this off a while," but he calls Quentin a slut. Yet now that the immediate danger is past, when Dilsey utters a reassuring word to Quentin once more and puts her hand on her, Quentin knocks it down, and shouts at Dilsey, "You damn old nigger." Caddy would never have spoken to Dilsey in these terms. The girl Quentin's family environment is much worse than what her mother's had been.

Thus Quentin has been more sinned against than sinning, and she is at least partially aware of how much she has become warped. Later that morning Quentin says to Jason that she wishes she had never been born, and more definitely, "I'm bad and I'm going to hell, and I don't care. I'd rather be in hell than anywhere where you are."

So much for Jason's role as head of the Compson household. How does he stand with the town, his business associates, and his fellow workers? Jason's own account of the events that occur on April 6 make very plain in what kind of esteem he is held.

We get a revealing glimpse later in the morning. Earl, who owns the store where Jason works, calls out to Job, a black man who also works in the store, and Job's name sets Jason off on a tirade against the blacks. "What this country needs," Jason opines, "is white labour. Let these damn trifling niggers starve for a couple of years, then they'd see what a soft thing they have."

Later, an out-of-town salesman comes in, and over a Coca-Cola Jason sounds off to him about the Jews. Cotton, he remarks, is a speculator's crop. The red-neck farmer gets no more than a bare living from it. What does he really work for? ". . . so a bunch of damn eastern jews," he begins, but noticing the expression on the salesman's face, Jason adds: "No offense. I give every man his due, regardless of religion or anything else. I have nothing against jews as an individual. It's just the race." Jason's grammar gets too scrambled here to allow us to make any precise sense of what he is saying. But the quality of Jason himself comes through clearly enough.

What does Earl think of Jason? We learn eventually. Jason has of late been leaving the store to send his broker a wire about his futures holdings and for other matters of his personal concern. When Earl makes an inquiry about where he had gone, Jason tells him a lie about having had to go to the dentist. Then he turns defiant. If Mr. Earl does not like the way he conducts himself, he knows what he can do about it. Earl replies that he has indeed known for some time what he could do about it, and that "If it hadn't been for your mother I'd have done it [dismissed you] before now, too. She's a lady I've got a lot of sympathy for. . . ."

Yet it is one of Jason's fellow employees in the store who describes most nearly the restless, malicious, mean-spirited nature of the man.

When old Job drives up with the delivery wagon, Jason teases him for having played hooky from his job by sneaking off to the afternoon performance of the visiting show that has come to town. Jason asks him, "Was it a good show?" Old Job replies: "I aint been yit. But I kin be arrested in dat tent tonight, dough." Jason persists in his charge that Job has just come from the show; yet he reassures Job by telling him that "You may can fool [Mr. Earl]. I wont tell on you."

Job replies: "Den he's de onliest man here I'd try to fool. Whut I want to waste my time foolin a man whut I dont keer whether I sees him Sat'dy night er not? I wont try to fool you.

You too smart fer me. . . . Aint a man in dis town kin keep up wid you fer smartness. You fools a man whut so smart he cant even keep up wid hisself" (pp. 311–12). And when Jason inquires who that man can be, Job replies, "Dat's Mr Jason Compson."

It is a discerning judgment and a true one. Jason is proud that he is not an impractical dreamer, not a person bemused by the past or by tradition, but a man who believes in nothing except the almighty dollar. Jason's rationality, however, is self-defeating. He does succeed in outsmarting himself. He turns out to be the most deluded dreamer of all, and the greatest of his delusions is the dream itself, which is not attractive but in reality ugly and stultifying.

In the critical commentary on Faulkner's work, there has been a persistent tendency to regard Jason with more sympathy than I am willing to allow him. It is argued that Jason, after all, is the person responsible for holding together the Compson family fortunes. He is the breadwinner, the head of the household, the person who is really trying to prop up the decaying walls of the house of Usher. Furthermore, he is the one member of the family who has accepted present reality and dismissed the enervating myth of the Southern past.

Jason does like to think of himself exactly in these terms. Listen to him on page 286: "I haven't got much pride, I can't afford it with a kitchen full of niggers to feed and robbing the state asylum of its star freshman. Blood, I says, governors and generals. It's a damn good thing [the Compsons] never had any kings and presidents; we'd all be down there [in the insane asylum] at Jackson chasing butterflies."

Yet an attentive reading of the novel makes clear that Jason's prowess as a breadwinner is not very great. He has retained his job in the hardware store because Earl is sorry for his mother. Jason's speculations in the market have shown no special shrewdness. On the one day that we see Jason in action, his account is sold out for lack of margin. His automobile has been bought with money got from his mother under false pretenses. An important amount of Jason's income is derived from funds that Caddy has provided for Quentin's clothes and upkeep, funds from which Jason is systematically stealing. Far from being the family provider, he is utterly selfish and quite cold-blooded in using for himself money that he has not earned.

One does not rail at Jason, however, because he is a poor provider. What condemns him is not so much what he does or fails to do, but what he is. His torturing of Quentin is pointless except as an indulgence of his hatred and contempt for her. Jason loves to torment any person in his power. Witness the scene in which he tantalizes Luster with tickets to the visiting show.

The novel opens with Luster's attempt to find the quarter that he has lost. This money was to buy his ticket to the show and Luster is simply dying to see it. Jason has been given a couple of complimentary tickets. He offers to sell one of them to Luster at a cut-rate price, though knowing all along that Luster does not have a cent to his name. Jason holds the tickets alluringly over the open lid of the woodburning stove. First, he drops one into the flames, and then having offered the other to Luster for a mere five cents, finally drops it in too. Dilsey reproaches him: "A big growed man like you. Git on outen my kitchen." There is a streak of sadism in Jason.

A far worse instance occurred at the time of Mr. Compson's death. Caddy, though by this time banished as a fallen woman from Jefferson by her mother and Jason, has secretly returned for her father's funeral. No one has notified her. She just happened to see the notice of it in a newspaper. But, of course, Caddy wants to see her baby and offers Jason fifty dollars if he will arrange it. He refuses, then she raises the amount. She will give Jason one hundred dollars if he will let her see the baby just for a minute, and she promises to leave town again—to go right away. Jason, always the business man, wants to be paid in advance, and when Caddy prefers to pay him afterward, asks her: "Dont you trust me," to which Caddy replies, "No. I know you. I grew up with you."

But Jason holds the whip hand now, so he is able to extort

payment beforehand. At last Jason agrees to let Caddy see her child: he gives her literally one glimpse of the baby. Caddy is waiting on a designated corner under a street light. Jason hires a hack and has himself, holding the baby in his arms, driven to where she is standing. He holds the child to the window for a moment and, as Caddy jumps forward to touch the child, orders the driver to hit the horses with his whip, and the hack goes past Caddy, as Jason himself says, "like a fire engine."

This is a truly devilish way to play with a mother's natural feelings, and Caddy properly insists on having another chance to see her child. This time she does not ask Jason's permission. She seeks Dilsey's help and gets it. Jason, learning of it later, is naturally furious with Dilsey, but Dilsey stands her ground: "I like to know," she says, "whut's de hurt in lettin dat chile see her own baby." And she remarks that were Jason's father still alive, matters would be different. "You's a cold man, Jason," she tells him, and adds a very significant clause, "if man you is."

Dilsey's is a very pertinent question. Is a being as mean-spirited and cold-hearted as Jason a credible human being? Or is he simply a libel on mankind, a monster, an unbelievable caricature because no human being could be so cruel? Human beings unfortunately *can* be so cruel. The events in our own century have done a good deal to restore our belief in the ultimate depths of human depravity. Yet our renewed realism about the possibilities for human evil do not exactly solve the problem for the artist. He has to do more than point to the record of history or to accounts of abnormal psychology. The novelist is concerned not merely with fact but with probable truth. He has to keep his character humanly interesting, which means in practice interesting to other human beings.

Though Faulkner pushes Jason close to the distortions of caricature, he does provide him with at least one interesting trait. Jason has a real ability to entertain us—even if we are entertained sometimes almost against our will. If Jason did not inherit his father's kindness, he did inherit something of Mr. Compson's wit. For instance, both father and son find Uncle Maury funny. Here, for example, is a young Jason describing Uncle Maury at Mr. Compson's funeral.

So he kept on patting [Mother's] hand and saying "Poor little sister," patting her hand with one of the black gloves that we got the bill for four days later. . . . He kept on patting her hand with his black glove. . . . He took them off when his time with the shovel came. . . . [Then a few minutes later] when I stepped back around the back I could see him behind a tombstone, taking another one out of a bottle. (Pp. 245, 249)

There is another sense in which we can make use of Dilsey's question about whether Jason is a real man, though it is a sense which Dilsey probably did not have in mind. Each of the three Compson brothers is incomplete. Obviously, Benjy is, but on reflection we have to concede that so is Quentin and so is Jason. Benjy is a man cut down almost to the level of mere sensation and instinct. Quentin is a man who is emotional, reflective, sentimental, and idealistic. He lacks stamina and judgment. Though Jason has his emotional side too—hatred and envy *are* emotions—he has consciously tried to make himself hard, detached, rational, and pragmatic. It is almost as if Faulkner had taken a normal man and separated his nature into three partial men. I dare say that Faulkner did not have this consciously in mind. Yet his turning the three brothers into partial men is an effective way of presenting the disintegration of a family. A number of other contemporary authors have used something like this technique as a way of dramatizing the breakup of civilization itself. One thinks immediately of James Joyce.

One further aspect of the third section of the book deserves mention at this point: as we read on into the novel, circumstances and events become clearer and clearer. For most readers Benjy's section is the most confused. Quentin's section has its difficulties, though the emotional patterns are more readily discernible and it is much easier to follow Quentin's shifts from past to present. Real daylight, however, begins to break upon the reader when he enters Jason's section. Jason's is a shallow mind essentially and he often does not understand what he thinks he understands perfectly. Throughout Jason's monologue, events and circumstances are burnished bright, and the colors are all primary. There is no haziness, no half lights, no clouds of mystery, in the mental world that Jason inhabits.

Even so, in Jason's section we are being presented with a very partial and biased account of events. (We can see this all the more clearly having already read Benjy's and Quentin's sections.) In sum, Jason, for all his vaunt of being a get-down-to-brass-tacks man, is just as obsessed as are his two brothers. Our view of the truth about Caddy and the Compsons in general will have to come, in part at least, from our ability to use the distortions in these accounts to cancel one another out and lead us to a conception that is self-consistent and that at least approximates the truth.

Such an effort receives further help from the fact that in the last section of the book the author shifts to third-person narration. We find ourselves for the first time now viewing characters and events not through the interpretations of one limited mind with all its biases and distortions, but peering into something that looks and feels like objectivity.

The date of the events narrated in the last section is April 8. It is Easter morning. It will be a momentous day for the Compsons. Of the three Compsons, however, only the idiot Benjy attends church services, and he does so, of course, because Dilsey takes him. Yet if the symbol hunter is desperate to find in this part of the book some Easter symbol, I'm afraid that he will have to be satisfied with the girl Quentin's empty room as reflecting ironically Christ's empty tomb on Easter morning. With readers who regard such a collocation as savagely ironic, even bitterly sarcastic, I shall have to agree. But if, as so many have proposed, it is Benjy who is to be regarded as a Christ-figure, such symbolism will have to be regarded as savagely ironic too: for Benjy's sufferings accomplish nothing and avail nothing. Besides, if we want to take into account Good Friday (April 6) it is the girl Quentin whose "crucifixion" we witness that day as Jason savages her. She is the consciously suffering victim, not Benjy who is scarcely aware of what is happening to him. But I am inclined to think that most commentators have tried to press the Christian symbolism further than it was ever meant to go, or will go.

The significance of the novel's paschal references seems to me to amount to not much more than this: the Compsons are generally bereft of Christian hope. Mr. Compson brought up his children, we are told, to believe that all men were just "dolls stuffed with sawdust swept up from the trash heap where all previous dolls had been thrown away the sawdust flowing from what wound in what side that not for me died not." Mrs. Compson believes in a kind of sentimental Christianity, but *believes* is really too strong a word. She simply likes to have her Bible (usually unopened) by her as a talisman.

She states her real creed when she tells Dilsey: "Whoever God is, He would not permit [the girl Quentin to bring one more scandal on the family by committing suicide]. I'm a lady. You might not believe that from my offspring, but I am." Poor Mrs. Compson, worried that her family was not as good as her husband's and in any crisis protesting to the bitter end that she is a lady. Jason, of course, mocks at Christianity. Dilsey is a believer, and her faith sustains her, but that is a different situation altogether.

Faulkner does not present Dilsey as a plaster saint. Her expression is "at once fatalistic and of a child's astonished disappointment"; that is to say that Dilsey rather expects to be disappointed though she has never become really reconciled to it. In short, hers is a fatalism that does not crowd out Christian hope, but hers is a chastened hope. She is constantly astonished that so many things go so badly, but she does not subside into despair.

Dilsey's faith puts her in a special relation to time. If Benjy lives in a virtual present, Quentin, having no future, lives in the past, and Jason, having repudiated the past, lives only in the future, then Dilsey's time includes the concept of eternity. She believes in an eternal order, and so the failures of the past, the daily disappointments, and her own meager prospects for the future, do not daunt her. Dilsey believes that goodness will prevail in time or, rather, in a realm outside time. She knows, then, what time is worth and what it is not worth, and so can properly evaluate time.

A number of people have pointed out the appropriateness of Dilsey's comment when her battered cabinet clock strikes five times. At that moment Dilsey announces that it is eight o'clock, for she can tell the time even when the clock has to be corrected.

The last section of the novel is not, as I have already indicated, a monologue spoken by Dilsey, nor is it entirely about Dilsey. Much of it concerns Jason in his futile chase after his niece Quentin. Yet somehow Dilsey does seem to dominate this section and, symbolically, this makes sense, for it is Dilsey who has tried to hold the doomed family together. It is she who has observed its comings and goings through the years and who is able to say, when the girl Quentin disappears, that she has "seed de first en de last."

When Quentin does not come down to breakfast on this Easter morning and when she will not answer a knock on her door, her uncle Jason properly fears for the worst. He demands the key from Mrs. Compson and when it is not immediately forthcoming, he drops all pretense of regard for his mother and bellows at her: "Give me the key, you old fool!" He takes the key from her roughly and enters Quentin's room. The description of the room provides an effective account of what poor Quentin's growing up in this household had made of her. A careful reading of the passage is the best testimony to Faulkner's brilliance as a writer. Here is the room:

It was not a girl's room. It was not anybody's room, and

the faint scent of cheap cosmetics and the few feminine objects and the other evidences of crude and hopeless efforts to feminize it but added to its anonymity, giving it that dead and stereotyped transience of rooms in assignation houses. The bed had not been disturbed. On the floor lay a soiled undergarment of cheap silk a little too pink; from a half open bureau drawer dangled a single stocking. The window was open. A pear tree grew there, close against the house. It was in bloom and the branches scraped and rasped against the house and the myriad air, driving in the window, brought into the room the forlorn scent of the blossoms. (P. 352)

The disappearance of Quentin galvanizes Jason into activity. He hurries to investigate the closet in his own room and finds that someone has forced the metal box that he had hidden beneath the closet floor, broken the lock, and taken out the cash. His hidden savings, most of it the money that he has, over the years, stolen from the sums that Caddy had sent for her daughter's expenses—all is gone. Jason at once calls the sheriff.

I have already hinted at what the Jefferson community thinks of Jason—what his employer thinks of him, what old Job thinks of him, and so on. Jason's meeting with the sheriff fills out the story. Jason reports that he is certain that Quentin has taken the money and eloped with a young man connected with the visiting show that had performed the night before in Jefferson. On Friday, Jason had seen Quentin in a car being driven by the same young man, who was then wearing a red tie. But the sheriff procrastinates. He cannot promise to drive to Mottstown where the show is to perform next and where Jason is convinced that Quentin can be found. Instead, the sheriff asks Jason what he was doing with three thousand dollars hidden in the house and whether his mother knew that he had that much money in the house. Moreover, the sheriff wonders what Jason intends to do with Quentin when he catches her.

Jason is furious that the sheriff would ask such questions. These matters are none of the sheriff's business. Technically, they may not be, but the sheriff knows what he is doing. "You drove that girl into running off, Jason," the sheriff says. "You drove her away from home. And I have some suspicions about who that money belongs to that I dont reckon I'll ever know for certain."

In conclusion, he tells Jason that if Jason had any actual proof that Quentin had stolen the money, "I'd have to act. But without that I dont figger it's any of my business." Jason, thus dismissed, sets out for Mottstown in his own car to try to find Quentin and the young man. The sheriff may have cut some legal corners, but the reader knows by this time that the sheriff has actually meted out a kind of rough justice. He knows further that Jason's general meanness and his persecution of his niece are suspected, if not positively known, in the community. Why should they not be, granted the compactness of the community and the concreteness of personal relationships in it?

Meanwhile, Dilsey, her son Luster, her daughter Frony, and Benjy have departed for Dilsey's church. Frony is somewhat disturbed by Benjy's presence and tells her mother frankly that she ought not to keep on bringing Benjy to church. "Folks talkin." But Dilsey says she knows what kind of folks, "Trash white folks. . . . Thinks he aint good enough for white church, but nigger church aint good enough fer him." Frony insists that folks will talk just the same, but Dilsey tells Frony to send such talkers to her. She knows what to tell them: ". . . de good Lawd dont keer whether he smart er not. Dont nobody but white trash keer dat." Dilsey's theology is sound. The Angelic Doctor could not improve on her statement.

The preacher for the occasion, imported from St. Louis, does not look like much to the assembled congregation and he does start off slowly. He "sounded like a white man." His sermon is a little formal, cold, even empty. But after a while he changes the rhythm of his speech and the quality of his voice. "It was as different as day and dark from his former tone, with a sad, timbrous quality like an alto horn, sinking into their hearts and speaking there again when it had ceased in fading and cumulate echoes." The change electrifies the congregation and the preacher, now a voice of power speaking to their condition, lifting up their hearts, moves on, up and up, from one climax to another.

His is a sermon about the crucifixion, about the shedding of the blood of the Lamb, and about the triumphant Resurrection. I can only allude here to its general theme and to its effect on the congregation. It has to be read in its entirety (see pp. 367–70). Brief excerpts will not serve.

Dilsey is much moved and tears run down her cheeks, tears that she makes no effort to wipe away, even when Frony warns her as they walk home that people are looking at her. For Dilsey, the sermon evidently has a special application to the Compsons. Dilsey knows that Quentin has run away, and in spite of Dilsey's quieting words to Mrs. Compson, Dilsey knows that Quentin is probably gone forever. Benjy, walking home beside her, is, of course, unaware of the excitement in the Compson household this morning and will probably scarcely notice her absence. So Dilsey feels the loss doubly, sorrowing for Benjy and with Benjy. No wonder she says, "Ive seed de first en de last. . . . I seed de beginnin, en now I sees de endin."

The Compson line has effectually ended. Jason will never marry. Neither he nor Benjy will have a child to carry on the line. Caddy has long since fled and now her daughter has also fled. But though Dilsey's words point to the ending of a family, she is obviously moved by considerations far deeper than the mere vanishing of a family name. She is moved by the spectacle of human waste, of promise that has come to nothing, of love and human concern that have been spilled on the ground, of potential goodness that did not fulfill itself.

Meanwhile, Jason's expedition in search of Quentin comes to nothing. He does get to Mottstown and locates the railroad cars in which the show travels; but when in his rage to find

Quentin he screams at a little old man in one of the cars, "Where are they?" and then when asked "Who?" barks out "Dont lie to me," the little man is infuriated, calls Jason a bastard, and manages to secure a rusty hatchet and tries his best to kill him. Jason is rescued by someone else connected with the show. His rescuer denies that the pair Jason is seeking are any longer with the show. Jason by this time is too much intimidated to call this man a liar, and he is still too shaken by the little old man's determined attempt on his life. Jason knows he is beaten and he finds himself in no condition to drive his car. He sits behind the wheel of the car, "with his invisible life ravelled out about him like a wornout sock." Finally, he succeeds in hiring a black man to drive him back to Jefferson.

At the Compson place, fourteen-year-old Luster is still reliving his night at the show, for Frony had given him a quarter for a ticket. Luster is as usual in charge of Benjy. It is now afternoon and, since it is Sunday, the golfers are out on the course which adjoins the Compson property. One golfer calls for a caddie, and Benjy begins to whimper. But on this day of Compson disaster, he must be kept quiet, if that is possible. Dilsey, in some desperation, decides to pacify Benjy by giving him his accustomed Sunday ride to the cemetery, even though T. P., another of Dilsey's sons, is not available to drive the surrey.

Luster, mischievous little Luster, who likes to tease Benjy, swears to his mother that he can drive the surrey and that he will be careful and drive it right. So, having cautioned Luster once more, Dilsey tells Benjy, "You's de Lawd's chile, anyway. En I be His'n too, fo long, praise Jesus." She buttons Benjy's coat and sends the pair off.

Benjy, once they are in motion, stops whimpering, but being in the driver's seat is more than Luster can handle. Once out of sight of the house, he breaks off a branch to serve as a switch, with a view to speeding up the journey. As they approach the courthouse square, he tells Benjy: "Dar Mr Jason's car. . . . Les show dem niggers how quality does,

Benjy. . . . Whut you say?" He gives old Queenie a taste of the switch and swings her to the left of the monument as he prepares to circle the square.

Suddenly Benjy begins to bellow his loudest. Why? Because the habitual route requires turning to the *right* of the monument. For Benjy to pass a familiar landmark in the wrong order is catastrophic. The whole structure of Benjy's world at once collapses. Luster is horrified at what he has done. But it is too late. Jason, now back in town and already in an ugly mood, rushes up and hits Luster over the head with his fist. He reaches back and strikes Benjy, ordering him to shut up, and then orders Luster to take Benjy home. But in reversing the direction of the surrey, the proper sequence to the cemetery is restored. Benjy stops bellowing. He sits in the surrey with eyes "empty and blue and serene again as cornice and façade flowed smoothly once more from left to right; post and tree, window and doorway, and signboard, each in its ordered place."

Proper succession in spatial arrangements is the kind of order that Benjy knows and values. Since Benjy is an idiot, human life is largely full of sound and fury, some of which Benjy himself can provide, but signifying very little besides certain functional associations and spatial arrangements. But Benjy's brothers are not in a much better case. Quentin killed himself because he had come to the conclusion that life was meaningless. What is the meaning of life to Jason? Nothing more than the accumulation of money and the achievement of respectability that Jason believes only wealth brings. Jason has tried to reduce every human relationship to its cash value. Even love itself becomes a bought-and-paid-for relationship. Small wonder that Jason declares that he has every "respect for a good honest whore." With such a woman, Jason knows where he stands.

None of these "faiths," including Mr. Compson's stoicism and Mrs. Compson's confidence that she is a "lady," are steady enough to see them through the disasters that befall them. But for Dilsey, in spite of her hardships, life does have meaning. Her religion, her belief in the eternal, rids her of some of the terrors of time and mortality. But for all the Compsons, not just Benjy, life is a tale signifying nothing.

Yet one ought to remark that Faulkner is writing a novel, not a moral tract. He does not insist that there be a moral. He does not flourish it in the reader's face. Furthermore, Faulkner is a realist. He is well aware that Dilsey's religion is not available to a great many people in our modern world.

The Sound and the Fury, it ought to be clear, is primarily a book about the modern world and only incidentally about the South. The Southern elements, to be sure, are very important. But the book is essentially about the disintegration of a family, of a tradition, and of a culture. The Southern setting perhaps renders these lesions and dissolutions more poignant simply because the South as a region is still family-centered, stubbornly traditional, and old-fashioned. But the disintegrating forces are not limited to the South; they are national and international. And the problems generated by the breakup of a culture are epidemic throughout the entire Western world. Maybe this is why this book, so markedly difficult in certain ways, has proved, nevertheless, the easiest of all Faulkner's novels for students of our present time to understand.

4 · AS I LAY DYING

As I Lay Dying is one of Faulkner's most accomplished works. He frequently referred to it as a tour de force, but his descriptive phrase was not very happily chosen. The novel is much more than a clever trick, a mere exhibition of skill. Faulkner probably meant to allude to the comparative ease with which he says he wrote it.

As I Lay Dying engages some of his most profound observations about human nature. This shortest of his novels makes an impact quite out of proportion to its length. The plot is one of Faulkner's simplest: as the novel opens, Addie Bundren is on her deathbed; she dies, the funeral service is held, her husband and children load her coffin onto a farm wagon, and what turns out to be a ten days' journey to the spot where she had insisted that she be buried begins. On that journey, they encounter all sorts of difficulties, but nothing deters them until Addie's body is at last underground.

In doing this, the Bundrens are not, as some careless commentators have thought, following the custom of the country. Their neighbors are actually appalled, and in view of what happens to an unembalmed body after a week's travel under the summer sun, their noses are gravely offended. But Faulkner's purpose is not to provide horror for horror's sake. He is a realist in this novel, as he is so often elsewhere, but we are mistaken if we read the tale of the Bundrens as an exposure of squalor and degradation. In *As I Lay Dying* the author provides his reader with an examination of quixotic idealism, including its folly as well as its genuine heroism. For the Bundrens' journey is indeed a quixotic quest. But the elaboration of these matters must wait upon some account of the way in which Faulkner has presented his characters.

If the plot of the novel is very simple, the technique of presentation is not. Nothing is told by the author in his own person and on his own authority. Instead, the novel is broken into fifty-nine segments, each assigned to a character in the novel. We are not told to whom the character is addressing his comments. Sometimes, in fact, he simply seems to be talking to himself.

Naturally, Faulkner is careful to have each person speak in character, but, since few of the people who figure in *As I Lay Dying* are very literate, Faulkner often endows them with a vocabulary that they do not in reality possess. This is a literary convention that the reader has to accept, and that acceptance, once made, pays handsome dividends. We are thus enabled to penetrate much more deeply into the complexities of their minds than we could otherwise, for we must remember that Faulkner has in this novel denied himself the privileges of an omniscient author.

On the other hand, when a character tells what he actually said to another person on this or that occasion, he always falls back into his vernacular speech. Thus, Vernon Tull will say to his wife Cora: ". . . I will help [Anse Bundren] out if he gets into a tight, with her sick and all. Like most folks around here, I done holp him so much already I cant quit now." Yet, a few lines earlier in this segment, this same unimaginative man can produce a bit of description like this: "[Anse's] eyes look like pieces of burnt-out cinder fixed in his face, looking out over the land." Or Dewey Dell Bundren, who addresses her father, her brothers, and everyone else in the authentic hill dialect of north Mississippi, is capable, when she tries to express her own feelings to herself, of using a very different sort of utterance. The girl is desperate with worry over her unwanted pregnancy: "I dont know whether I am worrying or not. Whether I can or not. I dont know whether I can cry or not. I dont know whether I have tried to or not. I feel like a wet seed wild in the hot blind earth."

Faulkner's technique of presentation bears directly on an important theme in this novel: the ultimate isolation of every human being from the rest of humanity. Perhaps in no other work does Faulkner stress so powerfully the final aloneness of the individual. Addie Bundren, for example, feels cut off from her husband and even from most of her children. She apparently had no close friend in the community in whom she could confide. Dewey Dell, her daughter, has no one about her to whom she can speak of her anxieties. Addie's son, Jewel, is close-mouthed, hugging his own problems to himself. The reader's sense of each character's isolation is strengthened by the fact that in reading the story of the Bundrens the reader is always inside some individual's mind —that person's memory of what was said or done on a particular occasion or his reflections on it or his inner meditation on his or her own plight.

Like *The Sound and the Fury*, this novel is centered on a family. Though the Bundren family represents a very different social class from that of the Compsons, there are a few resemblances. Addie Bundren, the strong-minded mother, is a very different sort of woman from the weak, complaining hypochondriac Mrs. Compson, but these two women in their very different ways exert an enormous influence on their families. Mr. Compson and Anse Bundren, though they stand at polar extremes in birth, breeding, and personality, are alike in failing to cope with their families' problems. In spite of obvious differences, there are also some resemblances among the children of the two families. Darl, who goes mad in the end, has much of Quentin's introspection and special insights. Whereas Jason Compson merely thinks of himself as practical, rational, and firmly based in reality, Cash Bundren is in fact a patient, practical man. Jason's claim to these virtues is fraudulent; he is at the mercy of his passions and impulses. Vardaman, the young Bundren boy, resembles, even if only remotely, Benjy Compson. Vardaman presumably will some day grow up, whereas Benjy never will.

Dewey Dell is too much the primitive, untutored girl to have any close likeness to Caddy Compson. She lacks Caddy's spirit and therefore feels even more desperately isolated than Caddy ever does. Jewel Bundren has no remote counterpart among the Compson children. He is high-spirited, resolute, instinctively brave, even foolhardy. As we shall find later, he is no son of the phlegmatic Anse Bundren. He is indeed his mother's child, with all of her contempt for mere words and her dedication to deeds. No wonder that he is her favorite child. Jewel is one of the least articulate characters in this novel, and significantly, Faulkner assigns only one segment to his thoughts. We see much of him and hear of him in some detail from other characters, but Faulkner, probably very wisely, does not permit him to try to express his thoughts and feelings directly to the reader.

Interestingly enough, Faulkner allows only one segment to Addie Bundren, though she seems to be fully articulate. Before her marriage to Anse she was a schoolteacher. Her one passage of direct speech is quite long and highly interesting.

Why did her creator not allow her a fuller utterance? Perhaps because Faulkner knew that a powerful human force can often be presented most effectively through an indirect method—letting that force remain almost as invisible as the wind and, like the wind, become apparent only by its influence as seen in tossing trees and unroofed barns. Addie, dead in her coffin, is, in a very real sense, the most dynamically alive being on the Bundren wagon.

To give Addie few words of direct expression is in conformity with her character. She is a bitterly disappointed woman, who feels that she has been cheated by the words offered her throughout her life, and thus feels a contempt for words. In the one passage assigned to her, she tells us how she came to distrust words:

I learned that words are no good; that words dont ever fit even what they are trying to say at. . . . And so when Cora Tull would tell me I was not a true mother, I would think how words go straight up in a thin line, quick and harmless, and how terribly doing goes along the earth, clinging to it, so that after a while the two lines are too far apart for the same person to straddle from one to the other; and that [the words] sin and love and fear are just sounds that people who never sinned nor loved nor feared have for what they never had and cannot have until they forget the words. (Pp. 163, 165–66)

In spite of her contempt for words, how well this woman can use them! In another passage she rises to poetry when she says that the "words that are not deeds . . . are just the gaps in peoples' lacks, coming down like the cries of the geese out of the wild darkness in the old terrible nights, fumbling at the deeds like orphans to whom are pointed out in a crowd two faces and told, That is your father, your mother" (p. 166).

Addie's distrust of words is an aspect of her total philosophy of life. She has not only been radically disappointed in her life, but also isolated from almost all the rest of humankind. She is a woman of furious intensity who is still unfulfilled, and now she is hopeless of finding any genuine fulfillment. Her husband, Anse, is surely the most contemptible character that Faulkner ever created. Her lover and the father of her son Jewel, the Reverend Mr. Whitfield (we never learn his first name), also proves unworthy of this fierce devotee to utter truth, though Addie does not live to hear her lover's final shameful retreat into vapid words.

When Whitfield learns that Addie is dying, he sets out for the Bundrens' to conduct her funeral service. He decides that at the service he must make a public confession of their adultery, but as he nears the end of his journey, he is told that Addie is already dead—and realizes that she has kept secret their guilty relationship. At once he tells himself that

God in His mercy has reprieved him: he will not need to confess to his parishioners, including Anse. God will accept his earlier sincere resolution to confess as sufficient, "will accept the will for the deed." Thus the unspoken words will be enough. Addie's cynicism is fully confirmed.

In dismissing words as meaningless, Addie has also given up what she regards as a spurious spirituality. One might call her basic philosophy a kind of transcendental materialism, for she has simply inverted the Christian doctrine. Since the soul is nothing, the body itself must be everything, and so, transcendentally important, for only the tangible is truly real. Addie tells Cora that "he" will save her from the fire and the flood. The conventionally pious Cora thinks at first that Addie is referring to Christ, but soon realizes that Addie is referring to her son Jewel, who in the course of the journey actually does save her decomposing body from both perils. Yes, the only savior in whom Addie can believe is not the Son of Man, but a son of man and flesh of her own flesh. Just as she can accept salvation only as something material and bodily, so with eternal rest. There is no Heavenly Father to whom to return. Thus, her overpowering wish is for her mortal body to rest beside that of her earthly father. If this wish also involves a slap at Anse and his people—in death at least she will be rid of their presence—that but adds to the vehemence of her wish. This act of separate burial has become terribly important to her. The possible contradiction involved in investing material things with an idealistic aura does not trouble her.

Some commentators on Faulkner have mistakenly interpreted Addie's demand of her family as vindictive in motive: she means to punish Anse and her children by imposing this burden upon them. But Addie, having spent her life with the fatuous trifler Anse, knows that it will cost Anse nothing. He will see to it that others do the work and take the risks. And surely she knows that if the task is to be accomplished, the burden will principally fall, as it does, on Jewel, her favorite child, possibly the only person whom she truly loves. Addie is a strong-willed woman, of the breed of Medea and Clytemnestra. If she really wanted to punish her husband, she would know how to do it in some way that would fully involve him.

Why, however, did the Bundrens honor her request? Or rather, when confronted with the difficulties that later developed, especially the river in flood and their team drowned in attempting a crossing, why did they nevertheless carry out her wish to the very letter? Let us deal with the easiest cases first. Vardaman, as a young child, had no voice in the matter. Jewel, who adored his mother, genuinely wanted to carry out her wishes, and when the difficulties of the journey developed, they did not daunt him but became exhilarating challenges.

As for Cash, it never occurred to him to do other than to accept what his mother asked. Cash is an unimaginative, apparently unemotional man, but there is no reason to believe that he did not truly love his mother. A son was supposed to love his mother, was he not? He had already expressed his love for Addie in his own way by working hard on her coffin to make it perfect, showing it to her as she looked through the window. In the ordeal of the river crossing, Cash's endurance and fortitude match Jewel's heroic action.

Dewey Dell also apparently loved her mother. At one point she says: "I heard that my mother is dead. I wish I had time to let her die. I wish I had time to wish I had." The girl would like to be able to mourn her fittingly, but she is now overwhelmed by the urgency of her own plight. She also has a pressing need of her own to get into town where, she believes, she can procure something to end her pregnancy.

Anse, as the reader discovers at the close of the novel, also has his own selfish reasons for getting to town. Yet, what about his reiterated assertions to all and sundry that he is determined to carry out Addie's wishes? Are we to dismiss them as completely empty? I think we should, for Anse knows full well that his promise to Addie will ultimately cost him nothing. His parade of virtue before his neighbors entails no real effort on his part, and even his neighbors can be trusted to help out. Haven't they always done so in the past?

The journey did in fact cost Anse the team of mules that were drowned, but by picking Cash's pocket of the money he had saved and by throwing in Jewel's horse as part of the deal, Anse manages to buy a team from Flem Snopes. Thus, he considerably lightens the expense to himself. Jewel is shocked when he hears what his father has singlehandedly done. His horse was his most prized possession, but he acquiesces. Jewel has moral courage as well as animal courage, and he truly wishes to honor his mother's wish.

The one Bundren who does not endorse the journey and at least twice tries to put an end to it is Darl. When the wagon bearing Addie's coffin tips over in the flooded river and the coffin is about to be swept away, it is saved by Cash and Jewel at great risk to themselves. Darl is on the wagon with Cash, but he contributes nothing to the rescue. Tull says, "Darl jumped out of the wagon and left Cash sitting there trying to save [the coffin]." Whether or not Tull is just to Darl, there is no question that later on Darl set fire to the barn in which Addie's coffin had been placed when the family camped out for the night. This attempt to destroy his mother's corpse was foiled when Jewel managed to get out of the burning building just before the roof fell in.

Why does Darl try to rid the Bundrens of their mother's corpse and thus stop the journey to her chosen burial place? Because he regards the whole enterprise as folly. Buzzards have begun to follow the evil smell that the coffin exudes. The people of the countryside are outraged by what is going on. Common sense and community opinion are certainly on Darl's side. The reader may well agree that Darl is right.

Yet on the whole, Darl's intelligence seems to be of a distinctly uncommon kind. He is highly intuitive. For example, he "knows" somehow that his sister has taken Lafe as a lover and that Anse is not Jewel's real father. The high-strung, inarticulate Jewel is repelled by Darl, as well he might be, since Darl continually tells him, apparently with a certain satisfaction, that Addie is going to die, or taunts him with loving his horse more than he loves his mother, or asks him who his father really is.

Darl's role is that of the keenly interested though detached observer. In fact, he represents the artist in his role of sensitive and knowing commentator on the people around him. More specifically, he is the *poète maudit*. None of his siblings, with perhaps the exception of the child Vardaman, feels close to him. They certainly do not understand him. He makes them uncomfortable with his uncanny knowledge of their secret thoughts and desires. Two of his siblings, Dewey Dell and Jewel, actually hate him. The attentive reader will not be surprised that it is this pair who, once their mother is safely buried, actually leap upon Darl and throw him to the ground to make sure that he cannot get away from the officers who have come to take him to the state's insane asylum.

Darl is an extremely good reporter of the Bundrens' activities. He is, however, much more than the merely accurate reporter. He can make the scene he describes come alive for the reader. No wonder that Darl is assigned nineteen of the fifty-nine segments of the novel—almost twice as many as Vardaman, who is easily second in the number of segments assigned to him.

Because Darl does observe so much and because his intuitions are so shrewd, some readers may assume that he is the hero—as well as the "intelligence"—of the novel, the character that they most admire and whose views and responses they may fairly claim reflect their own. Darl does indeed have his admirable traits, but there are less admirable ones in his very complex personality. He comes close to cruelty in his dealing with his brother Jewel. He shows less than a brother's concern with his sister's plight. Toward Addie, that fierce but much suffering woman, he shows far less tenderness than Jewel, who at his mother's death suffers a frantic, inarticulate grief.

Darl possesses the attractiveness of the artist, for Faulkner has dowered him with his own great gift of verbal expression. But he also has something of the artist's cruelty, what one is tempted to call a dispassionately technical interest in what he is rendering, a certain unfeeling dissection of the feelings of others. In creating Darl, Faulkner probably drew a bit on his own artistic personality; and if so, he included that part of himself that could express such sentiments as these: "[A writer] will be completely ruthless if he is a good one. . . . If a writer has to rob his mother, he will not hesitate; the *Ode on a Grecian Urn* is worth any number of old ladies."*

Darl, though only partially literate, is also something of a modern intellectual, a sceptic and a quasi-existentialist. In one of his meditations he says to himself: "I dont know what I am. I dont know if I am or not. Jewel knows he is [i.e., that he exists], because he does not know that he does not know whether he is or not."

Quite so. Jewel lacks Darl's self-consciousness and therefore never questions his own existence. Darl is all self-consciousness. He is a strange fish in this family of Mississippi hill folk. No wonder that his family and the whole community believe that he is a little "queer," as they call him, or an oddity. As such in this simple-minded and traditional society, he constitutes something of a subversive and even disruptive force. Faulkner was himself enough of an oddity in his essentially traditional society to be able to treat Darl with sympathy, though he is also well aware of how even Darl's family must view him.

The "modernity" of Darl accomplishes something quite important. It is a means for bringing the modern and the traditional worlds into juxtaposition. The matter is important, for Faulkner hints at or perhaps openly expresses such a confrontation in nearly all his Yoknapatawpha novels. He

*James B. Meriwether and Michael Millgate, eds., *Lion in the Garden: Interviews wiith William Faulkner, 1926–1962* (New York, 1968), p. 239.

uses local material, but he is almost always concerned with universal, even timeless, issues.

Early readers of *As I Lay Dying* sometimes made the mistake of assuming that it is a realistic and sociological study of deprived and somewhat depraved rustics. But *As I Lay Dying* is much more than that. Thus, Darl is intellectual and self-conscious man, sensitive, introspective, and questioning. Jewel is the unreflective man of action. Cash is the unimaginative, patient, methodical, quintessentially sober man. Faulkner has been content to treat Vardaman simply as the typical child in all the pathos of his inexperience and ignorance, and Dewey Dell as simply instinctual womanhood. But lest the reader assume that Faulkner is willing to reduce women to stereotypes, let him remember the presence of Addie. She is in some respects the most complicated and powerful character in this novel. Jewel may be her favorite child, but many of Darl's traits clearly derive from her.

Perhaps a more useful way in which to see how Faulkner uses limited and local material as his means for dealing with universal humankind, is to regard *As I Lay Dying* as a pastoral. We must begin, however, by dismissing any notion that a pastoral is necessarily about shepherds singing and dancing in a charming Arcadian landscape. Pastoral—I borrow the concept from William Empson—mirrors a more complex world, typically the world of the sophisticated reader, in a much simpler world. Since human beings are essentially the same the world over and through all the ages, the pastoral mode constitutes a means for dealing with universal problems by gaining a fresh perspective on them, as well as a proper aesthetic distance from them.

To be more specific, we have on the wagon carrying the Bundrens a representative microcosm of our far more complicated society. Some of life's perennial issues are there: among them, death ending a frustrated life, sibling rivalry, the strongly mixed motives which set us in motion toward our various goals, the consequences of a promise taken seriously, family pride, family loyalty and disloyalty, honor, and the nature of heroic action. I will limit my discussion here to no more than two of these: the interrelated matters of honor and heroism.

The reader rather expects that a Quentin Compson or almost any other descendant of the old Southern gentry will prove to be sensitive, sometimes hypersensitive, on the subject of his honor. But few readers will expect to find a concern for honor in such folk as the Bundren males. But the poorer Southern whites often fiercely defended their honor, for their personal honor was often the only thing that they could claim to own. The Bundrens, to be sure, were not abjectly poor. They owned a good house and a good farm. Anse was proud to possess not only property but, as he told Addie before their marriage, also a "good honest name."

One need not, of course, take Anse's pretenses to honor or anything else very seriously. But with Jewel or Cash, say, respect for the pledged word is a matter of deadly seriousness. They even embrace the traditional Southern code of male honor—pride in one's independence and valor in defending it. Witness Jewel's immediate response to what he deems an insult to his family. As the Bundren wagon nears the end of its journey, the smell emanating from the coffin causes some people whom they pass on the road to exclaim: "Great God, what they got in that wagon?" Jewel retorts with the ungrammatical but sufficiently insulting phrase, "Son of a bitches." Jewel is immediately challenged with the question: "What did you say?" Darl, well aware that the situation has suddenly become serious, explains to the stranger, "He dont mean anything, mister," but Jewel swings at the stranger, who draws his knife. Darl then intercedes once more: Jewel is ill, he is not himself, he explains, and then adds, "He thought you said something to him." This explanation opens a way for mutual accommodation, but in what follows the touchiness of the code of honor is nicely illustrated.

Darl promises that Jewel will take back the offending words but insists that the retraction must not be made under duress, for when the stranger demands that Jewel take back the words, Darl says, "Put up your knife, and he will." The stranger does so, and now Darl conjures Jewel to tell him "[he] didn't mean anything." "I thought he said something," Jewel says. "Just because he's—" But Darl hushes him and says: "Tell him you didn't mean it." And Jewel at last makes the necessary concession by saying that he didn't mean it. The angered man then remarks: "He better not. Calling me a—" But the Bundrens must not seem to concede too much and it is now Darl who quickly asks: "Do you think he's afraid to call you that?" Whereupon there is a slight retreat on the other side as the stranger cautiously replies: "I never said that." Jewel follows up the advantage with: "Dont think it, neither." But Darl, now that honor has been saved, orders Jewel to shut up and urges his father to drive on. This code of honor is quite as elaborate as that humorously described in the fifth act of Shakespeare's *As You Like It*. It has its own degrees corresponding to such niceties as Touchstone's "Reproof Valiant" and his "Countercheck Quarrelsome."

This contretemps, in terms of the plot of the novel, has little importance. But it reveals how protective of their honor people of the Bundrens' class can be. Even Darl shows that he is thoroughly familiar with the code and makes sure that the Bundrens in apologizing do not go too far in their concessions.

For the most part, Darl, like Shakespeare's Falstaff, recognizes the hollowness of honor. He understands all too well the motives that prompted Addie to demand to be buried among her own people, and when the costs of the journey become staggering, he denies the claims of the dead over the living. He regards it as ridiculous to take the long, roundabout journey, crossing a river in flood at the risk of life and limb, not to mention the consternation and disapproval they awake in the community through which they move.

Darl truly has traits of an artist and poet. But he is no sentimentalist, no idealist. His gaze is direct and incisive, and it can be withering. Like many a modern intellectual, he is antiheroic. He knows too much to believe very strongly in anything. Darl's affinities are not with any visionary romantic, but rather with Stendhal's Julien Sorel or Joyce's Stephen Dedalus.

Yet to say this is not to deny that a great deal of the poetry in *As I Lay Dying* occurs in the passages assigned to Darl. But then there is a great deal of poetry throughout the novel. Vardaman's thoughts and feelings, those of Dewey Dell, of Addie, of even the stolid and prosaic Vernon Tull can on occasion move into measured eloquence. This is how Tull describes the flooded river in which the Bundrens lose their team of mules and almost lose Addie's corpse when her coffin nearly slides off the wagon.

> The water was cold. It was thick, like slush ice. Only it kind of lived. One part of you knowed it was just water, the same thing that had been running under this same bridge for a long time, yet when them logs would come spewing up outen it, you were not surprised, like they was a part of water, of the waiting and the threat. (P. 131)

It would be a mistake to believe that we are to regard these eruptions into poetry as faults, as poetry out of place, as prettified speeches put into the mouths of prosaic people. They are not rhetorical embroideries upon ordinary speech, but penetrations into the depths of people's souls—the articulation of genuine feelings with words that do justice to the authenticity of those feelings. The poetry is no mere prettification, but a revelation of something really there. To see this is to approach an appreciation of the real significance of the novel.

At first glance, the characters would seem to represent most unpromising material: limited, rather coarse, only semiliterate country people. But Faulkner has deliberately chosen them, and not for their value as local color. He is not primarily concerned with their quaint and sometimes comic eccentricities, but with what they reveal about mankind everywhere and at all times.

Matthew Arnold wrote that "no one can deny that it is of advantage to a poet to deal with a beautiful world." But T. S. Eliot, by way of comment on this passage, puts the poet's true advantage in very different terms: it is "to be able to see beneath both beauty and ugliness; to see the boredom and the horror, and the glory."* This seems an excellent statement of what Faulkner has been able to do.

Very well, but to which of these qualities is it that Faulkner's gaze has been able to penetrate? To the boredom, the horror, or the glory of the life of the Bundrens? The perceptive reader will doubtless find all three. But in that case, how is the reader to relate them to each other? Are we dealing with comedy or tragedy? Do we want to praise Cash for enduring agonizing pain without complaint, almost as a suffering animal might? Or do we want to shake him hard for being so stupidly docile? Dr. Peabody, setting Cash's broken leg, asks his patient whether his manipulation of the leg hurts him, and Cash answers, "Not to speak of," though sweat drops "big as marbles" run down his drawn white face. The physician's next comment mingles pity, admiration for Cash's fortitude, and more than a bit of exasperation at Cash's acceptance of Anse's treatment of him. Peabody says: "About next summer you can hobble around fine on this leg. Then it wont bother you, not to speak of. . . . If you had anything you could call luck, you might say it was lucky this is the same leg you broke before." To which Cash replies: "That's what paw says."

If such a passage raises problems of what attitude the reader is to adopt, it is only one of many. Dewey Dell's encounter with McGowan, the druggist's clerk, is another. The treatment he prescribes for the girl's pregnancy resembles the kind of cruel humor that one finds in some medieval fabliaux. Are we to pity the plight of this ignorant and almost

*The Use of Poetry and the Use of Criticism: Studies in the Relation of Criticism to Poetry in England, ed. T. S. Eliot (Cambridge: Harvard University Press, 1933), p. 98.

inarticulate girl, or must our sympathy be qualified by our difficulty in believing that she could possibly be *that* stupid?

The ending of the novel may itself raise a further conflict of attitude. What are we to say when the unspeakable Anse, fresh from burying his wife and equipped with his new false teeth, returns to the wagon to introduce to his four remaining children (Darl having now been hustled off to the insane asylum) their new stepmother, a "duck-shaped woman . . . with them kind of hard-looking pop eyes"? Are we to take this as farcical humor? We have certainly moved far past the bounds of realism here. Could even Anse have arranged a marriage so expeditiously? Or even have been fitted with a set of false teeth in an hour or so?

I suggested earlier that *As I Lay Dying* might best be regarded as a kind of parable, a fable in which various universal types of human beings interact with each other in an endeavor that, in varying ways, involves all of them. But the reader may feel that Faulkner's story of the Bundrens' adventure is a very special kind of fable, a tall tale of the old Southwest, filled with quite unbelievable happenings and marvelous feats, but also with the boisterous frontier humor often found in such tales. In short, the reader may be driven to wonder whether this short novel possesses any unity of tone whatever. Whether it does will, of course, have to be determined by each individual reader. What follows represents one man's attempt to judge this point. But to present that judgment may be of some service if only to help the unpersuaded reader define why he believes that the novel finally falls apart.

The basic issue, as I believe Vernon Tull might put it, is as simple as this: are we to laugh or cry over the Bundrens' exploit and its sequel? Both are possibilities. The surface of the Bundrens' life shows squalor, crassness, selfishness, and stupidity, but beneath the surface there are depths of passion and poetry that are terrifying in their power. The very drabness of the surface is the guarantee of the genuineness of the passion below. These people are not rhetoricians who talk themselves into their transports. One of them has the poetry of madness; one of them, the poetry of the child. But the others are almost inarticulate, and the two brothers who dare most and suffer most lack the wordiness that their mother despised.

Faulkner has been concerned in all his books with what the human being can endure, what he can dare, what he can accomplish. The story of how the Bundrens managed the burial of Addie Bundren affords him a very special vantage point from which to contemplate the human capacity for both suffering and action. The heroic adventure involves a mixture of motives and a variety of responses. There is the child who only partially comprehends what is occurring and responds with astonishment and fear to what he sees. There is the young woman so much obsessed with her own problems that she can reflect upon the adventure only as a possible answer to her own need. There is the parasite Anse who does not even know that he is asking his children to be heroes and if he could understand it would not care. There is Darl who knows too much and feels too intensely to be able to take in more than the nauseating horror and fear that the act costs. There is the patient Cash, who never sees that he is doing more than his bounden duty. There is Jewel, perhaps the least reflective member of the group, violent and even brutal, whose heroism is so pure and unselfconscious that he is not aware that it is heroism. It burns like a clean flame that exhausts itself in the process, leaving no sooty residue.

As a commentary upon man's power to act and to endure, upon his apparently incorrigible idealism, the story of the Bundrens is clearly appalling—appalling but not scathing and not debunking. Heroism is heroism even though it sometimes appears to be merely the hither side of folly. Man's capacity to spend himself in a cause is always a remarkable thing and nowhere more so than when it springs from an unlikely soil. For a summarizing statement on this novel, one might appeal to one of the choruses in *Antigone*: "Wonders are many, and none is more wonderful than man." *As I Lay Dying* provides a less exalted but not unworthy illustration of Sophocles' judgment.

5 • THE HAMLET

The Hamlet (published in 1940) is a brilliantly written novel, especially with respect to its characters and its atmosphere. But it is a novel which has not always been well understood, and many readers have created problems for themselves by getting off on the wrong foot as they read it.

It is preeminently a novel about some of the poorer whites of Yoknapatawpha County. Like the Bundrens, they live in a small hamlet, Frenchman's Bend, in Beat Four. Families like the Sartorises and McCaslins and Compsons do not appear in the novel. Nor are there many blacks in Frenchman's Bend. The principal landowner, Will Varner, has one or two black servants, and the local blacksmith shop is run by a black man; but these are about all.

Most of the inhabitants own the land that they farm, but there are also a few sharecroppers, people like Ab Snopes and his family in the story "Barn Burning." (That story, by the way, was originally intended for the opening chapter of *The Hamlet*.) The principal figure in this novel is Flem Snopes, Ab's son. As the novel opens, Ab and his family have just arrived in Frenchman's Bend to farm on shares some land belonging to Will Varner.

A common misreading of *The Hamlet* begins with the assumption that Will Varner is an aristocrat. Varner is, as I have said, the principal landowner in Frenchman's Bend. He also owns the cotton gin, the sawmill, and the store. But if we think of him as a Southern aristocrat, we will start the novel with all the wrong associations. Will Varner knows his own worth, but he makes no pretensions to birth or breeding. We are told that "He was shrewd secret and merry, of a Rabelaisian turn of mind and very probably still sexually lusty. . . ." He has fathered sixteen legitimate children and there are hints that he may have some illegitimate children as well. In his business dealings he drives hard bargains which has led to his now considerable holdings; for they have not come by inheritance from royal land grants. He is hard, tough, and still very much a man of the people. Making all allowances for the relatively easy upward class mobility in the nineteenth-century South, and especially in northern Mississippi, which was still close to the frontier early in that century, in manners and attitudes Will Varner is more accurately described as a yeoman white who has acquired money rather than as a member of the old landed stock.

The Hamlet is, by the way, not to be read as a sociological study—not, that is to say, as a realistic novel. One can learn a good deal about Southern socioeconomic conditions from *The Hamlet*, but it is primarily a novel, and a rather special kind of novel at that. In the first place, Faulkner has pushed several of his characters almost to the limits of credibility. Flem Snopes, for example, is a man so completely committed to making money that one feels he is almost too good—or rather, too bad—to be true. A caricature of him would be a dollar sign walking around on two hind legs, quietly seeking whom it may devour. Though he grinds away interminably on his little wad of chewing gum, his only appetite seems to be for money. We never have a scene in which he seems to be enjoying a meal or savoring a drink or listening to someone tell a good story. His lust is a cold and almost abstract craving for money and nothing else.

Faulkner, nevertheless, has succeeded in making us accept him as a character. Indeed, so powerful has been his impact that Flem Snopes has already become a figure in American folklore, and "Snopesism" has become a common noun. Even so, Faulkner, in creating Flem, has almost created a mythical figure—a nearly nonhuman figure clothed in barely enough flesh and blood to allow us to accept it as a man.

Will Varner's youngest child, Eula, also comes close to being a figure out of myth. She is a beautiful and overpoweringly feminine woman. Even at the age of thirteen she impresses one as a goddess of fertility. When Faulkner describes her, he does not hesitate to pull out all the stops:

> . . . she was already bigger than most grown women and even her breasts were no longer the little, hard, fiercely-pointed cones of puberty or even maidenhood. On the contrary, her entire appearance suggested some symbology out of the old Dionysic times—honey in sunlight and bursting grapes, the writhen bleeding of the crushed fecundated vine beneath the hard rapacious trampling goat-hoof. She seemed to be not a living integer of her contemporary scene, but rather to exist in a teeming vacuum in which her days followed one another as though behind sound-proof glass, where she seemed to listen in sullen bemusement, with a weary wisdom heired of all mammalian maturity, to the enlarging of her own organs. (P. 55)

Faulkner takes a considerable risk in writing such flamboyant prose. But it works. We accept Eula as a sort of back-country Aphrodite—in part because she is completely unconscious of her beauty and utterly indifferent to the spell that she casts over men. She is not a mannered and self-conscious belle, out to make conquests. She is a kind of incarnation of nature, and like every other beautiful *natural* object, utterly unaware that she possesses beauty or power.

The third almost mythical character is Flem Snopes's cousin, Ike Snopes, one of Faulkner's several famous idiots. Faulkner was clearly fascinated with utterly natural man, man almost as deeply merged into nature as any mere animal. It is tempting to see in Ike something of the Greek faun, that creature with human features and arms and waist, but possessing goatlike thighs and hoofed feet, a creature that unites a human with an obviously animal nature. Benjy Compson is a faun, and in Faulkner's work there are others.

Both Benjy and Ike are indeed brought very close to the animal level. They have little sense of time; they are basically instinctual in their reactions; they have almost no sense of what society demands and prohibits. Yet they are both recognizably human, perhaps, *just* recognizably human, but sufficiently so to make Faulkner's essential point. Benjy is capable of receiving and giving love. Thus, he turns out to be finally more nearly human than his brother Jason, for Jason, in spite of his brittle rationalism, lacks the capacity to love. In the same way, Ike Snopes stands as a silent but eloquent witness to the essential inhumanity of his cousin Flem. For one could say of Flem, with the author of the Epistles to the Corinthians, that since he lacks love, he is no better than a "sounding brass or a tinkling cymbal" or a clattering adding machine. Yet it must be conceded that once again, in this novel, we have in Ike a character who presses humanity to its farthest limits.

In addition to these three characters that come so close to representing embodiments of natural forces, the country they inhabit sometimes itself takes on the quality of a mythical realm. My earlier warning against reading this novel as a realistic account of an actual society, or any reading that stresses its socioeconomic makeup, is very much to the point. The world that Faulkner sets forth in *The Hamlet* does have a close relation to his descriptions of Yoknapatawpha County. That has to be conceded. Nevertheless, in *The Hamlet* Faulkner has added a mythical dimension. He makes us see Frenchman's Bend as a countryside congenial to the presence of nymphs and fauns, a world in which the deities of nature have their place. The young schoolmaster Labove, though he is a north Mississippi boy, bred in the country, has begun to read the Greek classic poets, and Labove at least can imagine the Greek gods and demigods peeping out of the fields and woodlands of this backcountry region.

I had something of this sort in mind some years ago when I referred to the countryside depicted in *The Hamlet* as a "savage Arcadia." We need to remind ourselves that the province of Arcadia was for the classical Greeks also a backcountry enclave. It was far from cities. It was old-fashioned in its customs and ways. There the Greeks fancied the old nature gods still roamed: Pan, the god of Nature, and his troop of satyrs, fauns, and nymphs.

In any case, *The Hamlet* contains some of Faulkner's most evocative nature poetry. There are in *The Hamlet* wonderful accounts of dawn, of a summer rainstorm, of the onset of evening, and of a midnight in summer. Try reading aloud, for instance, the accounts of Ike Snopes's walks with his cow over the hills (found on pages 179–86) and you will gain some sense of how someone very close to nature, very much in harmony with nature, might experience the changing patterns of day and night.

This has been a long prologue to an account of a novel that is filled with human beings, many of whom are too, too human. Yet, since in a way, what Flem Snopes essentially does is to disturb this pastoral world, this savage Arcadia, by bringing into it the mercantile ethic, the huckster's guile, perhaps this long introduction is à propos after all. For, in one sense, the plot of *The Hamlet* has to do with the arrival of Flem Snopes into Beat Four and the story of how he became the financial power in the hamlet, swallowing up anything that was lying loose, introducing modern business methods, and, though only in a very humble and limited way, bringing the area under the sway of finance-capitalism.

These last comments may seem somewhat preposterous. How can one small operator, who does not scorn to lend five dollars at an interest of ten cents a week, how can one call him a finance-capitalist? Yet in reading the story of Flem's incursion into pastoral Beat Four, we are reading a parable. Flem's financial dealings are, to be sure, very small potatoes. But he does mirror what on a grander scale the so-called robber barons did after the Civil War. They literally looted a continent. For those who demand relevance, Flem's story is relevant, for it encapsulates what was done and essentially how it was done by the robber barons.

How did Flem, a poor sharecropper's son, get his first hold on Frenchman's Bend? By blackmail. When Ab Snopes—remember the story "Barn Burning"—came late in the season to find a landlord with whom he could farm on shares, Jody Varner, Will's ungainly and rather stupid son, thought it would be fine to take him on. Jody would let Ab plant and cultivate the crop, and then when it got close to harvest time, he would tell Ab that he knew all about Ab's past history as a barn burner. He was confident that Ab would take fright and be glad to leave the county in a hurry, his crop ungathered. It was a thoroughly unscrupulous scheme, but Jody in this instance had caught a Tartar.

Flem Snopes was just as unscrupulous as Jody Varner, but three times as intelligent, and by skillfully playing on the Varners' fears that their own barn might be burned, he manages to get himself installed as the clerk in the Varners' general store. With Flem in charge, the old easygoing ways disappear. Credit is restricted; careful bookkeeping is instituted; and the countrymen sense that they are now up against a new and ruthless force. Not that Flem ever does anything illegal; he is always careful to keep on the right side of the law. But he is pure ruthless efficiency, and in this easygoing old-fashioned community, such efficiency is new, and disturbing. Will Varner was a rascal, but at the same time, human. Flem is somehow inhuman.

On one level, *The Hamlet* is the story of Flem's rise to financial power as he becomes Will Varner's right-hand man, soon ousting Will's son and heir, Jody, not only from his place in the store, but from his place in the cotton gin and the other Varner enterprises, and finally acquiring valuable property in his own right.

For much of the time, the reader of *The Hamlet* views Flem's meteoric career through the eyes of V. K. Ratliff who is an itinerant sewing-machine agent making his rounds about the country, selling his machines to farmers' wives, but also carrying news and gossip and bartering and trading generally. Ratliff has a fund of good stories and he is an excellent teller of a tale. The art of storytelling in the South, by the way, is far from dead. Faulkner knew it firsthand, having listened to expert raconteurs exchanging their stories around a hunter's campfire or telling yarns on the front porch of a crossroads store or listening to an old Confederate veteran giving his reminiscences of the Battle of Shiloh.

One of the best individual stories told in *The Hamlet* is Ratliff's account of how Ab Snopes had become soured on the world by being soundly beaten in a horse trade. Ab had been foolish enough to take on the redoubtable Pat Stamper, of West Tennessee. In the various exchanges and tradings that go on between them, Ab has had fobbed off on him a horse that has been plumped up to look sleek and fat by means of a bicycle air pump; the valve that was inserted in his hide is discovered later, too late. Another of the horses worked off on Ab turns out to have been dyed another color. On Ab's way home, it rains, and the horse changes color before his eyes.

Ratliff, having heard of the newcomer Flem's prowess as a trader, decides to take him on, not so much in the hope of winning some money from him, but as a sporting proposition, as a challenge, as a way of vindicating his own skill and proving that he is still the champion trader in the community. Ratliff lays his plans carefully. It is to be a flank attack. He will let Flem score off him in the first instance, yielding a pawn in order to win a piece. Thus Ratliff makes sure that the word will get to Flem that Ratliff is in the market to buy goats. As he anticipates, Flem immediately buys up all the goats in the county, cornering the market.

Ratliff pretends to concede defeat. It looks as if he will have to pay Flem's price in order to get the goats needed to fulfill his contract. But then he springs on Flem a surprise. Ratliff has acquired and now presents for collection a note for twenty dollars which represents a claim on Flem from his cousin Mink. Ratliff will trade this note for the goats he needs. Flem readily agrees, and burns the note, for he prefers to burn the note rather than to refuse to pay it and risk having his barn burned by Mink.

Then Ratliff proffers a second note, one for ten dollars, which represents an obligation to another of Flem's cousins, Ike. How Ratliff obtained these two notes is a story too complicated to include in this chapter. Needless to say, Ratliff has laid his plans carefully. What is important to mention here is that in his bargaining Ratliff is a sportsman, more interested in exhibiting his skill than in the material reward. His basic motive becomes clear when he finds that one of the two notes constitutes a promise to repay money to Ike Snopes who is an idiot, hardly able to pronounce his own name. Flem had himself made Ike's guardian and is using Ike's meager capital, not for Ike's benefit, but to help finance his own speculations. Learning this, Ratliff himself burns the note so that Flem cannot continue to use Ike's little sum for his own selfish purposes and reaches into his own pocket to replace the value of the note with accrued interest. And then—adding to it the rest of his contemplated profit on the transaction—he deposits the whole sum with Mrs. Littlejohn, the person who really looks after Ike, as money to be used for Ike's welfare. In short, Ratliff contents himself with a moral victory over Flem.

One of the most interesting things about *The Hamlet* is the brilliant array of characters that Faulkner has assembled in one medium-length book. Some of them appear only briefly in the novel, but even so, are brought vividly to the reader's consciousness and are instinct with life and vitality. One of these is a young man named Labove. We never learn his first name. He is a hillsman whom the football coach at the State university has discovered to be an extraordinarily talented football player. Labove wins a football scholarship and by means of it and various odd jobs for one of the professors is able to work his way through college. I have deliberately chosen to say "work his way" rather than "play his way," for football to Labove is work. He takes little interest in the game. It is a chore, only a means to his chosen end. Labove is not even interested in the textbooks over which he pours with such earnest concentration. His great ambition is to be some day elected governor of the state. A professional education is his one means to that goal, and tearing to shreds the scrimmage line of the opposing team is his means to an education. It is all as simple as that.

Yet Labove is no heavy-handed oaf, no mere bundle of muscle. He entertains his private dreams and he lives by a rigid code of honor. For instance, he eyes with admiration the cleated football shoes supplied in quantity to the team. He soon learns that no one will notice if he helps himself to an extra pair. But he refuses to take a pair unless his team wins. If it does, he takes one pair to his all but barefoot family in their cabin back in the hills. But Labove is a truly formidable player, his team wins most of its games, and eventually even his old grandmother makes a clicking sound as she crosses the puncheon floor of her cabin, wearing the beautifully made cleated football shoes.

It is this young man that Will Varner seizes upon to become the master of the one-room school in Frenchman's Bend. A large consideration with Varner is to find a teacher who can keep order, for the older and wilder boys have paid little heed to the ineffectual old alcoholic who has been their schoolmaster heretofore. Labove does restore order and—however much modern education experts would frown at his methods—presumably he also does a decent job in teaching his charges to read and write and do a little figuring.

Labove is, whether he knows it or not, a good American Puritan and a believer in the work ethic. Faulkner describes his face thus: he has the "hungry mouth, the insufferable humorless eyes, the intense ugly blue-shaved face like a composite photograph of Voltaire and an Elizabethan pirate." But Labove's life soon becomes tormented, for his erotic nature is stirred to frenzy by the presence of one of his pupils, Eula Varner.

Labove does not want to marry Eula. He does not want a wife of any sort. But he is obsessed with a mania to possess her just once. As Faulkner puts it: "he just wanted her one time as a man with a gangrened hand or foot thirsts after the axe-stroke which will leave him comparatively whole again."

One afternoon when he finds Eula and himself alone in the schoolroom his mania overpowers him. He clasps Eula in his arms, but the intended rape does not come off. She repulses him, for she turns out to be surprisingly strong, exclaiming "Stop pawing me. You old headless horseman Ichabod Crane," and leaves the room. Eula's memories of "The Legend of Sleepy Hollow" are somewhat confused, for she is indeed not a star pupil. But she conveys clearly enough her contempt for the pedagogue of the Frenchman's Bend school.

Labove, like so many of Faulkner's yeoman-white characters, is a man of honor. He is convinced that once Eula has told her brother Jody of his attempt on her, Jody will come to the school prepared to execute condign punishment. So, man of honor that he is, he waits for Jody, scorning to run. When Jody in due time does not appear, Labove goes to the Varner store and only then it dawns on him that Eula has not even bothered to report his attack. He has made no impression on her at all. Labove is crushed. He borrows a nail from Jody, nails the schoolhouse door shut, and disappears from Frenchman's Bend forever. What happens to him? Well, my guess is that in due time, he became governor of Mississippi. His sort of determination must have won out, but that is another story and Faulkner never elected to tell it.

Within a few years, however, Eula's sexual awakening did occur: a young man named Hoake McCarron, from another part of the county, happened to see Eula one day and began to take her for buggy rides. The local youths, who had been congregating on the Varner front porch every Sunday afternoon in a kind of hopeless and tongue-tied courtship of the beautiful girl, resented McCarron. Though they had from time to time fought among themselves, they now combined against the handsome outsider. One night they ambushed him.

Faulkner very carefully sets the scene of the attack. He has earlier described the buggy rides

> through night-time roads across the mooned or un-mooned sleeping land, the mare's feet like slow silk in the dust as a horse moves when the reins are wrapped about the upright whip in its dashboard socket, the fords into which the unguided mare would step gingerly down and stop unchidden and drink, nuzzling and blowing among the broken reflections of stars, raising its dripping muzzle and maybe drinking again or maybe just blowing into the water as a thirst-quenched horse will. (P. 136)

This is prose written with superb fidelity to the fact, but it is poetry too, in which an atmosphere and a mood is beautifully caught.

It was on just such a night that five of the local youths ambushed McCarron and Eula at the ford. There was a violent encounter and "later, years later, one of [the youths] told that it was the girl who had wielded [the butt of the buggy whip], springing from the buggy and with the reversed whip beating three of them back while her companion used the reversed pistol-butt against the wagon-spoke and the brass knuckles of the other two."

In the encounter, McCarron suffers a broken arm, and when Eula and her beau return to the Varner house, her father Will, who was a practicing veterinarian, is asked to set the broken bone. McCarron explains that he was kicked by his mare.

After the older people have gone to bed, McCarron stays on, and, broken arm notwithstanding, has his reward. For the indolent and almost bemused girl is at last sexually aroused. She has to support McCarron's body with her arms. Even so, when he finally leaves for home, he will need to have the broken arm reset next morning.

In due course, the Varners discover that Eula is pregnant. Jody is outraged, though his mother and father take a realistic, not to say fatalistic view, of the matter. McCarron, who is not the marrying kind, has left the country, presumably for Texas, and apparently three others of the local suitors have also fled to Texas, each in the desperate hope that he might be credited with "the glorious shame of the ruin" that he had no part in accomplishing.

Now, Will Varner is a practical man. He suppresses Jody's choleric threat to avenge the blot on the family scutcheon. Instead, Will simply seeks out a husband at once for Eula, someone who can be the presumed father of the child that is on the way. The obvious man to fill this assignment is Flem Snopes. He has already ingratiated himself with Will Varner; he has proved to be an excellent business partner; and he will not have the slightest objection, provided of course that a proper settlement is made, to father vicariously Eula's child. Part of the settlement is a deed to the old Frenchman's place, which is a rundown and abandoned plantation house, on the porch of which Varner sometimes loved to sit, as monarch of all that he surveyed. Flem had somehow taken a fancy to it.

Flem and Eula are quickly married and hustled off to Texas for their wedding trip. They will remain in that distant state until the child is born and so conceal the fact that it will be arriving somewhat earlier than the schedule calls for. We are not told what Eula felt. We do not know what protests she may or may not have made. But we have been told earlier that Eula had never paid the slightest attention to Flem and that when it was necessary for her to let her father know that Flem had arrived and wished to see him, her habit was to refer to him as "that man," though sometimes "she said Mr Snopes, saying it exactly as she would have said Mr Dog."

Faulkner provides us with an unforgettable picture of the wedding party on the way to buy a marriage license. Here it is: "a lean, loose-jointed, cotton-socked, shrewd, ruthless old man [Will Varner], the splendid girl with her beautiful mask-like face, [and] the froglike creature which barely reached her shoulder. . . ."

V. K. Ratliff had also glimpsed the bride before she and her new husband leave the village. He looks at Eula's face. When he had last seen it, "It had not been tragic, and now it was not even damned, since from behind it there looked out only another mortal natural enemy of the masculine race. And beautiful: but then, so did the highwayman's daggers and pistols make a pretty shine on him. . . ." Even Labove, the schoolmaster, had had a premonition of the sort of man who would win Eula. This is what he imagines the creature would be: "He would be a dwarf, a gnome, without glands or desire, who would be no more a physical factor in her life than the owner's name on the fly-leaf of a book."

I remarked earlier in this chapter that in *The Hamlet*, Faulkner has pushed some of his principal characters nearly over the human limit, turning them into almost mythical characters. If so, we may think of the marriage of Eula and Flem as like that of Venus, the goddess of love and beauty, with Vulcan, the smith god, lame and somewhat soot-stained from his forge. This pair are ill-assorted indeed.

For Flem, of course, the marriage has nothing to do with love. It is a useful business arrangement. But it is more than that and Ratliff sees it as clearly symbolic. The shrewdest trader in the community, the peerless bargainer, has secured what many men would regard as the finest bargain of them all. Never mind the fact that Eula will be for him merely a beautiful possession. After all, millionaires who collect Old Masters are not always devotees of painting and the arts. If other men set a high value on what they possess, that fact is reward enough.

Ratliff seems to have been particularly struck by this brilliant climax to Flem's rapid rise to power. He celebrates Flem's prowess by putting him into a wonderful yarn, a kind of tall tale in which Flem is the demonic hero.

Ratliff begins in medias res. Without any introduction, he tells us about Flem's arrival in hell. But, as we get into the story, the beginning is easily inferred. Like Faustus of old, Flem must have made a compact with the devil. How else could he have achieved invariable success? Faustus signed away his soul to the devil in return for youth and seven years of good fortune. So Marlowe tells the story. But, according to Ratliff, Flem was a much better businessman than Faustus. He simply borrowed against his soul as collateral, leaving the soul on deposit in hell. Furthermore, Flem does not wait for the devil to come to him on earth to claim his soul. Instead, he has come to hell to check up on his collateral.

Flem refuses to be put off by the minor officials at this great, efficient establishment and insists on talking with at least the vice-president, a really big devil, the Prince of Hell himself. The Prince does not want to be bothered, but the minor devils plead that they just cannot do anything with Flem. But you will lose all the flavor of the colloquy unless you hear the way Ratliff makes these lesser devils speak:

'He says a bargain is a bargain. That he swapped in good faith and honor, and now he has come to redeem it, like the law says. And we cant find it,' they says. 'We done looked everywhere. It wasn't no big one to begin with nohow, and we was specially careful in handling it. We sealed it up in a asbestos matchbox and put the box in a separate compartment to itself. But when we opened the compartment, it was gone. The matchbox was there and the seal wasn't broke. But there wasn't nothing in the matchbox but a little kind of dried-up smear under one edge. And now he has come to redeem it. But how can we redeem him into eternal torment without his soul?'

'Damn it,' the Prince hollers. 'Give him one of the extra ones. Aint there souls turning up here every day, banging at the door and raising all kinds of hell to get in here, even bringing letters from Congressmen, that we never even heard of? Give him one of them.'

'We tried that,' they says. 'He wont do it. He says he

dont want no more and no less than his legal interest according to what the banking and civil laws states in black and white is hisn. He says he has come prepared to meet his bargain and signature, and he sholy expects you of all folks to meet yourn.'

'Tell him he can go then. Tell him he had the wrong address. That there aint nothing on the books here against him. Tell him his note was lost—if there ever was one. Tell him we had a flood, even a freeze.'

'He wont go, not without his——'

'Turn him out. Eject him.'

'How,' they says. 'He's got the law.'

'Oho,' the Prince says. 'A sawmill advocate. I see. All right,' he says. 'Fix it. Why bother me?' And he set back and raised his glass and blowed the flames offen it like he thought they was already gone. Except they wasn't gone.

'Fix what?' they says.

'His bribe!' the Prince hollers. 'His bribe! Didn't you just tell me he come in here with his mouth full of law? Did you expect him to hand you a wrote-out bill for it?'

'We tried that,' they says. 'He wont bribe.' (Pp. 149–50)

Ratliff's account rests upon a very firm basis here. There is a tradition, long established in the folklore of the Western world, that the Devil is a legalist, a stickler for the letter of the law, and that he usually wins his victories by holding careless men to the fine print in the contract. But Flem, in this story, turns out to be a sharper legalist than the Devil himself.

The Prince of Hell, however, is certain that any man can be bribed. Though he is told that Flem won't bribe, the Prince, still incredulous, asks whether Flem has been offered the various gratifications and vanities. He is told that Flem already has been offered them, and so the Prince, now thoroughly irritated, bursts out with "'Then what does he want? Paradise?'" And is aghast when the answer is, "'No. He wants hell.'"

Finally he consents to see Flem.

So they brought him in and went away and closed the door. His clothes was still smoking a little, though soon he had done brushed most of it off. He come up to the Throne, chewing, toting the straw suitcase.

'Well?' the Prince says.

He turned his head and spit, the spit frying off the floor quick in a little blue ball of smoke. 'I come about that soul,' he says.

'So they tell me,' the Prince says. 'But you have no soul.'

'Is that my fault?' he says.

'Is it mine?' the Prince says. 'Do you think I created you?'

'Then who did?' he says. And he had the Prince there and the Prince knowed it. So the Prince set out to bribe him his-self. He named over all the temptations, the gratifications, the satieties; it sounded sweeter than music the way the Prince fetched them up in detail. But he didn't even stop chewing, standing there holding the straw suitcase. (Pp. 151–52)

The sparring goes on between the two. I shall not quote the exchange further. Space does not allow for that. Besides, it will be better if you get out *The Hamlet* and read aloud to yourself the whole wonderful story.

The outcome of the contest, of course, is never in doubt. Flem proves more than a match for the Devil. He has better logic, a sharper interpretation of the law, and a more powerful grip on what is at stake. And the Devil quickly comes to realize it. In fact, the Devil, now completely shaken, screams out "'Who are you?'" as

choking and gasping and his eyes a-popping up at [Flem] setting there with that straw suitcase on the Throne among the bright, crown-shaped flames. 'Take Paradise!' the Prince screams. 'Take it! Take it!' And the wind roars up and the dark roars down and the Prince scrabbling across the floor, clawing and scrabbling at that locked door, screaming. . . . (P. 153)

Ratliff, as this tale shows, is a born storyteller, but his story about Flem is much more than a wonderful left-handed compliment to Flem's prowess as a manipulator. There is a cold-blooded deviltry in Flem, a meanness which is no joking matter, and Ratliff shows that he is thoroughly aware of it. Ratliff knows what Flem truly represents.

I have just discussed the first two sections of *The Hamlet*, those entitled respectively "Flem" and "Eula." We left Flem and Eula, now united in the bonds of holy matrimony, in Texas, where they had gone for their honeymoon. They will not return for some months, and the account of Flem's return and his renewed impact on Frenchman's Bend occupies the fourth part of the novel, that entitled "The Peasants." Meanwhile, in the third section of *The Hamlet*, which Faulkner calls "The Long Hot Summer," we have an account of some of the happenings in Frenchman's Bend while Flem was away. The third section, however, introduces matters that touch only peripherally on the story of Flem's rise to power.

After Flem gained a foothold in Frenchman's Bend, he had begun to import his kinsmen, other Snopeses, mostly his many cousins. Most of them are beholden to Flem for jobs and become his willing tools. Through them, Flem fastens his hold more tightly on Frenchman's Bend. There is I. O. Snopes, who succeeds Labove as schoolmaster; Lump Snopes, who becomes a clerk in the Varner store; Wallstreet Panic Snopes and Eck Snopes, and I am far from naming them all.

One of Flem's cousins, Ike, the idiot, occupies a prominent place in this third section of *The Hamlet*. Ike has found in a cow, his goddess, his love, his partner in sex, and now that the cow is penned up near where Ike lodges in Mrs. Little-john's boardinghouse, one of the Snopes clan is exhibiting Ike's performance with the cow as a spectacle.

When Ratliff discovers what is going on he takes steps to stop the exhibition. In fact, he tells several men who have come to the peep-show—a board, man-high, has been removed from the stable wall in order to look on—that "This here engagement is completed." He shoos the watchers away and takes steps to see that the closing of the show becomes permanent. But between Ratliff's discovery of the exhibition and his stopping it, Faulkner does something that is completely characteristic of his narrative methods. When the men start moving toward the stable, Ratliff asks: "What's this you all have got here now?" and is simply told "Go and see it." We do not learn until thirty-odd pages later what Ratliff's horrified reaction is. Having taken one look, he starts cursing, but he tells the spectators, "I aint cussing you folks. I'm cussing all of us."

Now the intervening pages that separate Ratliff's move toward the stable from his reaction consist of a long flashback in time. The flashback describes the coming of spring and the idiot's response to burgeoning nature and his wanderings over the hills with the cow as he companions her, saves her from a grass fire, steals feed for her, milks her, and at night lies down to sleep beside her. Why has Faulkner interposed these pages just before Ratliff sees the idiot's bestiality? Because Faulkner wants us to understand what the act means to Ike. These intervening pages are filled with some of the richest and most evocative prose-poetry that Faulkner ever wrote. Here, for example, is a dawn scene: the idiot

would hear [the cow] coming down the creekside in the mist. It would not be after one hour, two hours, three; the dawn would be empty, the moment and she would not be, then he would hear her and he would lie drenched in the wet grass, serene and one and indivisible in joy, listening to her approach. He would smell her; the whole mist reeked with her; the same malleate hands of mist which drew along his prone drenched flanks played her pearled barrel too and shaped them both somewhere in immediate time, already married. (P. 165)

Here is sunrise as the idiot experiences it. It seems to him that light is not "decanted onto earth from the sky" but rises from earth into the sky:

> It wakes, up-seeping, attritive in uncountable creeping channels: first root; then frond by frond, from whose escaping tips like gas it rises and disseminates and stains the sleep-fast earth with drowsy insect-murmur; then, still upward-seeking, creeps the knitted bark of trunk and limb where, suddenly louder leaf by leaf and disper- sive in diffusive sudden speed, melodious with the winged and jeweled throats, it upward bursts and fills night's globed negation with jonquil thunder. (P. 181)

As I remarked earlier, for Ike the cow becomes a kind of nature goddess, like the Egyptian cow-headed goddess Ha- thor, or like Hera (Juno was her Latin name), whom the Greeks called "ox-eyed."

> She stands as he left her, tethered, chewing. Within the mild enormous moist and pupilless globes he sees himself in twin miniature mirrored by the inscrutable abstraction; one with that which Juno might have looked out with, he watches himself contemplating what those who looked at Juno saw. He sets the basket before her. She begins to eat. (P. 182)

The idiot eats with her out of the same basket, "hulls and meal, and oats and raw corn and silage and pig-swill. . . ." There is an almost complete communion between them.

And to close the round of the day, there is a description of evening. The light drains from

> the sky and creep[s] leaf by voiceless leaf and twig and branch and trunk, descending, gathering frond by frond among the grass, still creeping downward in drowsy insect murmurs, until at last the complete all of light

gathers about that still and tender mouth in one last expiring inhalation. [Ike] rises. The swale is constant with random and erratic fireflies. (P. 186)

When the idiot reaches the cow,

she has already begun to lie down—first the forequarters, then the hinder ones, lowering herself in two distinct stages into the spent ebb of evening, nestling back into the nest-form of sleep, the mammalian attar. They lie down together. (Ibid.)

Why has Faulkner lavished so much of his nature poetry on the life of Ike and his cow—and remember that I have quoted only a few lines from a sustained description that is over thirty pages long? Certainly not because he is trying to justify the idiot's bestialism. I am sure that the horror expressed by Ratliff and by Houston, the owner of the cow, accords with Faulkner's own attitude. Faulkner's purpose is to suggest that even the almost mindless act of the idiot is, after all, an expression of love, not merely of sexual appetite. Ike Snopes is a man so deeply merged into nature that one is tempted to see him as no more than an animal. Yet, even he is capable of certain human cares and concerns. He dares to dash through the grass fire to rescue the cow. He tends her and feeds her. Even his sexual coupling with her is part of a total experience which involves his whole being; it is among other things an act of worship. For the idiot, the cow is an embodiment of nature itself. She is for him, as I have already intimated, a pagan nature goddess and, since the idiot is so deeply immersed in nature, an appropriate object of worship.

Faulkner's development of the novel thus far clearly invites us to compare Ike with his cousin Flem. Flem has been presented as the man with ice water in his veins. Ratliff, for example, sees him as the "cold and froglike victor" over the community. By contrast, Ike, with his poor stunted mind, nevertheless comes closer to real humanity. At least he can respond with his whole being to the beauty and fullness of nature. Flem seems interested only in possessing the whole natural world as an abstraction.

For a few incautious readers, Faulkner has succeeded too well—quite beyond his own intentions, I am sure. These few readers have recorded their blame of Ratliff for removing Ike's cow and thus putting a stop to his career of bestiality. In effect, they say that the world needs more love and accordingly assert that Ratliff has acted as an officious, self-righteous censor of morals. Perhaps we live in a permissive age, but how permissive should we get? Faulkner has used Ike positively to suggest the meaning of nature to this almost completely natural and uninhibited man; he has used Ike negatively to judge and condemn Flem's alienation from nature. But Faulkner himself, as this novel shows, is on the side of humanity. His ideal is the whole man who must love and even reverence nature, but who also inhabits a world that transcends nature, as man with his access to both past and future transcends the beast locked in his virtual present and into a pattern of instinctual responses.

The owner of the cow, Jack Houston, has his own story, and a curious story it is. Houston is now a widower. He had married rather late in life a girl who, from their days in grammar school together, had been in love with him. Houston resisted the whole notion of marrying and settling down with this girl or any other. He even left the country and stayed away for a number of years. But finally impelled to go home, he there found the girl from whom he had fled, still unmarried, still, in effect, waiting for him. He capitulated, and in his marriage found complete happiness. Houston built a new house and bought a stallion to ride. But Faulkner describes the purchase of this stallion as a kind of symbolic act, "as if for a wedding present to her, though he never said so. Or if that blood and bone and muscles represented that polygamous and bitless masculinity which he had relinquished, he never said that."

Whatever his motive, the buying of the stallion was fateful, for after some months of entire happiness, the stallion killed the woman. She was hunting a "missing hen-nest in the stable" though she had been warned that the horse was dangerous, but she was not afraid and did not take care. The frantic husband shot the stallion and resigned himself to living alone, but he was inconsolable and bottled up in himself a racking grief. Houston does not occupy an important role in this novel—he is simply the man who owned the cow that Ike worshipped and the man with whom Mink Snopes quarreled over a yearling bull. Yet Faulkner's vivid twelve-page account of his life makes him somehow an attractive figure. It certainly makes him come alive.

The story of Houston, though so briefly told, also points to an aspect of this novel that we have not mentioned so far. *The Hamlet* concerns itself, among other things, with the varieties of love. We have already witnessed some very different sorts of love. There is Labove's mad, hopeless, and of course unrequited, love for Eula. There is, as a negative case, the absolute lack of love for Eula (or for any other creature) by Flem, the man who actually marries her. There is Ike's horrifying association with the beast though, taking into account his poor limited mind, it has the characteristics of genuine love. And then there is the story of Houston who dreaded the full commitment that a married love entails, but who eventually made—and most happily—that commitment. But this is not all. There follows a brief account of Mink Snopes as a lover, and again it is the story of the most unlikely kind of marriage.

Mink had, as a poor young man, wandered into a lumber camp located in a stand of virgin timber. Most of the laborers were convicts leased out by the state. Yettie, the daughter of the man in charge of this lumbering enterprise, lives like a sultaness with a male harem. From time to time she would point out to the foreman a man that she wanted for her bed. In due course, Mink was summoned and, as Faulkner puts it, "entered not the hot and quenchless bed of a barren and lecherous woman, but the fierce simple cave of a lion-

ess. . . ." The experience, as Faulkner puts it, "made a mo-
nogamist of him forever" and, Faulkner might have added,
also made the woman monandrous forever. With the collapse
of her father's little empire five months later, Mink and the
woman walked to "the nearest county-seat and bought a
license" and were married by a justice of the peace.

Now on an early page of *The Hamlet* we find them living on
a hard-scrabble farm out from Frenchman's Bend with their
two little girls. Our glimpse of the way in which Mink treats
Yettie makes it difficult to believe that she was ever a lioness,
choosing her nightly companion from a whole camp of men.
Nevertheless, Yettie's present passionate devotion to her
fierce little husband is not left in doubt. In Faulkner's world,
love can become a transforming power. It can on occasion—
and between the most unlikely couple—set up an irrevocable
bond.

One of the several ironies in *The Hamlet* is that it should be
one husband indissolubly married to his wife who should kill
another husband just as fully and passionately wedded to *his*
own wife, although she is now dead. But so it is. Mink does
shoot Houston from ambush.

Mink is, as Ratliff puts it, a very special kind of Snopes, just
as the highly poisonous cottonmouth mocassin is a very
special kind of snake. Mink is made dangerous by the fact
that he has a sense of honor. His kinsmen, such as Flem or
Lump or I. O., are completely deficient in that dangerous
commodity. But Mink's honor comes close to being his sole
possession. Perhaps this is why he feels the need to protect it
so zealously.

Mink feels that Houston has besmirched his honor. Houston has not only treated him unjustly in the matter of the
impounded cow, but he has humiliated him before the community. When Mink does shoot Houston he would like, we
are told, to leave on Houston's body a printed placard reading: "*This is what happens to the men who impound Mink Snopes's
cattle,* with his name signed to it."

Yet how can one attribute a sense of honor to a man who

shoots from ambush? Well, I concede that Mink's honor is a rather soiled rag, but I think that one can show that it is nonetheless honor. For one thing, Mink makes no serious attempt to get away. He does not, to be sure, go to the sheriff with a confession that he did it, but he does refuse to leave the community, though his wife frantically begs him to go away and—obviously by prostituting herself—procures for him the money for his flight. Mink will not accept money earned by prostitution, and he refuses to try to get away.

Moreover, one of his wretched kinsmen, Lump Snopes, is incredulous when, under questioning, Mink tells him that he did not turn out the dead man's pockets—did not do so even though, as Lump tells him, it was common knowledge that Houston had fifty dollars on his person. Mink did not kill for money: the killing was in his eyes a proper retaliation. He had avenged an insult, had vindicated his own manhood.

Note that I attempt no defense of Mink. I grant that wretched little Mink's mind and soul were thoroughly warped. But it is important to try to understand his motives and to realize that he is capable of acting against his own self-interest, something of which his cousin Flem is simply incapable.

Mink was eventually caught and put in jail to await trial for murder. His one hope was that when Flem came back from Texas, Flem would see to it that he did not hang or go to the penitentiary for life. Mink reposes a confident hope in clan loyalty, and many of the community tended to agree that prosperous Flem would help his kinsman. Ratliff was not so sure, and Ratliff turned out to be right. Flem observes no code of abstract justice; he does not even respond to the primitive code of clan loyalty and obligation.

With the fourth and last section of the novel, Flem and Eula and Eula's infant have come back from Texas. Flem believes in making money out of everything, including his honeymoon. When he returns to Frenchman's Bend, he brings with him a string of Texas ponies, mean-tempered, wild, and unbroken. Flem hopes to sell them to the villagers for a profit.

They do not appear to be a bargain, for they are so vicious that they are strung together with barbed wire. A Texan named Buck Hipps takes care of them and the next day auctions them off.

As for Flem, he pretends that he has nothing to do with the horses. But the community is quickly convinced that they do belong to Flem and that such profits as are realized will go into Flem's pockets. But his ownership cannot be proved and so Flem is able to evade all responsibility for them.

Ratliff suspects that the horses do belong to Flem and makes it plain that he has no intention of bidding on these little devilish creatures. But, as we shall see, his warning is not heeded. The men of Frenchman's Bend are crazy about horses, and the Texan is a wonderful salesman. Long before the actual auction begins, he is busy showing off the ponies' good points. He says to the little crowd that has gathered: "'Them's good, gentle ponies,'" and proceeds to demonstrate. He grabs the nearest one by the head, "gripping the animal's nostrils, holding the horse's head wrenched half around while it breathed in hoarse, smothered groans. 'See?' [the Texan] said in a panting voice, the veins standing white and rigid in his neck and along his jaw. 'See? All you got to do is handle them a little and work hell out of them for a couple of days. Now look out. Give me room back there'" (p. 173).

The men do move back a little, and the Texan is able to let the horse go, which turns out to be as perilous as letting go a tiger. As he sprang away, "a second horse slashed at his back, severing his vest from collar to hem down the back exactly as the trick swordsman severs a floating veil with one stroke."

Finally, however, the Texan gets his horses into a fenced lot and, freed at last, "they whipped and whirled about the lot like dizzy fish in a bowl." But Buck Hipps keeps up his encouraging words: "'Pretty lively now,' he said. 'But it'll work out of them in a couple of days.'"

Earlier I commented on some of Faulkner's nature poetry.

Those scenes were generally static, or else show nature only quietly in motion—clouds floating across the sky or the slow failing of the light as evening comes on. In his account of the spotted horses, one finds brilliant descriptions of violent action. In fact, some of the best examples of Faulkner's celebrated power to catch and freeze the movement of exploding action occur in this episode. But Faulkner does not necessarily abandon his prose-poetry of nature, and one of the features of the powerful writing to be found in this part of *The Hamlet* is the juxtaposition of scenes of repose and scenes of frenzied commotion. For example, on one page we have the horses in the moonlight, rushing "fluid, phantom, and unceasing, to huddle again in mirage-like clumps from which came high abrupt squeals and the vicious thudding of hooves." But on the next page "the dreamy lambence of the moonlight" reveals a very different scene. It is a pear tree "now in full and frosty bloom, the twigs and branches springing not outward from the limbs but standing motionless and perpendicular above the horizontal boughs like the separate and upstreaming hair of a drowned woman sleeping upon the uttermost floor of the windless and tideless sea."

This is the poetry of stasis, of strange and occult beauty. It contrasts sharply with the poetry of violent motion, of shift and change which dominates the whole episode of the spotted horses. The pear tree passage makes a further contrast with the dominant tone of this section. The pear tree as a drowned woman lying on the floor of a tideless sea goes back to Faulkner's first great admiration—the poetry of Swinburne. This description is incantatory, evocative, richly decadent. But the prevailing tone of the section is comic, earthy, filled with solid folk humor. Ratliff in particular becomes a sardonic voice, quietly mocking the gullibility of his fellow villagers as he watches Flem bait his trap with which to catch them.

It is the combination of the nature poetry and the realistic but comic account of Flem's machinations that gives this section of *The Hamlet* its resonance: that is to say, the story is not merely one of rural high jinks, though it is that too. It becomes a kind of fable of what happened to the virgin continent of North America in the nineteenth century. Flem is not just a small, sharp trader, but a convincing symbol of big business as it proceeds to take over an essentially pastoral domain and to bilk a fundamentally decent but too gullible yeomanry. In short, the somewhat amusing tempest in this very small teapot mimics a larger storm that actually blew on the land with tremendous consequence for the American people.

The foregoing interpretation will or will not seem convincing to the reader. In any case, it certainly is not pressed by Faulkner. He makes no pretension to being a moralist, and if some of his episodes have symbolic meaning, he forbears to tag them with portentous labels. If the reader insists on a literal reading, *The Hamlet* can surely be taken as simply a story about a small-time rogue in a rural backwater, of a pretty country girl who found that she had to get married, of a string of wild Texas ponies, and of a group of countrymen who foolishly bought what they could not ride, could not harness, and indeed could not even catch.

In any case, of all Faulkner's novels, *The Hamlet* is the richest in examples of the tall tale tradition of the Old Southwest. There are three particularly fine examples: Ratliff's story of Ab Snopes's attempt to best Pat Stamper in a horse trade; Ratliff's account of how Flem Snopes went down to hell to redeem his soul; and the story, this time told in the third person, of the auctioning off of the spotted horses.

The Texan is quite an orator and quite a showman. Having trouble in getting the bidding started, he asks Eck Snopes to start things off with a ten dollar bid. But Eck very properly asks: "'What need I got for a horse I would need a bear-trap to catch?'" The Texan answers with a question of his own: "'Didn't you just see me catch him?'" But Eck, who has indeed witnessed that performance, replies: "'I seen you. And I dont want nothing as big as a horse if I got to wrastle with it every time it finds me on the same side of the fence it's on.'" But by *giving* Eck the horse in question on the promise that he will bid something on the next one, the Texan gets the bidding started.

Henry Armstid comes up just in time to hear the Texan give the first horse to Eck, and, in spite of the pleas of his wife, insists on bidding on the second horse. Mrs. Armstid protests that "'we got chaps in the house that never had shoes last winter. We aint got corn to feed the stock. We got five dollars I earned weaving by firelight after dark.'" But Henry bids that five dollars and insists that the Texan accept it.

The Texan, however, has no intention of taking advantage of such poverty. At the end of the auction, he hands a five dollar bill to Mrs. Armstid with these words: "'Get him on away, missus.'" And when Henry insists that he has bought the horse, the Texan replies: "'You don't own no horse of mine.'" But Henry, with a sure instinct that the Texan is merely Flem's agent, hands the five dollars to Flem. Flem takes it: he never refuses money.

When the Texan leaves the scene with Flem riding in the buggy beside him, the new owners have to take possession of their property, and Faulkner's prose rises to meet the occasion. The men enter the lot and advance on the horses; but when the horses, retreating before them, suddenly sense that they have moved back almost into that strange man-made contrivance, the barn, there arises among them "an indescribable sound, a movement desperate and despairing. . . . for an instant of static horror men and animals faced one another, then the men walked and ran before a gaudy vomit of long wild faces and splotched chests which overtook and scattered them and flung them sprawling aside." The horses rush on out through the gate that someone has left open and fill the lanes and thunder across the bridges of this whole end of Yoknapatawpha County. Their "brief and fading bursts of galloping hooves" resound through "the tremulous April night murmuring with the moving of sap and the wet bursting of burgeoning leaf and bud. . . ."

In the melee of horses and men, Henry Armstid receives a broken leg. More than ever, his wife is desperate to get back the five dollars that the Texan had told her Flem would have for her the next day. So the poor, beaten-down woman takes her courage in her hands and goes to Varner's store the next day. Flem is there and is equal to the occasion: "'I reckon [the Texan] forgot it,'" he tells Mrs. Armstid. "'He took all the money away with him when he left.'"

The hopeless woman has no recourse. "'I reckon it's about time to get dinner started,'" she says, and starts to leave. But Flem stops her. "'Wait a minute,'" he says, and going back into the store emerges in a moment with a little paper bag of candy. "'A little sweetening for the chaps,'" he tells her, and Mrs. Armstid is too browbeaten to throw it in his face. Instead, she says "'You're right kind,'" and moves toward home like "a gray and blasted treetrunk moving, somehow intact and upright, upon an unhurried flood." The store clerk suddenly cackles and slaps his thigh. "'By God, . . . you cant beat him,'" he exclaims. Flem has cancelled a five-dollar debt with a lie and five cents worth of cheap candy.

A little later Frenchman's Bend at large comes to acknowledge that Flem indeed cannot be beaten when he is brought into court by Mrs. Armstid and Mrs. Vernon Tull. The old justice of the peace, though he looks at Mrs. Armstid "with pity and grief," has to rule against her because one of Flem's cousins and allies, Lump Snopes, swears that he saw Flem give back the five dollars in question to the Texan. Lump owes allegiance to Flem and is quite willing to perjure himself.

Next, Mrs. Tull's case is called, and she is as belligerent as Mrs. Armstid was abject and defeatist. She remarks to Lump: "'If you think you are going to lie and perjure Flem and Eck Snopes out of—'" She means out of trouble, then he has another think coming. Mrs. Tull charges that one of the wild horses belonging to Eck Snopes ran up into the wagon in which she and Vernon and her daughters were riding. The horse caused their mules to run away, to the bodily injury of her husband.

Yet here again the law turns out to be ineffectual. As the justice puts it: "'The injury to your husband aint disputed. And the agency of the horse aint disputed.'" The only question is who owned the horse. Eck, almost the only honest Snopes, does not deny ownership. He volunteers that the Texas man gave it to him. But the old justice is forced to point out that there is no authentic document showing that the Texan transferred ownership to Eck, and that the fact that the Texan was heard to give the horse away is not enough to prove a transfer of ownership.

"'So I get nothing,' Mrs. Tull says. . . . 'My team is made to run away by a wild spotted mad-dog, my wagon is wrecked; my husband is jerked out of it and knocked unconscious . . . and I get nothing.'" But the justice interposes. She does get something: the law says that when the owner of the animal cannot or will not assume liability, "'the injured or damaged party shall find recompense in the body of the animal.'"

This final ruling is just too much for Mrs. Tull. "'The horse!'" she shouts. "'We see it for five seconds, while it is climbing into the wagon. . . . Then it's gone, God dont know where and thank the Lord He dont! . . . And he gives us the horse! Dont hold me [she says to her husband]. Get onto that wagon, fool that would sit there behind a pair of young mules with the reins tied around his wrist! Get on to that wagon, all of you!'" So, in raging disgust, she hustles her whole family out. What has happened is also too much for the justice of the peace. "'I cant stand no more,' the old Justice cried. 'I wont! This court's adjourned! Adjourned!'"

As happens too often, the law cannot protect the community. Part of Flem's power is his ability to stay just within the law. Even the representative of the law, the old justice of the peace, is confounded by the course of events. The only verdict he can render under the circumstances clearly runs counter to common sense and fundamental equity. Granted that the incident in question involves a little backwater community and the machinations of a very small-time rogue, the moral comes through plainly enough. All of which is not to say that Faulkner is a heavy-handed moralist: much of his telling of the "spotted horses" episode is hilarious. Besides, on the whole, not a great deal of damage is done. Certain farmers have lost some money and a good deal of self-esteem, but after all, no one compelled them to buy the devilish little ponies. Nevertheless, Mrs. Armstid is victimized—no laughing matter except for the likes of Lump Snopes. Faulkner, one observes, has been careful to include Mrs. Armstid in the story.

So Flem is triumphant once more. And he is to score one greater triumph before the book closes. He is to defeat even that honest and sagacious trader, V. K. Ratliff. He does it through one of the oldest tricks of all, the ruse of the salted gold mine. He so manages matters that Ratliff gets the notion that someone is digging for buried gold on the grounds of the Old Frenchman place. Ratliff takes the bait, raises what money he can, and is joined by a man named Bookwright, and Henry Armstid, who raised his share of the money needed by mortgaging his farm, "including the buildings and tools and livestock and about two miles of three-strand wire fence." Together they buy from Flem the Old Frenchman place and start digging for treasure themselves. In time they find silver coins all right; but a closer inspection indicates that they were minted long after the old Frenchman was alleged to have buried his wealth.

Some eyebrows have been raised at Faulkner's allowing Ratliff to be taken in by so obvious a trick. But Ratliff had long had a "thing" about the Old Frenchman place (look back on page 157). We are told that Ratliff "had never for one moment believed that [the Old Frenchman place] had no value." But there are more solid justifications for making Ratliff vulnerable in this case. Earlier, he had been jousting with Flem as a test of skill, as a vindication of his own shrewd judgment, not primarily for the money to be gained. One remembers that in his earlier victory over Flem he donated all his profits to the idiot Ike. But now his primary object is that buried treasure, and his judgment is consequently blinded. There is a further point: though in *The Hamlet* Ratliff becomes the conscience of the countryside, Faulkner does not mean to turn him into a saint. He is basically a decent and likeable man, but he is thoroughly human, and like the rest of us, he has his weaknesses. Flem knows how to play upon them, and, as a manipulator who is cold-blooded and absolutely single-minded, he is almost certain to win. Such men do usually win against people who have not become inhuman—against people who can be distracted, who value things other than just money, and who set a limit to what they will and will not do.

The last scene of the novel shows us Flem in his buggy on the way to Jefferson, which constitutes for him a new world to conquer. He stops the buggy on the road beside the Old Frenchman place where poor, crazy Henry Armstid is still —now in full daylight—digging for nonexistent treasure.

Ratliff and Bookwright quickly recover their poise and even their sense of humor, once they have discovered that they have been had. They try to persuade Henry Armstid to accept the bad news, but Henry has lost too much: he has literally gambled everything. Besides, Henry is a violent, passionate, warped little man. Now he is clearly demented. He spades the earth "with the regularity of a mechanical toy and with something monstrous in his unflagging effort." When Flem halts his buggy by the road, he sees his victim at his hopeless labor. Armstid "did not glance up at the sun, as a man pausing in work does to gauge the time. He came straight back to the trench, hurrying back to it with that painful and laboring slowness, the gaunt unshaven face which was now completely that of a madman." Flem turns away his head, spits over the wagon wheel, jerks the reins of his team, and puts them in motion. Flem's act of spitting here is eloquent: it signifies contemptuous indifference, a dismissal devoid of normal curiosity. Compared to it, Pilate's washing of his hands seems positively compassionate.

The Hamlet is a remarkable novel, and in my opinion, rarely given its proper due. I find it one of the richest of the novels in the Faulkner canon. It has the virtue that the Elizabethans loved: *copia*, amplitude, fullness. Where else can you find so many brilliant portraits of interesting human beings: Mink, Houston, Labove, Eula, Will Varner, Ratliff, not to mention others? Where else does Faulkner exhibit more powerfully his capacity to handle the tall tale? Or consider the varieties of love exhibited against that great bare background of sheer negativity and non-love represented by Flem Snopes. Consider, too, Faulkner's prose poetry, especially the celebration of nature. While such poetry occurs all through Faulkner's work, *The Hamlet*'s only rival among his novels, for either quality or quantity, would be *Go Down, Moses*. As for unity, there is surely a sufficiency. The narrative line is plain: the rise from rags to riches of a poor but dishonest young man, and for those who insist on the presence of a moral fable, that too is provided for, but without primness or overt manipulation. *The Hamlet* is a novel to be read again and again, and it is a wonderful text for reading aloud.

6 · GO DOWN, MOSES

To many readers *Go Down, Moses* seems merely a collection of stories, not a true novel at all. But Faulkner regarded it as a novel. It is really the story of the McCaslin family, both the white and the black McCaslins. However, the third section of *Go Down, Moses*, entitled "Pantaloon in Black," has in it no person of McCaslin blood. When this was pointed out to Faulkner he explained that Rider, the hero of the story, lived in a cabin rented from the McCaslins. We must take Faulkner's word for it, even though we are never given this fact in the novel itself. In any case, it is really a thematic unity that holds the novel together, and the account of the young black man and his bride, Mannie, does contribute to that unity. It is a perfect counterpoint to the story of Lucas Beauchamp, whose marriage to Molly is not broken by death until Lucas is an old man. Rider's story has the joyousness of youth and also its pathos. Lucas's virtues are those of sagacity and wisdom, hard-won through the years.

Actually, I shall not talk about "Pantaloon in Black" in my discussion of *Go Down, Moses*, for, as you will remember, I have already spoken of it in the second chapter. But you might keep it in mind as I talk about Lucas Beauchamp, who has a large role in one of Faulkner's very finest stories, "The Fire and the Hearth," to be discussed a little later.

In general, one character, Isaac McCaslin, born in 1867,

dominates the book. Even though Isaac has not been born when the opening narrative takes place—the year of that narrative is 1859—the first paragraph does introduce him as a man now well over seventy. Faulkner goes out of his way to tell the reader of the first section that what follows was related to Isaac years after the event actually occurred.

This opening section, entitled "Was," is the story of a manhunt after a runaway slave. McCaslin Edmonds, Isaac's cousin, is a young boy at the time and plays a role in the events. The subject sounds gruesome enough, but the tone of the account is comic. The slave who is being chased is Tomey's Turl; that is to say, his mother was named Thomasina, a name that became Tomey, and Turl's formal name was Terrel, now slurred to the monosyllable Turl. As the reader eventually finds out—for Faulkner seems in no hurry to tell him—Tomey's Turl is the half brother of his owners, the twins, Uncle Buck and Uncle Buddy. (Their baptized names, by the way, are Theophilus and Amodeus McCaslin.) Turl, then, is a kinsman as well as a slave, and Uncle Buck and Uncle Buddy are very peculiar slaveholders. Indeed, they are homemade, Southern-born abolitionists, who try to hold the institution of slavery at arm's length. Because their plantation house was built by slave labor, they prefer not to live in it, but instead house the slaves there. They themselves live as bachelors in a smaller house, really a large cabin.

It soon becomes plain that they are not doctrinaire abolitionists. They are not trying to have slavery abolished. But in a pragmatic way and in concrete terms, they are trying to ameliorate the condition of their slaves and to prepare them for normal citizenship. In creating Uncle Buck and Uncle Buddy, Faulkner has used the novelist's right to choose a special case and to exaggerate. Nevertheless, there was more of abolitionism in the Old South than the modern American is led to suppose; moreover, many a man who was not a slaveholder fought bravely and wholeheartedly for the Southern cause. After all, General Lee owned no slaves, having freed those that he had inherited, whereas the great commander on the other side, General Ulysses S. Grant, did own slaves, slaves that had come to him through his marriage.

I say all this to help the reader catch the spirit of "Was" and to enjoy the comedy. The reader will miss the point if he takes this story to be an attempt to whitewash slavery. Faulkner in his fiction makes it plain, over and over again, that slavery was a curse to the South—not merely a curse laid on the blacks but on the whites as well.

To return to the story at hand: Uncle Buck and Uncle Buddy pursue Tomey's Turl not with fire in their eyes and cold fury in their hearts and not primarily to recover valuable property. Rather, Turl is a kind of licensed rascal, but one who must not be allowed to create too much mischief. Uncle Buck is a great fox hunter and is exhilarated by the prospect of a good run with the hounds in pursuit of a particularly wily and cunning fox. He knows exactly where Turl is going. Turl is headed for the Beauchamp plantation to see his best girl, Tennie, a slave of the Beauchamps.

The McCaslin twins' real concern is not that Tomey's Turl will make it to the free states. Not at all. They want to catch him before he gets to the Beauchamps' because if they fail to do so, they can expect another visit from Hubert Beauchamp and his sister, Miss Sophonsiba. The visit would be made ostensibly just to return Tomey's Turl, but Miss Sophonsiba is eager to get married, and she clearly has her eye on Uncle Buck. Besides, the Beauchamps, if they came, would plan to stay, in the old Southern fashion, for a week or longer, as they did last time. The strain would be too much.

Uncle Buck and his nine-year-old nephew, McCaslin Edmonds (Cass), go off in pursuit of Turl. Uncle Buddy, who never leaves the place on any occasion, stays home. Uncle Buck and Cass fail to head off Tomey's Turl and arrive at the Beauchamp plantation where Hubert Beauchamp is somewhat less than cooperative. He persuades them to have dinner before trying to run Turl down. Miss Sophonsiba is very attentive to Uncle Buck, puts on all her fine airs, and treats his attempt to capture Turl as if it were a quest in the days of knight errantry—all of which makes Uncle Buck more and more apprehensive.

The complications of the story are very intricate; so I shall simply touch on two high points. Plainly, Mr. Hubert is as eager to marry off his sister as she is to get married. Even Tomey's Turl must be aware that Miss Sophonsiba is trying to prevent his being caught so that Uncle Buck will be compelled to stay with the Beauchamps as long as possible. Uncle Buck finds himself forced to spend the night. Hubert Beauchamp secretly shifts his sister into the room that Uncle Buck believes he is to occupy, and Uncle Buck falls into the trap. He and his young nephew slip quietly into the darkened guest room. They remove their trousers; then Uncle Buck "lifted the mosquito-bar and raised his feet and rolled into the bed. That was when Miss Sophonsiba sat up on the other side of Uncle Buck and gave the first scream."

She has been compromised. She will not listen to explanations. She simply keeps on screaming. Her brother will not listen to explanations either—not even when Uncle Buck pleads with him to be reasonable. Surely, had he "'tried to get into bed with her, would [he] have took a nine-year-old boy with [him]?'" But Hubert says that he is being reasonable. He would like a "little peace and quiet and freedom" himself. As he puts it "'[if I let you get off,] I would not only be unreasonable, I'd be a damned fool.'"

There is, however, one slim hope for escape. Mr. Hubert is something of a compulsive gambler, and Uncle Buddy, who has stayed at home, is a phenomenal poker player. While Uncle Buck is, in effect, being kept under house arrest, little nine-year-old Cass slips out the window and rides posthaste to bring Uncle Buddy to the rescue. (On this occasion Uncle Buddy will break his rule and leave home; after all it is a grave emergency.)

The plan works. Uncle Buddy plays a hand of poker for his brother's freedom. The betting gets more and more complicated, with raises joined to other conditions, entirely too complicated for anyone who is not a veteran poker player to follow. I am not a veteran poker player, and I will not attempt to go into details. To be brief: against what seem almost impossible odds, Uncle Buddy wins the hand, and the two old bachelor twins, the little boy, Tomey's Turl, and Tennie, his bride-to-be, ride joyfully home together. Tennie's transfer to McCaslin ownership had constituted one of the raises in the betting.

I asked Mr. Faulkner once how it came about that Uncle Buck and Miss Sophonsiba subsequently did get married and produce a child, Isaac McCaslin, in view of Uncle Buck's having been rescued from Miss Sophonsiba's clutches. Surely after this narrow escape Uncle Buck would have become even more wary, more gun-shy. Faulkner explained that he never got around to writing about how Uncle Buck was finally run to earth.

The next section of *Go Down, Moses* is entitled "The Fire and the Hearth" and takes place in about 1941. (The events of "Was," remember, occurred in 1859.) Buck and Buddy have long since died, but McCaslin descendants, both of white and of mixed blood, live on. One of those of mixed blood is Lucas Beauchamp, the son of Tomey's Turl and Tennie. When "The Fire and the Hearth" opens he is sixty-seven years old and has lived and worked all his life on the McCaslin plantation, which is now in the hands of Roth Edmonds, the grandson of the little nine-year-old boy who figures in the story "Was."

As this story begins, Lucas has been confronted with a problem. He has been running an illegal whiskey still for years, unbeknown to Roth Edmonds. Now Lucas has just discovered that George Wilkins, who wants to marry Lucas's daughter, Nat, is also running an illicit still and selling boot-leg whiskey. Lucas has no intention of letting this go on. George, a young man without discretion, will certainly get caught and when that happens every nook on the plantation will be checked over. In that search Lucas's own still might be discovered. Lucas does not "'want a fool for a son-in-law.'" Moreover, "'he [does not] intend to have a fool living on the same place he [lives] on.'" So Lucas puts in a night's work moving his own still to a safe place, burying it on the edge of an old Indian mound. With his own still well concealed, he plans to tell Roth Edmonds what George is doing and let the law take its course. This will be pretty hard on George and on Nat, but then Lucas is a ruthless old man.

Something has happened, however, to complicate the case further. In digging in the Indian mound to bury his still, part of the mound has collapsed, revealing a fragment of an earthenware vessel and part of its contents, a single gold coin. Lucas is immediately convinced that the old stories of buried gold on the place are true. He believes that if he can simply find the time to dig secretly he will locate the rest of the hoarded treasure.

He first thinks that he will let George off. He wants no sheriff's search for stills during the week or so that he will need to find the rest of the treasure. Besides, it might be useful to have George help with the digging. But he discovers that somebody has been watching him from a hiding place. It is Nat, and Nat will tell George that her father has been digging around the Indian mound. Lucas simply cannot afford to have George poking around, perhaps finding the treasure himself. So he hardens his heart once more. George must go. Lucas informs Roth Edmonds that George is running a still and tells him just where it is located. Roth immediately calls the sheriff.

Nat, however, proves more than a match for her father. She evidently suspects what is afoot, for the next morning Lucas is waked by his wife's screaming. She has discovered that Nat and George have taken George's still and his supply of white mule from its hiding place and piled it all on Lucas's porch. Before Lucas can destroy the evidence, the officers are there to seize it. Moreover, they have by this time located Lucas's own still down by the Indian mound. Not finding George's still at the place specified, they asked themselves what would be a good spot on the McCaslin plantation for hiding a still, and their guess pays off. Their discovery is made the easier, for Lucas had decided not to do any further digging in the mound. If law officers happened on the spot, he wanted them to find something quickly that would stop their looking further: the secret of the treasure had to be preserved.

So now the fat is in the fire. Both Lucas and George are under arrest, and the fact that Roth Edmonds, though furious, puts up bail for the pair and brings them back to the plantation is itself only a postponement of the day of judgment. There is not time to describe how they eventually get off, but three key scenes in this splendid, long story ought at least to be mentioned.

The first is a wonderful flashback. Just after Lucas mentions the name George Wilkins to Roth Edmonds, and before Roth can repeat "George Wilkins," Faulkner has inserted some fourteen pages of his best prose. The flashback takes us back to a day in 1898 when Lucas, the now aging and wily patriarch, was a passionate young man of twenty-four. It was the year in which Roth Edmonds was born. Roth's young mother was having a difficult childbirth, and Lucas was sent for the doctor. He had to swim a flooded stream to get the message through. Nonetheless, Roth's mother died. Molly, Lucas's young wife, who herself had recently given birth to her first child, moved into the white man's house to nurse the little white infant along with her own.

The arrangement persists for months, until Lucas, finding the absence of his wife intolerable and believing the worst about Molly's association with Edmonds, decides that his honor demands that he kill Edmonds. But he will not attack him from ambush in the dark: he awaits dawn to confront him. We learn a great deal about Lucas from this episode, about his manliness, his agonies, his pride in himself. He does try to kill Edmonds, but the pistol misfires. Honor is served; Molly returns to her husband's cabin; and the two little boys grow up as inseparable companions.

Lucas's overwhelming desire to find the buried treasure—he cannot be convinced that thousands of dollars are not just waiting for him to find—causes him to rent a magnetic metal detector. His handling of the white salesman who has come down from St. Louis is first-rate comedy. If Lucas has over-reached himself in his trying to manoeuvre George Wilkins into the penitentiary, in this episode he reestablishes his reputation as a man who knows how to manipulate others and to take care of his own interests. The white salesman is no match for him. In the end, it is not Lucas who is renting the machine from the salesman, but the salesman who is renting it from Lucas. Although Lucas bamboozles the sales-man by planting a few coins for him to discover, thus giving him a bad case of treasure-hunting fever, Lucas himself remains absolutely convinced that the gold is there to be found.

So when the exhausted white salesman finally gives up and returns to St. Louis, Lucas keeps up the search, and by this time it is more than his wife can stand. Molly comes to Roth Edmonds and tells him that she wants a divorce from Lucas. Lucas has become a changed man, she says. " 'He's sick in the mind now. Bad sick. He dont even get up to go to church on Sunday no more. . . . He's doing a thing the Lord aint meant for folks to do. And I'm afraid.' " Roth tries to reassure Molly that Lucas will not find any money and will finally give up. But Molly is not afraid that Lucas will not find it; rather that he will.

Lucas finally does give up his search. He brings the metal detector to Roth and asks him to get rid of it. When Roth asks, " 'For good?' " Lucas answers: " 'Yes. Clean off this place, where I wont never see it again. Just dont tell me where.' " Roth Edmonds, sensing how much the treasure means to the old man, suggests that he need not go that far, and offers to keep it for Lucas. " '. . . if you want to take that damn thing out now and then, say once or twice a month. . . .' " But Lucas is aware that it must be a clean break. He tells Roth:

"I dont want to never see it again. Man has got three

score and ten years on this earth, the Book says. He can want a heap in that time and a heap of what he can want is due to come to him, if he just starts in soon enough. I done waited too late to start. That money's there. . . . But I am near to the end of my three score and ten, and I reckon to find that money aint for me." (P. 131)

There is pathos and dignity in this moving final speech of the story.

"The Fire and the Hearth" has an amazing variety of effects. It contains some of Faulkner's most brilliant comedy and, in the person of Lucas, one of his most interesting characters. Lucas is distinctly not a stereotype of the black man—neither the old-fashioned stereotype nor the new. Lucas was to become a central character in a subsequent novel, *Intruder in the Dust*.

Isaac McCaslin is referred to in "The Fire and the Hearth," but he remains very much in the remote background. He does not appear at all in "Pantaloon in Black," which follows "The Fire and the Hearth," and does not emerge as an important character until we reach the fourth narrative, "The Old People." Yet the three sections that precede "The Old People" do provide important background material for this character who dominates "The Old People," "The Bear," and "Delta Autumn."

"The Old People" is a beautiful story which tells how Ike, at the age of twelve, killed his first buck, and how Sam Fathers, as a kind of priest of the wilderness, marked Ike's face with the hot blood of the deer. The story is thus really the account of an initiation and leads naturally up to the great hunting story, "The Bear." But if I am to do justice here to "The Bear," I shall have to forgo any further notice of "The Old People."

In "The Bear," the quarry is larger and more formidable than any deer. The object of the hunt is an immense bear that seems unkillable. He has been hunted for years and has become a local legend. Sam Fathers is the unofficial master of the hunt. Cass Edmonds is one of the Yoknapatawpha hunters, and so it is not surprising that Ike, from the age of ten, has been taken each December to the camp in the big woods to hunt the bear that has come to be known as Old Ben.

I referred to Sam Fathers earlier as a kind of priest of the wilderness, and in the course of the story Faulkner suggests that the annual hunt is a kind of ritual, a mere ceremony, since no one really believes that they can bring the great animal to bay and kill him. Faulkner refers to Ike as entering "his novitiate to the true wilderness" and that it seemed to Ike "at the age of ten he was witnessing his own birth."

Sam makes it plain that Ike must learn to discipline himself, to control his actions and even his expectations. Once or twice he hears Old Ben running before the hounds before he is even vouchsafed a glimpse. He longs to see the great animal, and Sam Fathers places him where, if he remains quiet, he may catch sight of him. But though Ike sensed somehow "that the bear was looking at him," he could not see it.

Finally, after another failure, Sam explains to Ike what he must do if he hopes to see Old Ben. " 'It's the gun,' Sam said. 'You will have to choose' "—that is, choose between divesting himself of the gun and having a sight of Old Ben, or being armed and unable to see him.

The next time, Ike leaves his gun in camp. But once in the wilderness he realizes that he must give up more; he must meet nature on its own terms. "He was still tainted" by civilization, and so he hangs his watch and his compass on a bush. Ike realizes that he must take the chance of not being able to find his way back to camp—of being lost in and at the mercy of the wilderness. He moves on, and sure enough, discovers that he *is* lost. But he does not panic; he does what Sam had told him to do under such circumstances: he begins to circle. Suddenly he sees Old Ben's tracks, the print of his trap-wrecked foot in the wet ground. Before his eyes the track is beginning to fill with water; so the bear is close at hand. Ike follows the tracks and suddenly the wilderness coalesced. . . . the tree, the bush, the compass and the watch glinting where a ray of sunlight touched them. Then he saw the bear. It did not emerge, appear: it was just there, immobile, fixed in the green and windless noon's hot dappling, not as big as he had dreamed it but as big as he had expected, bigger, dimensionless against the dappled obscurity, looking at him. Then it moved. It crossed the glade without haste, walking for an instant into the sun's full glare and out of it, and stopped again and looked back at him across one shoulder. Then it was gone. It didn't walk into the woods. It faded, sank back into the wilderness without motion as he had watched a fish, a huge old bass, sink back into the dark depths of its pool and vanish without even any movement of its fins. (P. 209)

It is as if Old Ben had vouchsafed him an audience, had allowed it to the human being who was willing to come into his mansion without fear and in humility.

The next part of "The Bear" is primarily concerned with the coming of the great mongrel dog that the hunters named Lion. He is a wild predator and kills one of Major de Spain's colts. Sam traps him, patiently tames the great beast, and teaches him who is master. It is the kind of dog that Sam has said all along they must have if they are ever to hope to bring Old Ben to bay. Ike at this time is thirteen, and we are told that he "should have hated and feared Lion." Why? Because a part of Ike does not want Old Ben killed and does not want the annual hunt to end. This is a topic to which Faulkner recurs, and I shall say more about it a little later. In the meantime, something ought to be said about Ike's experience with another dog—an experience which also taught him something about bravery, about himself, and about Old Ben.

Ike owns a little fyce. A fyce is a small mongrel dog with a good deal of fox or rat terrier in its makeup. It is quick, nervous, and its tendency to do a great deal of yapping and frenzied barking may conceal the fact that it really has a great deal of courage. Ike wants to try an experiment: he carries his fyce with a sack over its head into Old Ben's haunts, and Sam brings along two hounds on a rope leash. They "lay down-wind of the trail and actually ambushed the bear."

Old Ben turned at bay though Ike later concluded that he did so not out of alarm but out of sheer amazement "at the shrill and frantic uproar of the fyce." The bear "turned at bay against the trunk of a big cypress, on its hind feet; it seemed to the boy that it

> would never stop rising, taller and taller, and even the two hounds seemed to have taken a kind of desperate and despairing courage from the fyce. Then he realized that the fyce was actually not going to stop. He flung the gun down and ran. When he overtook and grasped the shrill, frantically pinwheeling little dog, it seemed to him that he was directly under the bear. He could smell it, strong and hot and rank. Sprawling, he looked up where it loomed and towered over him like a thunderclap. It was quite familiar, until he remembered: this was the way he had used to dream about it. (P. 211)

The bear suddenly disappears, leaving the boy and the little dog unharmed. Sam asks Ike why he did not shoot. "'You've done seed him twice now, with a gun in your hands,'" Sam says. Ike returns the question to Sam: "'You had the gun. Why didn't you shoot him?'" But he gets no answer. Sam does not seem to have heard him. Instead, Sam turns his attention to the little dog. "'You's almost the one we wants,' he said. 'You just aint big enough.'" But Sam predicts that some day, somebody is going to get the right dog. Ike replies: "'I know it. . . . That's why it must be one of us. So it wont be until the last day. When even he [the bear] dont want it to last any longer.'"

This passage is interesting. For all their passion for the hunt, neither Sam nor Ike seems eager to kill the bear and bring the annual hunt to an end. Unconsciously, they talk of the hunt as if it were a great ritual, the climax of an august action that is to be achieved in its proper way and at its proper season. Or, it might be like a great drama fulfilling itself, or a religious ceremony, and indeed, for them, it obviously is. The killing of Old Ben takes on the character of a solemn sacrifice. But these terms, I hasten to say, are mine. Sam Fathers's language is different and of course so is the language of the boy.

The fyce episode foreshadows the arrival of Lion, and the account of how Sam captured it, broke it to his command, and trained it. Boon Hogganbeck, a half-Indian, half-white man, becomes the special companion of Lion and actually shares his bed with the dog. In the first hunt in which Lion is used, there is a lively chase. Old Ben kills two of the hounds, but Lion manages to stop Old Ben and hold him for a few moments. Of the hunters, only Boon arrives in time to get a shot, and Boon is a notoriously poor marksman. As he tells it ruefully that evening: "'I missed him five times. With Lion looking right at me.'" So Old Ben breaks free, gets into the river, and escapes. That night Boon does not bed down with Lion. In his mortification, he says, "'I aint fit to sleep with him.'"

Yet the performance of Lion makes it plain that the hunt next year will probably be successful. To Ike it is like "the last act on a set stage. It was the beginning of the end of something, he didn't know what except that he would not grieve. He would be humble and proud that he had been found worthy to be a part of it too or even just to see it too."

Part three of "The Bear" tells the story of the next year's hunt. Lion is able to bring Old Ben to bay. The bear rears up on his hind feet with his back to a tree and Lion leaps for his throat. The bear catches the dog, as Faulkner describes the scene, "in both arms, almost loverlike, and they both went down." Boon is the first to get to the scene of the struggle, but this time he tosses away his gun and, as the bear stands up erect again with Lion still clinging to his throat, Boon leaps on the bear's back and with his knife probes for the bear's heart.

With Old Ben's death, Sam Fathers collapses. He has

suffered no injury. He appears simply exhausted, not only physically but emotionally. As for Lion, the great dog has been almost disemboweled. Boon declares that he is going to the nearest settlement for a doctor. Major de Spain, one of the hunters, alluding to Boon's torn ear and claw-shredded arm and leg, says that Boon needs a doctor himself, but Boon is concerned only for the dog. "'Damn that,' Boon said. . . . 'Cant you see his goddamn guts are all out of him?'" But De Spain sends Tennie's Jim for the doctor and Boon stays at the camp where the dog and Sam Fathers have been brought.

The doctor arrives and sews up Lion as best he can. As for Sam, the doctor can find nothing really wrong. He is simply to be kept in bed for a day or two. The doctor's final diagnosis is that Sam has just "quit," and he goes on to explain: "'Old people do that sometimes. Then they get a good night's sleep or maybe it's just a drink of whisky, and they change their minds.'" But, as we shall find later, Sam has no further reason to live now. He will not change his mind. He is old and tired and he wants to go home—to join his lost people.

It is one of those "windless Mississippi December days which are a sort of Indian summer's Indian summer," to quote Faulkner's own beautiful phrasing. Since the weather is mild, Boon has Lion moved out to the front gallery of the house into the sunlight; Lion had never liked to be shut inside a building. By sundown Lion is dead.

The hunting party prepared to break camp and go back to town. Boon will remain with Sam Fathers at Sam's little wilderness house here at the boundary of the big woods. Ike wants to stay with Sam too, and, after General Compson intercedes for him, Cass, Ike's elder kinsman, raises no objection. Missing a couple of days of school will not be that important. This is a Thursday. Somebody will come back for Ike on Sunday.

Cass and Major de Spain start back to the camp on Saturday evening and after driving all night arrive at Sam's house before daybreak on Sunday morning. Some distance away is the mound that marks Lion's grave. The men see close by it a platform of freshly cut saplings bound to four posts, and on it a blanket-wrapped bundle. It is an Indian-style burial. There they find Boon and Ike "squatting between the platform and [Lion's] grave."

The almost inarticulate Boon is frantic with grief. He has his gun with him and is guarding the grave. As Cass walks toward him, he shouts "'By God, you won't touch him. Stand back, McCaslin.'" But Cass continues to walk slowly toward him and gets his hand on the gun. He says quietly, "'Turn it loose, Boon.'"

Boon tells them: "'This is the way he wanted it. He told us. He told us exactly how to do it.'" And Boon explains why he and Ike have been keeping a vigil by the grave to keep the wild animals away. By this time Cass has quickly taken the shells out of Boon's gun and dropped the gun behind him, all the time keeping his eyes on Boon.

Then Cass puts the question that he should not have put: "'Did you kill him, Boon?'" It is almost too much for Boon. Like a drunken man, he stumbles toward the tree, catching at it, then turning his back toward it, like Old Ben himself, now at bay. Cass puts the question again, keeping his eyes fixed on Boon's "wild spent scoriated face and the tremendous heave and collapse of his chest."

Boon's reply is "'No! No!'"

"'Tell the truth,' McCaslin says. 'I would have done it if he had asked me to.'" This inquisition is too much for Boon and too much for the boy.

> Then the boy moved. He was between them, facing McCaslin; the water felt as if it had burst and sprung not from his eyes alone but from his whole face, like sweat.
>
> "Leave him alone!" he cried. "Goddamn it! Leave him alone!" (P. 254)

It is a magnificent ending to the account of Sam Fathers' death. If Faulkner had been interested only in the story of the annual hunting of Old Ben, this would have made a smashing ending. But Faulkner had other things to tell us in "The Bear," and so there are parts four and five still to come.

The "present" of the fourth part of "The Bear" is 1888. Ike is now twenty-one and, having come of age, he has an important decision to make. Most of the substance of this part is taken up with his attempt to explain his decision to Cass Edmonds, his elder kinsman who, along with old Sam, the half-Indian, has stood as a father to Ike.

Ike is the last living male descendant of Old Carothers McCaslin through the male line. Old Carothers was his grandfather. Ike is therefore the legal heir to the McCaslin plantation. His cousin Cass is only the great-grandson of Old Carothers, and besides, he descends through the female line, for Cass's grandmother was Uncle Buck and Uncle Buddy's sister. Remember that Ike was born very late in his father's life, a circumstance that accounts for the fact that though he is only two generations distant from Old Carothers whereas Cass is three generations removed, Ike is sixteen years *younger* than Cass.

By law and custom, Ike, now that he has come of age, should take possession of the plantation, and his cousin Cass expects him to do so. More than that, he urges him to do so. But Ike has decided to repudiate his inheritance, and this is essentially what his long colloquy with Cass, which occupies most of part four, is about.

Ike gives two reasons for renouncing his inheritance. The first has to do with what he learned from Sam Fathers, the great hunter and priest of the wilderness. The primary lesson was that since nature belongs to all men, no man can own it. Cass, however, has the better of the logical and practical aspects of the argument. For example, he asks the younger man how he can believe that he must repudiate what he has inherited from his father and grandfather if he really believes that his grandfather never owned the land in the first place, or that the Indian who sold the land to his grandfather ceased to own it the moment that he thought of it as something that could be sold. If land is something that cannot be bought and sold, since it cannot be possessed by any one individual, then why is Ike's act of repudiation necessary?

It soon becomes apparent, however, that Ike is speaking out of a deep mystical conviction. As Ike confesses a little later in his talk with Cass, he does not himself fully understand what it is that he is trying to articulate. But his conviction *is* deep, and he is not to be deterred by the logical contradictions that Cass discovers in his argument. It very quickly becomes clear that Ike is not merely concerned with a universal principle, but with a profound personal commitment. Thus, though he says that no man can take possession of this or that portion of God's earth, he is not trying to persuade Cass to join him in repudiating the ownership of land. Ike seems to take it for granted that Cass will in fact continue to operate the plantation as he has through the years during which Ike has been a minor—and, with Ike's blessing, take legal title to it. Let Cass inherit the plantation. Ike simply insists that he himself cannot accept ownership.

Ike's rather mystical view of the matter is involved with his conception of America and the American dream, and also with his concern for the injury done to the black man in enslaving him. As we listen to Ike talk, we come to understand that Ike is a deeply religious man. True, he has his own interpretation of Christianity, but there is no question that he has committed himself whole-heartedly and fervently to certain tenets of the Christian faith and that he means to conform his life to them.

How is his view of America related to his view of the world? In order to offer a new chance to men living in "the old world's worthless twilight," God allowed Columbus to discover the New World. Note that Ike does not believe in the concept of the Noble Savage. The Indians who already possessed the New World had failed to build a just society. The land was already accursed, "already tainted before any white man owned it." It needed new blood and a new start.

But the white men failed too. They brought with them, almost as soon as they came to the Americas, the curse of black chattel slavery. The curse was so heavy that God foresaw that it would take time—perhaps a long time—before even "some of His lowly people" could be set free.

When Cass points out that one could find texts in the Bible itself that seemed to justify slavery as the proper condition of black men, Ike is ready with an answer. He tells his cousin that "There are some things [God] said in the Book, and some things reported of Him that He did not say." Besides, Ike argues, the Holy Scriptures were written to be "read . . . by the heart, not by the wise of the earth because maybe they dont need it or maybe the wise no longer have any heart." The Scriptures were written to be read "by the doomed and lowly of the earth who have nothing else to read with but the heart." The men who wrote the Bible "were writing about truth and there is only one truth and it covers all things that touch the heart."

This long colloquy between Ike and Cass reveals also that Ike has been much influenced not only by Sam Fathers but by his own father and his uncles, Buck and Buddy, those undoctrinaire abolitionists, who deplored slavery and gave their own slaves as much freedom as they could.

Yet there was still another circumstance which I judge was an even more powerful influence in forming Ike's decision to repudiate the McCaslin land. Ike had leafed through the commissary ledgers, reading in the fading handwriting of his father and uncle the business transactions of the plantation and the records kept of the slaves, including their births and deaths. In the course of such reading Ike discovered something that shocked him.

There were certain rather cryptic entries that made it plain to him that Old Carothers, his grandfather, had begotten a child of Eunice, one of his slaves. The child was a girl named Thomasina, who later died in childbirth, though her child, a boy named Terrel, survived. The fact that Old Carothers in his will left Terrel $1000 and that Eunice, Thomasina's mother and Terrel's grandmother, drowned herself some six months before Terrel's birth, allows only one explanation: Old

Carothers had not only begotten a child on one of his slaves, but he had been guilty of father-daughter incest with that child. So Tomey's Turl of the story "Was" turns out to be Thomasina's Terrel of the ledgers. It is a dark and terrible secret. Ike, who was sixteen when he found it out, had been deeply and permanently affected.

Ike's repudiation of his inheritance, then, derives not only from a rather mystical vision of what should be, but from a desire to expiate his grandfather's sin.

The ledgers, it should be said, are much more than a dark chronicle. They include their comic elements, and they even record good deeds, for instance, the emancipation of slaves by Uncle Buck and Uncle Buddy on the very day on which their father, Old Carothers, was buried. Clearly, Carothers's sons, Theophilus and Amodeus, in their own way, also repudiated their father's wickedness.

In this fourth part of "The Bear," we learn further about the seriousness with which Ike attempted to fulfill his grandfather's legacy to Tomey's Turl, and through him, to Turl's three surviving children.

To return to the long colloquy between Ike and Cass, they eventually get on to the subject of the Civil War, as any two Southerners talking together in 1888 must have done. Ike has his own interpretation of the War. He sees slavery as a curse, and has to rejoice in its destruction, and yet he is proud of the fight that his native section put up, though so heavily outnumbered, outgunned, and blockaded. How does Ike make sense of his position? By boldly arguing that the hand of Providence is to be seen in the fact that the War was fought at all.

God saw to it that the South would lose the War—in spite of its gallantry. In effect, Ike says: Look at the almost incredible falling out of events—for instance the Battle of Antietam, when Lee's battle orders were dropped on the floor of a tavern, picked up by a Yankee soldier, and brought to his commander just after Lee had divided his army in the face of the enemy. Look at Stonewall Jackson, shot down by his own men in the gathering darkness at the great victory of Chancellorsville. Look at Longstreet, Lee's other great lieutenant, also shot by his own men under similar circumstances only a few months later.

Ike sees such disastrous accidents as in fact no accidents at all. In them he sees the hand of God. God wanted the South to lose. Why? Because he loved the Southern people but realized that they could "learn nothing save through suffering, remember nothing save when underlined in blood. . . ." To bring on the War and provide that the South should lose was the only way to break the hold of slavery on the South.

Ike argues that it was almost incredible that the War was fought at all, what with the great differences that existed in the North between the New Englanders on the one hand and the farmers of Iowa and Illinois on the other. So much for the essential disunity of the North. Turning to the other side, there was the incredible temerity of the Southerners who really believed that all that was "necessary to conduct a successful war" against a power of infinitely greater resources was "just love of land and courage."

So the fact that the War was fought at all was in itself a minor miracle. God ordained it because He "still intended to save [the South] because He had done so much for it." Therefore, He raised up old John Brown, brought on the War, and saw to it that the South was beaten and the institution of slavery was destroyed. "Whom God loveth, He chasteneth."

I do not expect many readers of *Go Down, Moses* to find this a reasonable thesis. But that is not the point here: what is the point is Ike's pride in his own people, in spite of his hatred of slavery and his trust that the course of history is directed by God's providence.

There is much more in this long and sometimes rather tangled argument that is worth discussing if only time permitted, but time does not permit, and I must try to summarize what remains in a few sentences. Ike persists in the renunciation of his claim to the plantation, and his elder kinsman is compelled to acquiesce in his decision. But Ike apparently feels that through his renunciation he has come out from under the shadow of slavery. "I am free," he declares. What about the black people, Cass asks. Did the outcome of the Civil War really free them? Are they now truly free? Ike has to admit that it will be a long time before they become truly free; but matters will come out all right in time, "because they will endure. . . ."

Somewhat earlier in their dialogue, Ike had enumerated the virtues of the blacks. They possess "pity and tolerance and forbearance and fidelity and love of children whether their own or not or black or not." But their great virtue, as Ike believes, is their capacity to endure. His view of the matter, however, is not that they will simply have to wait it out since they cannot do anything else. Obviously, Ike associates his giving up of his inheritance with their cause. He has freed himself, and his freedom from property is one way of promoting the black man's freedom.

I put it badly, however, when I say that Ike has freed himself. That is not the way Ike puts it. He tells Cass: "Sam Fathers set me free."

Ike buys carpenter's tools and plans to live by his own effort, emulating Jesus of Nazareth, the carpenter's son. But soon Ike falls in love and marries and, humanly and normally, looks forward to having a son. Thus, in taking the vow of poverty, he failed to take the vow of celibacy as well. His young wife, as I read the story, is not a coarse or unfeeling woman. She is scarcely to be blamed for wanting a home, an established place in which to bear her children. She cannot understand why her husband refuses to accept an inheritance which is legally his. So she tries to persuade him to reverse his decision. She even uses her sex to try to compel him. But she cannot change his mind, and, as it happens, no son is born. The marriage breaks up, and Ike becomes the person who is described in the opening sentence of the novel: "a widower now and uncle to half a county and father to no one."

So ends the fourth part of "The Bear." Yet this is not quite the note on which Faulkner wanted to end his great story of this idealistic young man, who learned under the tutelage of Sam Fathers to love the wilderness to the point of veneration. How, then, does Faulkner end it? He does a very bold thing. The time of the action recounted in the fifth and final part of the story takes us back three years. In the fourth part we had listened to a young man of twenty-one on the day of his coming of age. But in the fifth part, Ike is only eighteen. Two years have elapsed since the hunt in which Lion and Old Ben had died.

Ike is preparing to go back to the big woods and visit the graves of Lion and Sam Fathers. But change is already in the air. Major de Spain had some years earlier sold his wilderness holdings to a lumber company, and the company had run a narrow-gauge railroad line into the property. Now, at last, the company is making ready to cut timber and haul it out.

Ike asks Major de Spain whether he would not like to join him in his return to the scene of the great hunt, but the Major begs off. Though he has consented to the destruction of the wilderness and will make money thereby, he evidently dreads to see the beginning of the destruction. To Ike, he simply pleads the press of business, but it seems plain that he has a deeper reason.

Ike does make his visit into the woods, noting the half-completed planing mill, the great piles of stacked steel rails, and the passage of the little locomotive on the narrow-gauge line. He is reminded of the story of a half-grown bear that, on the locomotive's first trip into the woods, had been terrified and climbed a little ash tree close to the railroad line. It "clung there, its head ducked between its arms as a man (a woman perhaps) might have done."

When Boon Hogganbeck had heard about it, he sat under the tree all night to prevent anyone's shooting it. Major de Spain had the logging train stop its runs until the young bear, after almost thirty-six hours in the tree, came down and made off into the woods.

Why is this little story placed just here? Presumably to show the vulnerability of the wilderness world to man's machines. But surely also to dramatize a second point. Boon Hogganbeck, the man who jumped on Old Ben's back and killed him with a hunting knife, protects the half-grown bear, and Major de Spain, the chief organizer of the annual hunt for Old Ben, stops his business enterprise out of pity for the half-grown bear. The action relates to the hunter's code. Old Ben can take care of himself. He is a proper foe. But the hunter will not take advantage of the fright of a young animal, a panic that renders it an easy mark. And, as we shall see in the next section of this novel, "Delta Autumn," when it comes to deer hunting, you shoot bucks, not does.

Back to Ike's visit to Sam's grave. As he walks into the woods, he reflects on the wonder of nature and the procession of the seasons: "summer, and fall, and snow, and wet and saprife spring in their ordered immortal sequence, the deathless and immemorial phases of the mother who had shaped him if any had toward the man he almost was." That mother is, of course, nature herself.

Ike readily locates Lion's grave and the buried tin box holding Old Ben's "dried mutilated paw, resting above Lion's bones." Sam's grave is close beside Lion's, and on a nearby tree Ike finds the other now empty axle-grease box and puts in it a "twist of tobacco, [a] new bandanna handkerchief, [and a] small paper sack of the peppermint candy which Sam had used to love."

There follows another of Faulkner's great prose hymns to nature. As Ike thinks of Sam, he is overwhelmed by a conviction of nature's immortality. He knew that

there was no death, not Lion and not Sam: not held fast in earth but free in earth and not in earth but of earth, myriad yet undiffused of every myriad part, leaf and twig and particle, air and sun and rain and dew and night, acorn oak and leaf and acorn again, dark and dawn and dark and dawn again in their immutable progression and, being myriad, one: and Old Ben too, Old Ben too; they would give him his paw back even, certainly they would give him his paw back: then the long challenge and the long chase, no heart to be driven and outraged, no flesh to be mauled and bled. . . . (Pp. 228–29)

Yet Faulkner remains the realist. He breaks off Ike's reverie by his sudden discovery that a rattlesnake is almost at his feet. Nature contains death as well as life and serpents who carry death in their fangs. Ike salutes the snake in Indian fashion: "Chief, Grandfather," for death is part and parcel of nature's total life.

Then something occurs that runs counter to Ike's sense of nature's vitality and peace. He hears an intolerable racket. As he approaches the source of the noise, he finds that it is Boon, whom he had planned to meet at just about this spot. Boon's gun has jammed and he is frantically hammering on it, trying to get it back into working order. Boon is under a tree which stands alone in a little clearing, and the tree is full of squirrels which are as excited as Boon is. The relative isolation of their tree of refuge keeps them from escaping; but they are wildly leaping about in its branches.

As Ike comes up he notes that Boon is "hammering the disjointed barrel against the gun-breech with the frantic abandon of a madman. He didn't even look up to see who it was. Still hammering, he merely shouted back at the boy in a hoarse strangled voice: 'Get out of here! Dont touch them! Dont touch a one of them! They're mine.'"

Boon's actions and words have puzzled a good many readers. One popular, but I think erroneous, interpretation is that even Boon, that half-barbarian, child of the wilderness, has succumbed to greed. The wilderness is doomed because everybody wants to exploit its resources: Major de Spain at one end of the scale and Boon at the other.

This explanation is, for me, too simple, and it does not take sufficiently into account the fact that Boon is a man of strong passions, but is so inarticulate that he cannot express them properly. Remember the scene which ends part three, where Boon, standing beside the blanket-wrapped body of Sam Fathers, threatens to shoot McCaslin Edmonds as if he thought he had to defend Sam's body from him.

I suggest that Boon, like Major de Spain and Ike, feels acutely the impending doom of the wilderness. Its spoliation is now clearly at hand. Ike is not without means to cushion the shock and has a richness of sensibility that will allow him to continue to believe in the rich immortality of nature even though this portion of the wilderness is soon to be lost. But how can Boon respond? How except in a fierce defensiveness: these are my squirrels; don't you try to take them away from me. It is a defensiveness so violent, so manic, that he means to include every intruder. He does not even look up to see that it is his young friend, Isaac McCaslin, that he is threatening.

Before moving on to the next section of Go Down, Moses, I should like to say something further about Ike's nature worship and his Christianity. For him, they do not really contradict each other. Ike has little, if anything, to say of the Christian afterlife. Rather, Ike feels that being gathered back into nature, as the body of Sam Fathers has been gathered back, is to be gathered back into life itself. It is to be merged fully once more into immortal nature where the death of an individual plant or bird or beast is simply a dying back into an ongoing life.

Yet Christianity has also influenced Ike. I am thinking here not merely of Ike's wishing to imitate Jesus the carpenter, but of his knowledge that the wilderness is not the Garden of Eden. Ike clearly sees that Adam's original rapport with nature was long ago ruptured and can never again be restored.

It is true that on his visit to Sam's grave two years after Sam's death, Ike has his vision of complete harmony with nature, in which the hunters would give back to Old Ben his paw, a day in which there would be "no heart to be driven and outraged, no flesh to be torn." Yet that vision is a remembrance of a golden age long since lost, or of some far off apocalyptic future. The realist of the here and now knows that man must prey upon nature: the hunt must go on. Man is now in the state of fallen Adam: somewhere there occurred a fatal break between man and nature.

Man cannot simply act upon his instincts. He must learn self-control, how to toughen his muscles, but also how to discipline his will. The training that Sam gave to Ike was not merely how to survive in the wilderness, but how to respect and to love the wilderness; not merely how to kill, but when to refrain from killing. In short, the wilderness wisdom that Ike acquired involved a discipline of the mind and emotions as well as the body.

If man must perforce prey upon nature, he must beware of gorging himself on it greedily or destroying it wantonly. He must learn to reverence and love the very thing that he is condemned to violate. Thus, Ike's worship of nature is not mere nature worship. His view of man involves something very like the Christian doctrine of Original Sin. When that high priest of nature, Sam Fathers, baptized Ike into man-hood, he did not anoint his face with water from a woodland spring, or even with the juice of some berry or fruit; it was with the hot smoking blood of Ike's first deer.

The next section of *Go Down, Moses* is entitled "Delta Autumn." It is a grave and beautiful story, and it gives us a view of Ike as an old man. The time would be about 1941. The United States had not yet entered World War II, but the fighting in Europe had begun and Ike and his friends talk about it.

The word "Delta" in the title refers to a place and many readers will naturally assume that the delta of the Mississippi is that triangular fan of alluvial mud below New Orleans through which the great river enters the Gulf of Mexico. But our story has to do with what in the state of Mississippi is called "the Delta." It is the triangular northwestern part of the state bounded by the Mississippi River on the west, one of its tributaries, the Yazoo River, on the east, and the Tennessee state line on the north.

The Big Woods in which Old Ben was hunted was in this Delta, but as the woods were cleared, the forest retreated further and further south toward the confluence of the Yazoo and the Mississippi rivers. Once Jefferson was not far northeast of the Big Woods. Now in 1941 it is a long trip, even by automobile, to what is left of the woods. But Uncle Ike each autumn still joins the hunting party of much younger men there.

Among them is Roth Edmonds, the grandson of Cass Edmonds. Roth obviously has something on his mind. He seems a much more sardonic and even brutal man than he did in "The Fire and the Hearth." He is bitter and even rather short with the old man who is his elder kinsman.

During the hunt there is a great deal of joking about hunting does and knowing remarks about Roth's having a doe that he can hunt season after season. Early in the morning after their first night in camp, the jesting is accounted for, when Roth hands Uncle Ike an envelope enclosing a thick sheaf of banknotes and asks him to give them to someone who will call on him a little later. Roth asks Ike to hand the person the envelope and tell her "no." So the old man knows what to expect when a little later a young woman does come into the tent asking for Roth. What he is not prepared for, however, is the young woman's saying, "You're Uncle Isaac." It turns out that she is the granddaughter of Tennie's Jim, and thus the great-granddaughter of Tomey's Turl. She has with her her infant son, whose father is Roth Edmonds.

So Old Carothers's sin which had caused Ike to repudiate his inheritance appears once more. Ike's repudiation has been of no avail. The latest descendant of Old Carothers has begotten a child on the latest descendant of the slave woman, Eunice, whom Old Carothers had ravished so many years ago. True, Roth's sin is scarcely incest, and as the young woman admits, Roth had not promised her marriage. She indicates that Roth does not know that she is related to him. She has not told him. But she could not keep herself from coming to the hunting camp to see Roth once more, in the hope, the desperate hope, that he would return to her.

It is a bitter meeting for the old man, and his anguish makes him seem harsher and less feeling than he really is. Most bitter of all for him is to hear her say that his very relinquishment of the plantation to Roth's grandfather has made Roth what he is, for she tells Uncle Ike: "'I would have made a man of him. He's not a man yet. You spoiled him. You and Uncle Lucas and Aunt Molly. But mostly you.'"

When he incredulously says "'Me? Me?'" she answers "'Yes. When you gave to his grandfather that land which didn't belong to him. . . .'" This is hardly fair. If persons other than Roth himself are responsible for his character, it would surely be Roth's own father or his own grandfather, not Ike. Besides, giving people property does not necessarily mar them. It may hold dangers, but the sons of wealthy men are not inevitably bad, just as the sons of poor men are not always virtuous.

Dramatically, of course, it is proper that the young woman should voice the reproach. For whatever reasons, Roth has become an insensitive and callous man. She is hurt and bitter and cut to the heart. But her reproach does raise an important question: did Isaac McCaslin act properly in relinquishing the plantation? Never mind the excellence of his intentions; he has paid a heavy price personally by rendering himself poor: he thereby lost his wife and his hope for a son.

The question that I have put, however, must nevertheless be faced. Power in itself is neutral: it can be used for good as well as for ill. In giving up his property, Isaac McCaslin gave up his power to do good. In setting himself free, Ike has also shirked his responsibilities. He can now only look on helplessly at the young woman's grief and his own sense of shame at a kinsman's guilt.

I have a friend who knows twice as much theology as I do, and he tells me that he does not regard Ike's resignation of responsibility a Christian act at all. He may well be right. Yet one must try to be fair to the old man, now crushed by the girl's plight and his inability to do anything about it. For even if he had retained the plantation, it is by no means certain that he could have helped. When he hands Roth's money to the girl, she says "That's just money." What she wants is something very different, Roth's love, and that is something that is not in Ike's power to give. It is fatuous to say, as some have, that had Ike remained owner of the plantation he could have forced Roth to behave. A careful reading of the story will make it plain that few people could have made Roth do anything—and certainly not his seventy-five-year-old, remote cousin.

What the helpless old man does have to give is his most precious possession, the hunting horn that General Compson had left him in his will, the horn covered with deerhide and bound with silver. He hands it to the girl as a gift for her infant son. It is a recognition of kinship, and more. Roth has broken the hunter's code and lost his honor. If I interpret correctly old Ike's intention here, he is saying that honor now has to go to the branch of the family represented by the child. In any case, since Ike is childless, and so is Roth, both these family lines have come to an end.

The last sentences of "Delta Autumn" underline the fact that Roth has broken the hunter's code. Old Ike lies on his cot, associating in his sorrowful rage the destruction of the wilderness that he had loved with Roth's treatment of the girl, both of them violations. Then someone comes into his tent to pick up Roth's knife. His explanation is that they've got a deer on the ground. Ike asks whether Roth had killed a deer. The answer is "'Yes. . . . Just a deer. . . . Nothing extra.'" Ike says to himself "'It was a doe.'"

The last section of the novel may at first glance seem to have little reference to the larger issues presented in *Go Down, Moses*. Isaac McCaslin does not appear in it at all; Lucas Beauchamp and Roth Edmonds are present only in the remote background. Yet this concluding story does touch on several of the novel's dominant themes, though here they are muted. Faulkner often ended his stories and novels on a quiet note—or, to use a favorite phrase of his, "with a dying fall."

The plot of this concluding story is simple. A grandson of Lucas and Molly Beauchamp is executed in Illinois for killing a Chicago policeman. Molly somehow divines that he is in trouble, and appeals to Gavin Stevens, a white attorney in Jefferson, for help. She does not go to Roth Edmonds, though of course she and Lucas live on his plantation. She does not because Roth Edmonds had ordered her grandson off the plantation after he caught him trying to rob the commissary store. The boy had then moved to town, had fallen into evil courses, moved to Chicago, and finally got into the numbers racket, committed murder, and was executed.

Stevens is touched by the old woman's concern. With the help of his friend, the local newspaper editor, he learns from the wire service what has happened and arranges for the local paper not to report how and why the young man died. Molly will simply be told that he had died and been buried up North. But that is not enough to satisfy Molly. She wants his body brought back home and given proper burial in his native soil.

Stevens and his friend, the newspaper editor, raise the money needed to bring the body home and to provide a decent burial. That is the story. It is simple enough, but it touches upon a number of the themes dramatized earlier in the novel. Let me mention one or two. The old Southern patriarchal system is now breaking down, but elements of it remain. Miss Worsham, whose grandfather had owned Molly's grandparents and who grew up with Molly, is sincere when she tells Gavin Stevens that " 'It's our grief.' " The "our" is neither diplomatic nor condescending. She truly means to include herself. Moreover, Gavin Stevens, though he lacks the ties that bind Miss Worsham to Molly, has been genuinely touched by Molly's faith and her plight. There is, of course, no sentimentalizing of the patriarchal system. In this novel we have not been allowed to forget the wickedness of a bad master like Old Carothers or the callousness of his descendant Roth.

The title of this story and of the whole volume is taken from the Negro spiritual: "Go down, Moses, and set my people free." What are the prospects for the freedom of the black man? Ike had told his cousin in 1888 that the freeing of the former slaves would take a long time. How right he was. The novel reaches the 1940s, and the black man enjoys only a limited freedom in the South. But escape into the North does not necessarily guarantee freedom either. It presents its own temptations and perils. The fate of Samuel Worsham Beauchamp, whose body has just arrived in a casket from the Illinois State Penitentiary, is eloquent testimony to this fact. The freeing of the black people is still unfinished business.

7 · LIGHT IN AUGUST

Light in August is technically one of the most brilliant and daring of Faulkner's novels—so much so that the first readers were unsure that the novel possessed any real unity. For example, the two principal characters never meet, though the juxtaposition of their lives has everything to do with the meaning of the novel.

Light in August opens with one of these two characters walking along a Mississippi country road. It is Lena Grove, a simple country girl, obviously pregnant. When she is offered a ride by a country man, Henry Armstid, who is driving a wagon, she explains that she is on the way to join her husband. They arrive at Armstid's house and his wife takes Lena in for the night. Mrs. Armstid clearly does not believe Lena's story about being married; nevertheless, she breaks her china piggybank and tells her husband to give the coins to Lena.

In the morning, Lena catches another ride into Jefferson, where she inquires for her husband, whose name, she says, is Burch. Nobody knows a man by that name, but there is a Mr. Bunch who works at the planing mill just outside Jefferson. Lena is accordingly dropped off there, but the quiet, methodical little bachelor named Byron Bunch is not the man she is looking for. Byron has a shrewd suspicion that a certain Joe Brown may be the man who has begotten Lena's child.

Brown had come to the mill some months before, long after another stranger also began work at the mill. This stranger's name is Joe Christmas, and he and Brown contrast sharply with each other. Brown has a "weakly handsome face," and he reminds one of the other workers of a "worthless horse. . . . Runs fast, all right, but it's always got a sore hoof when hitching-up time comes."

Joe Christmas is a very different sort of person. There is "something definitely rootless about him, as though no town nor city was his, no street, no walls, no square of earth his home." He holds himself aloof; on his first day at the mill he coldly rejected Byron Bunch's overtures of friendship.

Later, the word gets around that Christmas and Brown are making and selling moonshine. They have taken up quarters in a cabin on the old Burden place on the edge of town. By the time that Lena arrives in Jefferson, both Brown and Christmas have stopped working at the mill, and on the Saturday afternoon on which Lena arrives at the planing mill nobody is at work there save Byron Bunch, whom all work and no play have made a very dull boy indeed. Byron, shy and timid, especially with women, nevertheless finds women attractive, and almost instantly falls in love with this girl who obviously needs help—all the help she can get. He takes Lena to his boardinghouse and finds a room for her there. The next evening, troubled in spirit because he is afraid that he has let slip to Lena that the man she is seeking is a bootlegger, Byron goes to call on one of the few people in town with whom he can talk, a defrocked Presbyterian minister, Gail Hightower.

Before Faulkner lets us overhear Bunch's conversation with the Reverend Mr. Hightower, Faulkner informs his reader who Hightower is, and explains why he was ousted from his church. It is a grim story, and one that can tell us a great deal about Hightower. It can also tell us a great deal about the nature of the community into which Lena and Joe Brown and Joe Christmas have come.

Hightower's Christianity is of a most peculiar sort. He was delighted to accept a call from a church in Jefferson, and for a very special reason. Jefferson was the town in which his grandfather, a Confederate cavalryman, had been shot and killed, and from boyhood this flamboyant ancestor had become Hightower's special hero. In fact, Hightower does not seem in the least interested in the living people to whom he has ostensibly come to minister. All of his energies are absorbed in a dream of past glory. His obsession even gets into his sermons. His parishioners are somewhat puzzled, but give him the benefit of the doubt. Eventually, however, they begin to shake their heads.

In neglecting the living, Hightower neglects his wife. "After about a year in Jefferson, the wife began to wear that frozen look on her face. . . ." One Sunday morning, she goes to pieces during his sermon, rises from the pew, and shakes "her hands at [her husband] and God."

The wife is sent to a sanitorium, and when she returns, the people of the church hope for the best. But soon things become much worse. Finally, the city newspaper headlines the fact that she "had jumped or fallen from a hotel window in Memphis. . . . There had been a man in the room with her."

It was a Sunday morning when the news broke.

The congregation were horrified to see the back pews filled with newspaper reporters, but they could not believe their eyes when they saw Hightower himself walk in and actually go into the pulpit as if nothing had happened. The ladies [in the church] got up first and began to leave. Then the men got up too, and then the church was empty save for the minister in the pulpit . . . and the Memphis reporters. (P. 62)

Hightower was asked to resign but refused. When he entered the church the next Sunday the "congregation as one rose and walked out." At long last Hightower agrees to resign, and, as Faulkner puts it, "the town was sorry with being glad, as people are sometimes sorry for those whom they have at last forced to do as they wanted them to." They believe that Hightower will now go away, and his congregation makes up a purse to provide moving expenses. Instead, he buys a little house on a back street and the people of his church and of the town are furious at him once more.

One night some men tie him to a tree and beat him until he is unconscious. But Hightower refuses to identify his assailants. Note again how Faulkner puts matters: "The town knew that that was wrong, and some of the men came to [Hightower] and tried again to persuade him to leave Jefferson, for his own good." They offer to prosecute the men who beat him if he will only name them. But he is adamant. He simply wants to be left alone. Then, and I quote Faulkner again, for he is here rendering for us what the nature of a small provincial community is: "The whole thing seemed to blow away, like an evil wind. It was as though the town realized at last that he would be a part of its life until he died, and that they might as well become reconciled." The neighbors again begin to send him dishes of food, not, to be sure, the kind that they sent to him earlier when his wife was away in the sanitorium, rather the sort that "they would have sent to a poor mill family. But it was food, and wellmeant." This, then, is the man whom Byron Bunch uses as a kind of father-confessor and to whom he goes to talk about Lena Grove's arrival in the town and the plight she finds herself in.

At this point, it may be useful to review the situation. Into this provincial, Protestant smalltown community, one that has its prejudices and limitations but also its own virtues of kindliness and human sympathy, have come three strangers: Joe Christmas, who rejects sympathy and carries with him the aura of a conscious pariah-hood; the worthless Joe Brown, a feckless scamp, who does not want to acknowledge that he has got a young woman with child; and, most recently, Lena Grove, the young woman herself. But consider further: among these strangers and aliens, there is Gail Hightower, who lives in a kind of cultural cyst—within the community, but not really of it. We have seen how the community tried to expel him and failed.

There is also Byron Bunch. He has no close tie with anyone, unless it be with Hightower. The woman who runs the boardinghouse regards him as a good, even admirable man. His fellow workmen at the mill respect him, but also detect a certain aloofness in him. Bunch is one of Faulkner's model Puritans—abstemious, methodical, no sour bigot, to be sure, but without one shred of glamorous youth. He lives only on the fringe of the community.

When Bunch sits down with Hightower, the reader learns of another alien in the community, Miss Joanna Burden. She is the daughter of abolitionist parents who had come to Jefferson right after the Civil War to educate and help the blacks. The Burdens were resented as people from the outside who had come to stir up racial trouble and in general to remake the society according to their outsiders' notions. For years, now, Miss Burden has lived alone, literally, as well as metaphorically, on the edge of town, or better still, like Hightower, walled off in a cultural cyst.

In fact, both Joanna Burden and Hightower can be regarded as special victims of their Civil War ancestors. Hightower has wilfully locked himself into the past in his worship of his grandfather's heroic image. Joanna's loyalty to her grandfather's precepts has played its part too in preventing her from having any real part in the living community about her. But of course, in her case, far more than in Hightower's, it is the community that has actually turned the key in the lock.

Let's turn back, however, to Bunch's Sunday evening visit to Hightower: how does Joanna Burden come into the conversation? Because she was found murdered the day before. Her lifeless body was discovered inside her burning house.

Faulkner has used that burning house very adroitly in the opening chapters of *Light in August*. At the close of chapter 1, the man driving the wagon on which Lena is getting her ride into Jefferson calls her attention to a tall yellow column of smoke and says, " 'That's a house burning.' " Toward the end of chapter 2, Bunch, talking with Lena at the planing mill about Christmas and Brown, tells her that some say that they are selling whisky and that they keep it out there "where that house is burning." Chapter 3 contains no mention of the burning house because, as we have seen, it is devoted to an account of Hightower's past, but chapter 4 begins with a mention of the burning house, and as we listen to Bunch we get a detailed account of the discovery of the fire and are allowed to make a pretty sound conjecture as to who set the fire and why.

It seems that on Saturday morning, a country man on the way to town discovered that the house he was passing was on fire. He rushed into the house to give the alarm, and met a man, later identified as Brown. The man acted as if he were drunk, and kept insisting that there was no one inside. Despite Brown's attempt to keep him from going upstairs, the country man forced his way in and, in an upstairs room, found Joanna Burden's body, with her head "cut pretty near off." He jerked a cover off the bed, rolled the body onto it, and, catching up the corners, swung it onto his back, carried it outside, and laid it on the ground.

Then, as Bunch tells it, " 'he said that what he was scared of happened. . . . Because the cover fell open and she was laying on her side, facing one way, and her head was turned clean around like she was looking behind her. And he said how if she could just have done that when she was alive, she might not have been doing it now.' "

Is this an attempt at macabre humor? Either on Bunch's part or on the country man's part? I do not think so. The country man has behaved admirably and has no need or disposition to mock at Joanna's lifeless body. Nor is it in Bunch's nature to do so. This realistic but laconic reporting of an incident does carry, as most understatements do, a latent humor. But the point of importance is that the country man believes that someone had crept up on Joanna when her back was turned. We shall find out later that it was quite otherwise.

Though Brown had set fire to the house presumably in

order to conceal the fact that Miss Burden had been murdered, now that this fact cannot be further concealed, and after he has heard that a $1,000 reward has been offered for the discovery of the culprit, he reports to the sheriff that Christmas was the murderer. He tells him of having seen Christmas get up at dawn on Saturday morning, go out of the cabin, and then return saying "I've done it." When Brown asked "Done what?" Christmas had told him "Go up to the house and see." (As we shall learn later, Brown here is substantially telling the truth.) When the officers express scepticism, Brown plays what he obviously believes is his trump card. He says that Christmas has confessed to him that he possesses some Negro blood. (Brown again, we shall find, is speaking the truth.) Brown must have gone on to say that surely they will take a white man's word rather than a black man's. Whether the officers believe Brown fully or not, they do begin the search for the missing Joe Christmas.

So ends chapter 4. With chapter 5, Faulkner makes a brilliant technical move. He takes us back to the early hours of Friday morning—Miss Burden died just after midnight on Saturday morning—and lets us see Christmas close up, this time not through the eyes of either Bunch or Brown, but directly, as the omniscient author himself reveals what happened.

Christmas had been unable to sleep. After midnight Brown comes in drunk, chattering and laughing. He will not stop. When Christmas puts his hands around his throat, Brown tells him to take his black hands off him: "You're a nigger. . . . You said so yourself." Then Christmas starts to choke him in earnest, but when he slackens his grip, Brown promises to be quiet and soon is asleep.

As for Christmas, he says to himself: "Something is going to happen to me. I am going to do something." He starts to reach for his razor, but his "thinking" tells him "This is not the right one" and so he refrains.

A little later he says aloud to himself "Its because she started praying over me. . . . That's it. Because she started praying over me." He begins to curse this woman who started praying over him. He leaves the cabin and moves to the nearby abandoned plantation stable. He asks himself: "Why in hell do I want to smell horses?" And then immediately finds the answer: "It's because they are not women. Even a mare horse is a kind of man."

In the stable he is able to go to sleep. After perhaps two hours, he returns to the cabin to pick up a cheap magazine and his shaving kit. He walks to a little valley in which a spring rises. He makes a fire, sleeps for more than two hours this time, and then shaves. From a small store not far away he buys some crackers and potted meat, returns to the spring and eats his breakfast. Then he starts reading the magazine straight through as if it were a novel.

We have before us an obsessed man who knows that he is committed to doing something but feels curiously passive about it. Hence, his saying, "Something is going to happen to me." We have been presented also with the perfect emblem of a man killing time. He is going through the motions of living: eating, shaving, reading a magazine, not because he has the least interest in it, but simply to pass the time.

A little later we see Joe as a man tidying up his affairs. He digs out of the side of a sandy ditch six metal tins of whisky. He punches holes in the cans, pours out the whisky, and reburies the cans. He will not be selling any more whisky henceforward.

At nine that evening, having eaten his supper in a restaurant, Joe is standing in the street, continuing "to look more lonely than a lone telephone pole in the middle of a desert." He walks through the streets hearing the "fecund-mellow voices of negro women" and we are told that he felt as if he had been returned "to the lightless hot wet primogenitive Female." He feels so smothered that he runs until he finds himself in the white section of the town. People are playing bridge on a veranda; their "white faces intent and sharp in the low light." A little later he nearly gets into a fight with a group of black people. The little flurry passes over; the group disappears; but Joe finds that he has unconsciously taken out his razor and is holding it in his hand. "What in hell is the matter with me?" he asks himself.

By ten o'clock that evening he is sitting in the ruined garden of the old Burden place. Sitting there, he hears the courthouse clock two miles away strike eleven, and then twelve. He gets up and moves toward the house. But we are told that he does not go fast and that he does not even think now that *"Something is going to happen. Something is going to happen to me."*

So ends chapter 5, with the reader watching Joe make his way toward the house with his razor. The reader, of course, already knows what the passing country man will find in that upstairs bedroom next morning. But why did Joe cut Joanna's throat? Why did she seal her death warrant when she started praying over him? Why was Joe so fearful of the female principle? The careful reader has been given in these first five chapters enough hints to cause him to ask the forgoing questions, but no more than that. He knows absolutely nothing about Joe's relationship with Miss Burden. In short, he does not have a whodunit murder mystery before him. He knows the identity of the murderer. What he does not know is the motive. That is what Faulkner now undertakes to tell us, but he will do it in his own way.

That way involves a long continuous flashback that will give the crucial facts of Joe Christmas's life from his early babyhood until he entered Miss Burden's garden and waited for the clock to strike twelve. Thus, for nearly the whole of the next seven chapters we shall see nothing further (or almost nothing) of Lena, or Byron Bunch, or Hightower. It is a daring strategy, and Faulkner's use of it has caused some readers to believe that *Light in August* lacks essential unity as a novel. We shall deal with that problem later. It is enough for the moment to invite the reader to embark on this tremendously effective account of the various forces that twisted Joe Christmas away from womankind, away from normal involvement in the human community, and almost away from nature itself.

Joe was left as an infant at the door of an orphanage in

Memphis on Christmas day. This accounts for the surname that he was given. By the age of five, Joe has from time to time been eating the toothpaste that he finds on the washstand in the bedroom of the orphanage dietician. One day she comes back unexpectedly and the child retreats into a clothes closet. He hears the woman's voice and that of a man, but, completely innocent of any knowledge of sex, does not know what is going on. But he has eaten too much of the pink toothpaste and so, "in the rife, pinkwomansmelling obscurity behind the curtain he squatted, pinkfoamed, listening to his insides, waiting with astonished fatalism for what was about to happen to him."

The noise of his vomiting causes the dietician to snatch back the curtain. She seizes the child and cries out, "'Spying on me! You little nigger bastard.'"

She remains in a state of panic fear. She tries to bribe the child not to tell, though the child has no notion of what it is that he is not to tell aside from his stealing her toothpaste. Then she tries to have him removed to a black orphanage, insisting to the matron in charge of the orphanage that Joe is really a black child.

This is the first of the damaging experiences with women that Joe undergoes. There was an earlier one, not damaging, but indicating plainly what Joe needed and did not get. In the orphanage was a little girl, older than Joe, who had taken a fancy to him and mothered him. When Joe was three years old, the little girl, then twelve, was leaving the orphanage to live with a foster family, and woke Joe up to tell him goodbye. When she woke him he was "a little annoyed, never full awake, suffering her because she had always tried to be good to him. He didn't know that she was crying because he did not know that grown people cried," and to him a girl of twelve was grown. It is a tiny scene, but touching and important, for it makes plain how little mothering of any sort Joe ever got in his whole life.

A little while after the toothpaste episode, Joe is placed with a childless couple named McEachern. Mr. McEachern declares Christmas to be a heathen name and an instance of sacrilege. He will give the child his own name. But the child pays no attention: he knows that his name is not and never will be McEachern.

When Joe is eight years old, Mr. McEachern demands that Joe memorize the catechism. Joe refuses. His stubbornness more than matches that of his foster father. The ordeal begins before breakfast on a Sunday morning and goes on past suppertime. Joe has no food, and, lying in his bed, wonders why he feels "weak and peaceful." Later that evening, his foster mother slips up the stairs with a tray of food. She tells Joe that her husband does not know that she is bringing it. What does the boy do? He takes "the tray and [carries] it to the corner and [turns] it upside down, dumping the dishes and food and all onto the floor." Then he silently gets back into bed. Long after she has gone, he kneels above "the outraged" food and "with his hands ate, like a savage, like a dog."

The incident constitutes a paradigmatic model for all of his relations to his foster parents. He is resigned to his foster father's rigid code of action but he is repelled by every timid attempt of his foster mother to show him kindness or to bind him to her with tenderness. Faulkner puts it thus: "The man, the hard, just, ruthless man, merely depended on him to act in a certain way and to receive the as certain reward or punishment, just as he could depend on the man to react in a certain way to his own certain doings and misdoings."

To sum up, it was not "the hard work which [Joe] hated nor the punishment. . . . He expected no less, and so he was neither outraged nor surprised. It was the woman: that soft kindness which he believed himself doomed to be forever victim of and which he hated worse than he did the hard and ruthless justice of men." He believes that his foster mother is trying to make him cry and that if she could do so, she would have a hold on him.

Such was the distinction that Joe made between his foster father and his foster mother. One can, of course, put the difference in other terms. Joe felt comfortable with justice, not with mercy or love. Mr. McEachern did better with teaching the catechism than he knew. In his own terms, Joe becomes as rigid a Puritan as McEachern himself: harsh, fatalistic, and according to his own lights, just.

Faulkner treats Joe's adolescence and young manhood in great detail, in more detail than I can discuss here. Joe is curious about sex but repelled by his first sexual encounter. His first real love affair is with Bobbie Allen, a waitress in a little restaurant in Jefferson where she is also a part-time prostitute. Joe is shy and awkward, and his very innocence makes him attractive to Bobbie. He learns to climb noiselessly out of his room at the McEachern's and spends the night with her. The tough man and woman who run the restaurant tease Bobbie about her shy lover, but the relation lasts for a while. One night he confides to Bobbie that he thinks he has got some Negro blood. He adds that he does not know, he simply believes that he has. Bobbie says she thinks he is lying and then that she does not believe it, and Joe says "'All right.'"

Why does Joe feel compelled to voice this suspicion? One remembers that he will later on voice it to Joe Brown and to Joanna Burden. I suggest that he does it to see whether it would really make any difference to his lover or his friend. Evidently he wants terribly to believe that they would continue to love and esteem him no matter what his racial heritage.

He plans to go to a dance with Bobbie and waits out on the highway where she picks him up in a car. But McEachern has become suspicious, is on the alert, and hears the car stop. He saddles his horse, rides to the schoolhouse where the dance is being held, bursts into the room, and denounces Bobbie as a Jezebel and a harlot. Joe picks up a chair and shatters it on McEachern's head. Then he orders the crowd to stand back and tells Bobbie to drive on back to town; he will follow. But Bobbie is beside herself with rage, not only at Joe's foster father, but at Joe himself. As she gets into the car she begins to beat him in the face.

Joe mounts McEachern's old horse, rides back to the McEachern place long enough to pick up the little hoard of money that is hidden under a plank in his room, and then rides post haste into town to join Bobbie. When he arrives, Max and Mame, who run the restaurant where Bobbie works, and Bobbie herself are already packed to leave town. They do not want to get mixed up in a murder case. All they want to know is whether Joe has killed the old man, and Joe honestly does not know. Then, why, they ask him, has he come here?

Joe is stunned. He repeats the question "What did I come for? I came to get Bobbie." He is going to take her away. He has plenty of money. They will go away and be married.

But Bobbie is still in a furious rage. She screams reproaches; Joe has told her himself that he is a nigger. This nigger son-of-a-bitch wants to get her in a jam with the clodhopper police. So Joe's money is taken, most of it, that is; he is beaten up and left lying on the floor; and Max, Mame, and Bobbie set out for Memphis.

With this disillusioning end to his love affair and with his need to get away before he will be arrested for murder, Joe Christmas begins his wanderings down a long street which we are told ran into Oklahoma and Missouri, as far south as Mexico and as far north as Chicago and Detroit. He started down the long street when he was eighteen years old and moved down that street for fifteen years. He was a laborer, miner, and prospector. He worked for a while in a gambling house. He enlisted in the army, served for a few months, deserted, and was never caught.

He slept with many women. Sometimes he told them that he was a black man and was berated and thrown out of the establishment; sometimes he was beaten unconscious. One night he told a woman that he was a Negro, and she was undisturbed. She asked "'What about it? . . . Say, what do you think this dump is, anyhow? The Ritz hotel?'" Joe's response to her indifference was to beat her up. "It took two policemen to subdue him. At first they thought that the woman was dead."

In an earlier time he had teased white men into calling him a Negro so that he could fight them. Now he fought any black man that would call him white. For a time in the North he lived with black people, shunned all whites, and lived as man and wife with "a woman who resembled an ebony carving." Indeed, he tries hard to become a black man. But the experiment fails.

For Joe, the problem of whether he is white or black is a question that keeps him restless, a question that cannot be put to sleep. For him it is inextricably bound up with the question "Who am I?" Joe's identity crisis is permanent. He has honestly tried to become a black man and in his own terms failed, not that the blacks have refused to accept him, but because he cannot accept the role himself. He has no trouble in passing as a white man, either in his earliest days or in the very last years of his life. But there is the nagging uncertainty that continues to corrupt his sense of security.

How did the nagging uncertainty arise? When the dietician called him a "little nigger bastard"? When some of the children at the orphanage teased Joe by calling him a nigger? Before we try to answer this second question, it will be well to remember who tells us that the other children call Joe a nigger. It is the dietician who tells this to old Doc Hines who works as a janitor at the orphanage. In relating this exchange between the dietician and Hines, the author tells us that the dietician was half mad with fear that her sexual affair would be exposed and that old Doc Hines was quite mad too. Faulkner, in describing the pair, uses the phrase "mad eyes looking into mad eyes, mad voice talking to mad voice."

We are not told that the child Joe reacted in any way to the taunt of nigger. What the author does tell us is that Joe felt that he was "different from the [other children]: because [the old janitor was] watching [him] all the time."

At any rate, very early Joe came to feel that he was a being somehow apart from the other children, and very early he also became conscious of the fact that whites were somehow different from blacks. One of the most horrifying scenes in the novel is that in which the child Joe accosts a black man who is working in the orphanage with an innocent but urgent question. The child asks him "how come you are a nigger?" The black man asks the child "who told you I am a nigger, you little white trash bastard?" When the child replies "I aint a nigger," the black man says, "you are worse than that, you dont know what you are. And more than that, you wont never know. You'll live and you'll die and you wont never know."

The black man turns out to be a true prophet. Joe Christmas does not know and, if I read the novel correctly, he never does learn. Yet there is something deep in him that demands to know who he is; he can never cease trying to find out. It is the one thing that destroys him and yet, in a sense, it is the noblest feature of his character: his insistence on pursuing the search for his identity to the very end. One remembers that it was the same sort of insistence that doomed Oedipus.

If the novel makes one fact entirely plain it is that Joe never had any difficulty in being accepted as a white man. Joe's problem is a spiritual problem, a deep restlessness of the soul, a lesion in the psyche itself, not a matter of biology. In short, what is at stake in *Light in August* is not Joe's possible possession of a few Afro-American genes, but his *belief* that he may possess them. The issue is the way in which he thinks of himself and the way the community thinks of him.

All of this is not to say that Faulkner does not think racial attitudes are important. On the contrary, it is the attitudes that are important, and that this is so is underscored when, as we read the rest of the novel, we discover that the evidence that Joe has any Negro blood at all is flimsy indeed. As presented in this novel, Joe's fate would have been precisely the same if his father had had not a drop of Negro blood, and actually was, as he claimed to be, a Mexican. Faulkner has, to be sure, used his cultural setting superbly for his purpose. But we must see what his true purpose is: to present the tragedy of a man who belongs to no community, who is a kind of modern Ishmael, who believes that every man's hand is raised against him, who does not know who he is, who has no memories of a mother or of being mothered, and not even the sense of nature itself as a kind of fostering mother. He is repelled by the feminine principle. His natural stance is to have his fist clenched and ready to strike back.

Joe Christmas is Faulkner's version of the completely alienated man, and the problem of alienation is one of the dominant themes of our century. One thinks at once of such writers as Joyce, Kafka, and Camus. *Light in August*, then, is not merely a study of racial prejudice in the Southern states. In the story of Joe Christmas, that local and provincial theme has been elevated to, and fused with, one of the great international themes of our epoch.

Thus far, I have commented on Joe's wanderings as he moved from one city to another and noted his experiments in living as a black man and as a white man. These wanderings began in earnest after his affair with Bobbie Allen ended and continued for some fifteen years. Thus, at the age of thirty-three, the street down which Faulkner says Joe had been rather aimlessly traveling "had become a Mississippi country road." One afternoon, Joe was put "off a southbound freight train near a small town." He did not know its name nor did he care "what word it used for a name."

Instead, he makes a few inquiries of a local black boy and finds out that the large house nearby is owned by a Miss Joanna Burden, who lives alone. After darkness falls, Joe goes to the kitchen of the Burden house. He climbs in through a window and in the darkness finds a dish of food, field peas cooked with molasses, and begins to eat.

In a moment a woman carrying a candle enters the room. Her face is "quiet, grave, utterly unalarmed." She looks at his face for a full minute and finally says: "If it is just food you want, you will find that." Her voice is "calm, a little deep, quite cold." So begins a meeting that is to have such portentous consequences for both people.

As one would suppose, the relationship between Joe and

Joanna was a strange one. They talked together very little, even after they had become lovers, and they did not become lovers until some time after Joe had taken up residence in a cabin on the Burden place. Joe well remembers "the hard, untearful, and unselfpitying and almost manlike yielding of [Joanna's] surrender" to him.

> There was no feminine vacillation, no coyness of obvious desire and intention to succumb at last. It was as if he struggled physically with another man for an object of no actual value to either, and for which they struggled on principle alone. (P. 222)

Joanna's special appeal to Joe at once becomes manifest. Though Faulkner makes it entirely clear that Joe is not a homosexual, he has made equally clear that Joe is thoroughly put off by all female softness and intrigues. He is pleased with Joanna's manlike fortitude, strength, and directness. Yet he is shocked too: "My God," he later thinks to himself, "it was like I was the woman and she was the man."

The whole relationship is, as one would guess, troubled and ambivalent. For example, the night after they had become lovers Joe goes into Joanna's house, not in eagerness but in quiet rage. He goes upstairs to her bedroom, and though this time she does not resist, he tears the clothes off her body. Later, he tells himself, "Now she hates me. I have taught her that, at least."

The next night Joe has resolved to be off, but when darkness falls, he finds himself moving toward the Burden house. This time he finds to his surprise that the door is locked and bolted. Curiously enough, however, the kitchen door is unlocked, and Joanna has set out food for him on the table. But even this he takes to be an insult: the door giving access to the bedroom bolted; yet food carefully *"Set out for the nigger."* In his fury, he hurls dish after dish against the kitchen wall. The next day he goes to work at the planing mill. One recalls that in chapter 2, we already had a detailed account of Christmas's first day there.

Joe does not desert his cabin on the Burden place, but from this day on in the spring time he sees nothing of Joanna until September, when, completely to his surprise, he returns one afternoon to his cabin and finds her sitting on his cot waiting for him. Joanna's psychic reactions are quite as unpredictable and complicated as are Joe's. She wants to talk with him. She wants now to tell him about herself.

Though she was born on the Burden place and has lived on it for all of her forty-one years, and never been away from Jefferson for more than six months at any time, and though even these absences have been few, her speech and accent remain thoroughly New England in character. She lives in, but is not of, the Jefferson community. In that New England accent she tells Joe the story of her abolitionist ancestors.

It is a story worth hearing. Her grandfather had brought up all his progeny to hate two things: hell and slaveholders. The Burdens had come into Jefferson soon after the Civil War to uplift the black man. They had paid for it bitterly. Joanna's father once took her as a child of four to see the graves of her grandfather and her brother who had been killed by Colonel Sartoris in a Reconstruction election campaign. Showing her the graves was meant to commit Joanna to her inherited mission. She can never lift the shadow of the black man to her level, her father insists, but neither can she escape the responsibility of trying to do so.

This colloquy between Joe and Joanna in the gathering darkness probably represents the closest that they were to come together in spiritual communion. Almost spontaneously, they put their deepest concerns to each other. Thus, Joe asks Joanna why her father had not revenged himself on Colonel Sartoris for having killed his father and his son. Joanna takes a little time to arrive at an answer, but at last she comes up with a most revealing one. She tells Joe that her father was French, half-French at least, with enough French blood "to respect anybody's love for the land where he and his people were born and to understand that a man would have to act as the land where he was born had trained him to act. I think that was it." And whereas she does not thereby condone what Colonel Sartoris did, she sees his firing his pistol as something more than an act of common murder.

But before she tries to answer Joe's question, she puts a question of her own to Joe. Apparently à propos of nothing, she asks Joe, "her voice almost gentle now, 'You dont have any idea who your parents were?'" Joe says no, "'Except that one of them was part nigger,'" and when she asks him "'How do you know that,'" Joe comes out with the truth: "'I dont know it.'" But in a moment he speaks again, "his voice now [having] an overtone, unmirthful yet quizzical, at once humorless and sardonic: 'If I'm not, damned if I haven't wasted a lot of time.'" The uncertainty, the nagging doubt, the need to know, yet the impossibility of ever knowing, all find expression here.

If this alienated, warped, and desperate pair had had more such talk, had had sufficient trust in each other to elicit more such confidences, perhaps their story might have had another ending. There might even have developed a true marriage. But Joanna's warping of spirit was at least as deep and as incurable as Joe's. She had repressed too much in her forty-one years, and so there began in their relations what Faulkner calls the second phase: Joanna's desperate attempts to crowd a lifetime's sexuality into a few months. Joe feels that he has fallen into a sewer, though the sewer "ran only by night. The days were the same as they had been," with Joe at work at the planing mill and she, the business-like, quiet old maid. But at night all repressions were swept away, and Joe experienced "the abject fury of the New England glacier exposed suddenly to the fire of the New England biblical hell."

In time, the second phase gradually gives way to a third. Joanna tells Joe that she is pregnant and begins to talk of their child to be born in a few months. The last thing that Joe Christmas wants is a child. But worse soon occurs. Joanna reverts to the prim spinster who means to take him in hand and to try to regulate his life. Worst of all, she reverts to her puritanical evangelism, and begins to pray over him. In doing so, she unwittingly signs her death warrant, for the moment that she becomes determinedly possessive or femininely motherly, she arouses all the old hostilities that through the years have conditioned this badly warped and twisted man.

Nevertheless, so stable a relationship had developed between Joe and Joanna that Joe cannot break out of it blindly and violently. For example, one evening when he returns to his cabin, he finds on his cot a note from Joanna, and before he has read it, tells himself that Joanna has come to her senses—that the old sexual relationship between them is about to be resumed. As Faulkner puts it: "He saw only himself once again on the verge of promise and delight. . . . 'All that foolishness,' he thought . . . 'all that damn foolishness! . . . thinking how they would both laugh over it tonight, later, afterward, when the time for quiet talking and quiet laughing came: at the whole thing, at one another, at themselves.' " But the note, when he finally reads it, conveys quite another message.

Miss Burden thinks that it is high time that Joe make something of himself. She plans to send him to a school in Memphis where he will learn some law and take over her business in helping the blacks. Joe is stunned and furious; but, even so, he does not break with her immediately. Instead, he continues to come to her room every night to be argued with and prayed over. It is a situation of deadlock. "Neither surrendered; worse: they would not let one another alone; he would not even go away." But by its very nature the strain imposes a limit on Joe's endurance. And so, some three months later, we find Joe sitting in the ruined garden of the Burden place, hearing the courthouse clock two miles away strike first ten and then eleven, and saying to himself: "*I had to do it*" already in the past tense; "*I had to do it. She said so herself.*"

Two nights before Joanna had said it. She had once again asked him to kneel with her and pray to God for forgiveness, and he had once again refused. Then she had said to him:

"Then there's just one other thing to do" and he had interpreted her statement correctly, knowing that she meant there is nothing for us now except to die.

On this night—it is a Friday—Joe hears the clock strike midnight and mounts the stairs to Joanna's room. He enters the room and she tells him to light the lamp, but Joe tells her that " 'It wont need any light.' " But at her insistence, he does light the lamp. She is sitting up in her bed, her back against the headboard, and she has draped a shawl over her shoulders. Once again she asks him to kneel with her, and again he refuses. Then he "saw her arms unfold" and sees her pull from beneath the shawl an old Civil War cap-and-ball pistol. He sees—and we see through his eyes—its shadow on the wall. He was watching "when the cocked shadow of the hammer flicked away."

We do not hear the pistol fire. Indeed, we are whisked away from the house to the middle of the road where Joe hails a passing automobile. The occupants, a youth and a young woman, with terror on their faces, let Joe into the car. He wonders why they seem so scared, but later, after he has asked them to stop and has gotten out of the car, he understands. Joe had forgotten that he still had the old cap-and-ball pistol in his hand. The car roars away and Joe inspects the pistol, noting the cartridge on which the hammer had fallen but which had failed to explode. Then he sees that the pistol holds a second live cartridge, on which the trigger had not been pulled. " 'For her and for me' " he says to himself as he throws the pistol into the underbrush. This last episode provides a beautiful example of Faulkner's mature narrative technique.

Let us review matters briefly. At the end of chapter 5, Faulkner has left Joe just outside Miss Burden's house. In another moment he will begin to mount the stairs that lead to her bedroom. Some one hundred and forty pages later, we actually watch Joe climb the stairs, but in the intervening pages we have learned so much more about him that we can understand why he feels that he must kill her. Then, three pages later, we see in shadow the hammer of the pistol fall, but we do not have to be told that Joanna failed to kill Joe and that Joe had cut her throat. After all, Byron Bunch, back in chapter 3, has told us what was found in the Burden house the next day. Furthermore, it is dramatically more effective for the reader to share in the blackout that evidently overwhelmed Joe, and to learn with him, only after he has got out of the car, precisely what had happened back in Joanna's room. Joanna had evidently planned to kill Joe and then with the second cartridge to kill herself, but Joe had been saved by the fact that the cartridge was defective.

There is a further value in Faulkner's way of handling his presentation. Thomas De Quincey many years ago defended a comparable technique employed in Shakespeare's *Macbeth*. Immediately following the scene in which we learn of Macbeth's murder of King Duncan, there is a scene of shockingly different character. It is filled with the bawdy talk and drunken jests of the porter who takes his time about opening the castle gate to the new arrivals who are demanding admission. The contrast between the eerie and almost hallucinated scene of the murder and the earthy bawdiness of the porter's ramblings is extreme. But De Quincey's point is that we need this drastic change of tone. We have dwelt so long in the special atmosphere of Macbeth's haunted imagination that we need to be reminded that the everyday world still exists—even if that realization comes with a shock.

Faulkner has used a similar psychology. We have for so many tense pages followed the obsessed minds of Joe and Joanna that we need to be reminded how special their world is. We need to be reminded that in the little town of Jefferson an ordinary young man may take his best girl to the movies or out for a ride on a pleasant August night. But of course Faulkner's method yields a special dividend. Joe himself is so keyed up, so beside himself, that he does not even notice that he is still carrying the pistol that he took away from Joanna. We could be told about it, to be sure; but how much more effective it is to see that only the terrified young people in the car were aware of the gun, not Joe.

With the account of Joe's murder of Joanna, many matters broached earlier in *Light in August* begin to make sense: Joe's relation to Byron Bunch and to Joe Brown and to the town generally. But, of course, *Light in August* is not only about Joe Christmas. Lena, heavy with child, is there in Jefferson too, as is Byron already hopelessly in love with Lena, though, because he is a man of honor determined to see that Joe Brown marries her. And there is Gail Hightower, whose story we already know in part. Of this whole cluster of strangers to the Jefferson community and alienated from any community at all, only Joanna Burden's fate has been decided.

In some sense Joe's story is the most important of all, nevertheless some of the other characters have important stories too, and we must understand them if we are fully to understand Joe himself. For characters who have little or no direct relation with each other may have very important relationships to the theme of the novel.

With chapter 13, the chapter that immediately follows the account of Miss Burden's death, there is another of Faulkner's characteristic time shifts. In this chapter, we revert to an earlier scene where the crowd has gathered around Miss Burden's burning house and where the sheriff is beginning his investigation. Joe has of course escaped and will not be jailed for a full week after the murder. What occupies the novelist's special attention at this point is Hightower, especially in his relation with Byron Bunch.

Hightower winces at the news Byron Bunch has brought him, especially the news that Miss Burden is dead and that her suspected murderer is reported to be a black man. Hightower fears that there may be a lynching especially in view of the gruesome circumstances of Miss Burden's death. But he is also worried that Byron may be taking too much interest in Lena.

Hightower is a man who believes that he has been badly injured by life and has no wish ever to become involved again in its dangerous crosscurrents. Faulkner tells us in so many words that Hightower thinks that he is "not in life anymore" and a little later Hightower declares to himself " 'I have bought immunity. I have paid. I have paid.' " Hightower tells himself that "I just [want] peace," to be left alone, to observe life with horror or compassion or weary irony, but not to have to take responsibility for it. This former Christian minister does not, as St. Paul did, ever expect to say with joy "I have finished my course, I have kept the faith." Instead, he means to watch the race course from some quiet vantage point on the side lines.

He is genuinely fond of Byron Bunch and recommends to him a like passivity. He cautions Byron against becoming involved with Lena. The child she is soon to bear is not Byron's child. Yet obviously Byron has fallen in love with Lena and now that he has settled her temporarily in the cabin lately occupied by Brown and Christmas, Byron may find it impossible to avoid assuming responsibility for Lena's future. Byron's hope that Brown can be induced to marry Lena is, in Hightower's eyes, a desperately foolish hope. He regards his quietly methodical little friend as a Don Quixote, gentle, compassionate, honorable to a fault, but afflicted with an idealistic folly.

Hightower is as fully cut off from the community as is Joe, but whereas Hightower's isolation is sought for and his attitude toward the community is passive, Joe is fiercely combative. Only during his last days of life, while he is hiding from the sheriff's posse, does he show any desire for something like Hightower's quiet retirement from the world. After some days of solitude and enforced fasting—for there is no food available to him—there comes over Joe a sense of "peace and unhaste and quiet." He feels "dry and light." For this embattled spirit, it is a new and strange experience. His whole life heretofore has shown him to have taken up arms against the world. Joe's battle with the world is just that: not warfare against a limited adversary, but general war that is deep-seated and rooted in a basic philosophical disagreement with it.

Thus, readers who wish to interpret Joe's actions as a black man's heroic defiance of the oppressive white community ought to take note of the fact that during the week in which Joe is a hunted outlaw, his most violent actions are directed against the black community, not the white. Joe enters a black church where an evening service is being held. He strides up the aisle, catches the preacher by the throat, hurls him out of the pulpit, knocks down a seventy-year-old man, cracks the skull of a young black man who approaches him with a "razor nekkid in his hand," and escapes.

The action is that of a possibly demented man, certainly that of an obsessed man. But the reader ought to know by now what the nature of the obsession is: an alienation so complete that Joe believes every man's hand is raised against him. If that hand is not immediately raised, that very fact seems an act of provocation. But clearly the psychic forces now at work in Joe have a long history—they go back to his childhood itself—and in these last days of his life are simply coming to a head, or, one might say, coming into focus.

Joe does not perhaps fully come to an understanding of himself in these closing days, but the reader by now ought to understand more fully the compulsions that account for Joe's conduct and the special warping that circumstances have given to his psyche. Let us try to take this understanding a little further.

Faulkner has shown us in the long flashback into Joe's earlier life how his relation to womankind has been corrupted. This corruption has everything to do with Joe's relation to the human community. Lena, on the other hand, comes into Jefferson and the community responds positively. True, the good women look askance at her unwed pregnancy, but Jefferson, with all its faults, is a true community, and as such, senses instinctively that women bearing children are the care of any community and it therefore moves to shelter and protect them.

Conversely, Joe's antagonism toward women and the female principle causes him to reject anything that threatens his individualism or challenges his essential isolation. Joe's rejection of the female principle reaches to a deeper level still: he has never had any real rapport with nature, the nurturing mother of us all. As Joe hides out in the woods, avoiding the sheriff's posse, he suddenly becomes aware of a desire "to see his native earth in all its phases for the first or the last time." Note the phrase, "for the first . . . time." It is significant, for Faulkner tells us that though Joe had grown to manhood in the country, he had done so without "learning anything about its actual shape and feel. For a week now he has lurked and crept among [nature's] secret places, yet he [has] remained a foreigner to the very immutable laws which earth must obey."

Joe does, as I have earlier remarked, experience a sense of peace and quiet, and at first believes that such beatitude comes from his discovery of nature, "until suddenly," we are told "the true answer comes to him." He has decided to stop running away—to accept the end of his life. He hails a wagon and catches a ride to Mottstown, and Faulkner tells us that in doing so "he is entering again . . . the street which ran for thirty years. . . . Though during the last seven days he has . . . traveled further than in all the thirty years before. . . . And yet he is still inside the circle." He acknowledges that he has "never broken out of the ring of what I have already done and cannot ever undo."

Joe is a fatalist. He believes in a God of justice but not of mercy, in a God who judges but does not forgive. In spite of Joe's early refusal to memorize the catechism, he has learned more from his old Presbyterian foster father than he realized. And he finds a kind of peace in accepting the fact that he must now pay for what he cannot ever undo. He can at least face up to his doom like a man. Joe Christmas is neither the first nor the last of Faulkner's company of stoics.

Joe Christmas, however, has his own way of ceasing to run from the sheriff. He does not call on him and say I am the man you want: arrest me. Instead, he visits the barbershop, buys a new shirt and tie and straw hat, and then walks the streets of the town until someone recognizes him. When that person asks whether his name is Christmas, he does not deny it. He puts up no resistance when they take him to Jefferson and jail him to stand trial for the murder of Joanna Burden.

Faulkner now proceeds to fill in another gap in the life of Christmas. In Mottstown live old Doc Hines and his wife, and Doc Hines is the former janitor in the Memphis orphanage where Joe Christmas began his life. Now we learn that it was Doc Hines who left the infant Joe on the orphanage steps, and that he was the grandfather of the child. The whole terrible story at last comes out: how Milly Hines, their daughter, had slipped off with one of the employees of a visiting circus; how the fanatical Doc Hines was certain that the man was a Negro, and so shot and killed him; and how, when Milly's child was born, he saw to it that Milly had no physician to help her through the ordeal, as a consequence of which she died. Later, not telling his wife what he had done with the baby, Hines left it at the Memphis orphanage.

Faulkner depicts among his more fanatical Protestants some pretty extreme cases, several of whom are to be found in *Light in August*. Of these, surely old Doc Hines is the worst. By comparison, he makes Mr. McEachern look almost gentle, almost benign. In anyone's terms, Hines is a madman. When Joe is captured, Hines tries to incite the crowd to lynch him, though aware that Joe is of his own flesh and blood. Surely no child was so damned from the very cradle by the people with whom he came in contact, including his own kin.

Byron Bunch meets Mrs. Hines, hears her story, and on the Sunday evening after Joe's capture, brings the Hineses to Hightower's house. Mrs. Hines has one request to make of the ex-minister. She wants Hightower to furnish Joe with an alibi. The only real evidence against Joe is the worthless Brown's word. If Hightower were willing to testify that Joe spent the night of the murder at Hightower's house, the case against Joe would collapse. Byron tells Hightower: "'Folks would believe you. They would believe that, anyway.'" Byron here is awkwardly frank. He means that at the time of

Mrs. Hightower's death, ugly rumors circulated to the effect that Hightower was a homosexual. Besides, Byron goes on to plead: the people of the town would not do anything to him, not anything that would really hurt him. "'And I reckon you are used to everything else they can do.'"

Byron does not mean to be cruel. But it is in his character to be fully caught up in Mrs. Hines's plight. What Byron proposes is too much for Hightower: to tell a lie to acquit a double, perhaps a triple murderer, and worst of all, to throw himself once more into the whirlpool of life after he had thought he had removed himself from it forever. He refuses, and tells them all to get out of the house.

Early the next morning Byron is back at Hightower's house. He wakes him with the word that Lena is already in labor. Will Hightower rush over to the cabin while Byron hurries for the doctor? Hightower does go to the cabin and actually delivers Lena's child, for the doctor is late in getting there. The incident rather sets Hightower up. "'I showed them!'" Hightower thinks. "'Life comes to the old man yet . . .'" and walking home Hightower "moves like a man with a purpose. . . ." When he passes the Burden house, charred by the recent fire, he thinks "Poor, barren woman. To have not lived only a week longer, until luck returned to this place. Until luck and life returned to these barren and ruined acres."

A basic theme of the book surely now begins to come clear. Lena is a simple country girl and one who, in the old Victorian phrase, has proved to be no better than she should be. But she embodies nature: young, innocent, with healthy instincts and impulses, and her presence, though it is an almost passive presence, has begun to pull some of the outsiders and pariahs back into life once more.

Byron Bunch clearly has come to feel, through his attraction to her, life and love. Even Hightower begins to be drawn out of his death-in-life. This is not to say that Lena can save all the pariahs and the alienated or that she is consciously trying to save any of them. But the way in which she affects two lives calls attention to what she has come to represent.

Joe Christmas has done some plea bargaining for a sentence of life imprisonment, but as he is being removed from the jail to the courthouse, he unaccountably makes a break for freedom, and succeeds in getting as far as Hightower's house. During his break for freedom he secures a pistol. He rushes into Hightower's house, strikes the minister on the head with the pistol, and barricades himself behind an overturned kitchen table. Yet when the first peace officer, a young man named Percy Grimm, bursts into the room, Joe refuses to fire at him. Grimm, on the other hand, puts five bullets into Joe and then, with a kitchen knife that he has snatched up, proceeds to emasculate the dying man. The next peace officer to burst into the room vomits at what he sees Grimm doing.

This violent scene has been often misunderstood, even though Faulkner has gone to some pains to point out its significance. It is not a lynching. Percy Grimm is technically a duly commissioned law officer who is confronting a dangerous man known to be armed. Few could blame him for firing first in what amounts to hot pursuit. What is completely atrocious is the mayhem that Grimm visits on the dying man. No wonder the second peace officer begins to retch at what he sees.

Actually, in Percy Grimm we meet one more alienated character. Faulkner is very specific about Grimm's alienation. Percy Grimm was just a little too young to take part in World War I. His dream of glory—to serve his country by wearing its uniform and even to die for it—has been thwarted. His father did not understand him, thinking him lazy and worthless, when in reality the boy was suffering what Faulkner called a "terrible tragedy," and yet having no one to whom he could talk, no one "to open his heart to." His becoming a member of the state's National Guard offers him a uniform, at least on a part-time basis, and some consolation.

When Joe is first captured, Grimm volunteers his services: he and men like him will see to it that there is no lynching and that Christmas has a fair trial, even though it is all too plain that he is Joanna Burden's murderer. There is in reality no disposition to lynch Joe; the wise and practical old sheriff is quite right about this. But Grimm will not be put off; the fair name of Jefferson is in danger, it must not be stained. Grimm finally carries the day and gets himself and a group of other young men sworn in as special deputies. Was Grimm sincere? I think so. In fact, *Light in August* would become a poorer and thinner novel if one were forced to think otherwise. I believe that Grimm was a dedicated peace officer until, in the heat of the chase, his blood up, all his latent sadism suddenly bursts forth, for like Joe, Grimm has a great deal of violence in his nature.

Grimm is in reality Joe's mirror image. Joe is outside the community and wants to remain outside it. He defies it. Grimm feels himself an outsider from the community, but is desperate to have it accept him, not merely as a member, but as a leader against its foes. He insists that the community's good name is in danger, even when it is clear to others that it is not.

Faulkner makes the point very neatly when Hightower, later that day, believing that he is dying, has a vision of all the people that he has known in his life. He sees very clearly the faces of old friends and former parishioners. But one face is blurred: it seems to be a mingling of two different faces. Faulkner tells us that Hightower "can see that it is two faces which seem to strive . . . to free themselves one from the other, then fade and blend again." The two faces belong to Joe and to Percy Grimm.

Hightower learns something further in this final vision and meditation: not only are Joe and Percy Grimm brothers under the skin, but he himself and Joe are also brothers in crime. For if Joe is guilty of the death of his paramour, Joanna, Hightower has been just as guilty of the death of his own wife. By withholding love, he forced her into her loneliness, her madness, and her shameful death. It is a truth which up to this point Hightower has refused to accept. Now he does accept it.

The reader too learns something about Hightower that he may have guessed but could not have known certainly. In one of Faulkner's most brilliant flashbacks, we are told of Hightower's childhood and early life, and how his psyche had been warped almost as decisively as Joe's had been. Hightower ruefully comes to accept the fact that in hero-worshipping his grandfather, he had failed to live in the present at all. To live merely in the past is not to live. Hightower had in effect died with his grandfather's death years before he had actually been born.

What, in the meantime, is happening to Lena Grove? And to Byron Bunch? Byron had seen to it that a deputy sheriff brings the wretched Brown to the cabin where Lena lies with her newborn baby. But though a horse can be led to water, he cannot be made to drink. When Brown becomes aware that the rear window is unguarded, he leaps through it and is last seen hopping a ride on a fast freight leaving town. But the indomitable Lena does not give up her pursuit of the father of her child. In our last view of her, some weeks later, Lena is on the road again. This time she has a baby at her breast and is accompanied by the indefatigable Byron Bunch. We see them through the eyes of a secondhand furniture dealer who has given them a ride north, a ride long enough to include two night stops. The furniture dealer is now home, lying in bed with his wife and telling her of his odd and amusing adventure.

Some readers have found it rather disconcerting that Faulkner should suddenly introduce an entirely new character in the last chapter of the novel. But Faulkner had his reasons. In the first place, this new narrator, the furniture dealer, is a shrewd observer, with sound judgment and a good sense of the comic. Moreover, the fact that he is no Gavin Stevens with his Phi Beta Kappa key, but instead a plain man of the people, is important in lending credibility to his interpretation of the events on which he is reporting; that is, his estimate is typical and representative of that of the community at large.

He is not deceived about Lena's motives. As he tells his wife: "'I think she was just traveling. I dont think she had any idea of finding whoever it was she was following. I dont think she had ever aimed to. . . . I reckon this was the first time she had ever been further away from home than she could walk back before sundown in her life. . . . And so I think she had just made up her mind to travel a little further and see as much as she could, since I reckon she knew that when she settled down this time, it would likely be for the rest of her life.'" That is, Byron will eventually persuade her to settle down with him and he will be the father of the rest of her children. But in the meantime, the furniture dealer finds Byron's clumsy attempts at courtship amusing, as is Lena's evident certainty of her hold on Byron and her serene confidence in life itself. The furniture dealer takes a real pleasure in describing Lena's face: ". . . it was like it was already fixed and waiting to be surprised, and [as if she knowed] that when the surprise come, she was going to enjoy it."

So the novel has a happy ending after all—not that Lena's quiet triumph cancels out Joe's death, or the failure and heartbreak in the lives of Joanna Burden and Gail Hightower. Life can be tragic, and Joe is allowed the full dignity of his defiant attempt to assert and maintain his lonely identity. But life also contains its instances of quiet happiness and is constantly starting over, renewing itself. The fact that the babe at Lena's breast was born on the very day that Joe Christmas died has its significance.

8 · ABSALOM, ABSALOM!

Many readers have come to regard *Absalom, Absalom!* as Faulkner's most powerful, and perhaps the greatest, of all his novels. Technically it is one of his most ambitious. But there is no vain display of technical virtuosity. The means used are necessary to give proper development to Faulkner's theme.

Some expositors of *Absalom, Absalom!* have seen not one story but two: the story of Thomas Sutpen and the story of Quentin Compson. Thomas Sutpen's story may be summarized in this way: he had come to Yoknapatawpha County in the early 1830s, had acquired a great plantation which he called Sutpen's Hundred, and eventually married a local girl and established himself as a power in the community. But his origins were always somewhat mysterious. He arrived in Jefferson out of nowhere with a group of French-speaking black slaves. People wondered where he had acquired the money to buy his one hundred-square-mile tract of land and to build his grandiose plantation house. Moreover, his personal habits and manners attracted attention, even a measure of suspicion. For example, he would, on occasion, strip to the waist and fight with one of his slaves, not by way of discipline or punishment, but apparently to prove that he was indeed their master, not merely in terms of custom and law, but physically, in a bloody, no-holds-barred fight.

The neighboring plantation owners who were invited to

attend these events certainly did not engage in bare-fisted fights with their slaves. No wonder that they regarded Sutpen as outrageously strange, and that he became something of a legend in the community which had to regard him as different from themselves. If the difference compelled a certain respect, it also created apprehension.

These disturbing differences caused Sutpen to be arrested in the early days of his sojourn on suspicion of theft. When he came back to town one day with four ox-carts laden with mahogany furniture, crystal candelabra, and such, the townsfolk were certain that his gains were ill-gotten; they simply had to be. But two well-known and highly respected citizens, Goodhue Coldfield, a small merchant, and General Compson, a planter, came to Sutpen's rescue. Later, through his marriage to Coldfield's daughter, Sutpen even achieved a certain respectability. When the Civil War broke out, Sutpen became a colonel and proved a brave and resourceful soldier. Thus he eventually became a pillar of the community and its trusted defender. But he remained in an important sense different, not fully understood, a man of mystery.

For instance, there was the curious circumstance of Henry, his son and heir, quarreling with his father and suddenly leaving his father's house with one of his college friends who had come to Sutpen's Hundred for a Christmas visit. A story got out through the black servants that there had been a family quarrel and that the two young men had gone off together to New Orleans, the city that Charles Bon, Henry's friend, called home. Charles, so it was thought, had fallen in love with Henry's sister Judith, and Judith, with him.

Soon after this the Civil War began, and not only the elder Sutpen but Henry and Charles Bon went off to war, though the young men, of course, did not serve in Sutpen's regiment. When the War ended, and before Thomas Sutpen had come home, Henry and Charles made their way back to Sutpen's Hundred, and then, strange to tell, Henry shot Charles dead, at the very gates of the plantation. The two young men had been inseparable friends for years, had fought side by side through the four years of war, and had traveled back to Mississippi together. Then, inexplicably, one had killed the other and fled the country.

Judith, Sutpen's legitimate daughter, and Clytie, the offspring of Thomas Sutpen and one of his slaves, buried Charles in the family graveyard on the plantation. During the War, Judith's mother, Ellen Coldfield Sutpen, had died, and so had Ellen's father, Goodhue Coldfield, leaving a young daughter, Rosa. Rosa moved out to join Judith. There, the three women, Judith, Clytie, and Rosa, awaited Thomas Sutpen's return.

Years later, Sutpen was killed by a poor white, his retainer and henchman. Still later, Judith died in a yellow fever epidemic. The only Sutpen now left (since Henry had disappeared) was Clytie, who continued to live in a cabin near the great manor house which was beginning to fall into ruin. So ended Sutpen's great bid for prestige and power.

This much was known generally about the Sutpens, but much was left cloaked in mystery. What had caused the quarrel between father and son? The cause must have been serious to compel Henry to abandon his home and his prospects as heir to a great estate. More mysterious still was Henry's killing of his best friend. What possibly could have been his motive? The situation resembles that in *Light in August*, where the murderer is clearly identified but his motive is hidden. In both novels the exploration of the motive is very important; but here the resemblance between them abruptly ends. Henry and Joe Christmas are very different men, and in *Absalom, Absalom!* Faulkner's way of penetrating the mystery is very different from that employed in *Light in August*.

The Sutpen legend and its surrounding mysteries were the possession of the whole town of Jefferson. But Faulkner has made them impinge with special force on Quentin Compson, who, as the novel opens, is a young man of about nineteen or twenty, and is just preparing to leave for his first year at Harvard. The time is late summer. Somewhat to his surprise,

Quentin is asked by Miss Rosa Coldfield to call upon her. He does so and hears from her an account of Thomas Sutpen, her brother-in-law.

Miss Rosa has bottled up in her diminutive body an undying rage against Sutpen. She sees him as a demon. His presence in Jefferson has amounted to a curse on the Coldfield family. She is convinced that Sutpen married her sister, Ellen, only to gain respectability, which, as a scapegrace, he knew that he needed. She insists that Sutpen had no family background, indeed, "had no past at all." He was no gentleman, and the only virtue that Miss Rosa can accord him is courage. She admits that he was brave. But in her eyes his bravery was simply an aspect of his destructive force.

As for Henry Sutpen's murder of his best friend, Charles Bon, Miss Rosa has no idea why it occurred, except that Sutpen was a demon and that his progeny were thus doomed and accursed. Beyond this, Miss Rosa can offer no explanation nor does she attempt any.

All the strange and violent events seem to Miss Rosa completely irrational. Thus, she tells Quentin that she saw "'Judith's marriage [to Charles Bon] forbidden without rhyme or reason or shadow of excuse,'" the forbidder, of course, being Thomas Sutpen. On her deathbed, in the year 1863, Ellen had begged Rosa to try to protect her "remaining child." (She calls Judith her remaining child since Henry had, as Miss Rosa tells Quentin, "repudiated his home and birthright.")

Miss Rosa also tells how in 1865 Henry had practically flung "the bloody corpse of his sister's sweetheart at the hem of her wedding-gown." Her explanation, however, goes no further than that Sutpen had "created two children not only to destroy one another and his own line, but my line as well. . . ."

Miss Rosa, then, does not help much with the problem of motivation, but she does indicate the depth of her fury, and she is frank about the fact that she has a personal grievance. After his return from the war, Sutpen had asked her to marry him and, as she confesses, she had accepted him. But the marriage did not take place. She gives no explanation here beyond the cryptic comment that her "life was destined to end on an afternoon in April forty-three years ago," that is to say, in 1866, a year after the War had ended. Later we shall learn what happened that afternoon.

This is then the end of the first chapter. In the next chapter we learn why Miss Rosa had summoned Quentin to her cottage. It was because she wanted him to drive her out to Sutpen's Hundred after dark, for a particular reason of her own. So in this second chapter, we find Quentin sitting on the veranda of the Compson house, talking to his father about Miss Rosa and waiting for the time to pick her up for the twelve-mile drive in a buggy out to the ruinous Sutpen mansion.

Quentin's father, Mr. Compson, knows a great deal about the Sutpen story, and he has his own theories about why what happened did happen. In *Absalom, Absalom!* Mr. Compson makes a rather different impression on the reader from that made in *The Sound and the Fury*. Though *Absalom, Absalom!* was published five years after *The Sound and the Fury*, it depicts events that occurred prior to those related in *The Sound and the Fury*. One way to account for the reader's different impression of Mr. Compson is to assume that, by the time Faulkner came to write *Absalom, Absalom!* he had rethought the character and had changed his conception of him. But there is another possibility: in *The Sound and the Fury* we saw Mr. Compson largely through Quentin's eyes—that is to say, largely through the eyes of a young man who had resolved to commit suicide. What Quentin dwells on there is his father's defeatism and even cynicism.

In *Absalom, Absalom!*, however, Mr. Compson is presented more objectively, in third-person narration except for a few specifically labeled statements made by Quentin to his roommate Shreve. Moreover, the Quentin whom we see and hear in *Absalom, Absalom!* is the Quentin of September 1909 and January 1910, not the Quentin of June 2, 1910, the day on which, in *The Sound and the Fury*, he has so committed himself to death that he is already a living dead man.

To get back to the conversation between Quentin and Mr. Compson as they wait for darkness to fall: Mr. Compson can fill in some of the gaps in Miss Rosa's frenzied and rather incoherent account. He also can look at events with a detachment that Miss Rosa obviously lacks. He is aware of some of the ironies involved in the story and he is on the whole a rather shrewd observer. Also, Mr. Compson has a great deal of information about Sutpen, for *his* father, General Compson, was almost the only friend that Sutpen had in Jefferson. As we shall find out later in the novel, Sutpen had told General Compson things about his early life that he had confided to no other person in the community. Indeed, it soon becomes plain that Mr. Compson knows much more about Thomas Sutpen than Sutpen's sister-in-law, Miss Rosa, does. Yet, as we shall find a little later, there is much about Sutpen's story that is puzzling even to Mr. Compson, and some of the hypotheses that he offers as explanations of certain happenings turn out to be wrong.

Nevertheless, it is very helpful to the reader, fresh from Miss Rosa's hot imprecations and furious repudiations of her demonic brother-in-law, to be provided in chapters 2–4 with a cool, rational, and coherent review of the Sutpen story. Mr. Compson's account of Sutpen's arrival in Jefferson in 1833 in particular is brilliantly set forth and filled with penetrating observations, many of which had been passed down to him by General Compson. The General had early discerned that Sutpen was already "completely the slave of his secret and furious impatience." The General had also taken note of Sutpen's "gaunt and tireless driving." There is also the telling comment that when Sutpen decided to marry, he came "to town to find a wife exactly as he would have gone to the Memphis market to buy livestock or slaves."

General Compson also passed on to his son a significant comment on Sutpen's self-confidence. Though he was clearly underbred, he believed that Sutpen had so "painfully and tediously" drilled himself in the formal rituals of society that though a Compson or "Judge Benbow might have done [what was required] a little more effortlessly than he, . . . he would not have believed that anyone could have beat him in knowing when to do it and how." Mr. Compson also reveals an ominous aspect of Sutpen's character. Anyone looking at Sutpen would have to say: "Given the occasion and the need, this man can and will do anything." In sum, what General Compson had observed were the lineaments of a self-made man of great force and indomitable will. Yet his having come so far and having accomplished so much with little more than his bare hands makes him overconfident of his own powers. He is guilty of hubris. Thus, his self-confidence may prove to be his undoing. For the discerning reader these perceptions should furnish significant hints of what is to come.

Mr. Compson's long conversation with Quentin develops in great detail some matters that Miss Rosa's monologue had only touched on, for example, the building of Sutpen's great house, Sutpen's attitude toward his slaves, his relations with his neighbors, his marriage to Ellen Coldfield, and his relations with his father-in-law.

Mr. Compson is very interesting on the subject of the father-in-law, Goodhue Coldfield. Coldfield is a storekeeper, not quite a merchant. He is one of Faulkner's more austere southern Puritans. He is a pillar in the local Methodist church and is regarded as a model of probity and a monument of respectability. It was his respectability that caused Sutpen to pay court to his daughter, Ellen. Miss Rosa is at least right about that. For Sutpen, seeking to establish himself as a great landowner in a plantation society, might normally have been expected to seek a wife from among the daughters of the planter class. But he does not. He needs respectability badly, and since he thinks of it as a commodity, his courtship takes him to the household that seems to him to have the largest lump of it, and the lump of finest purity.

This point is worth making, not only because it tells us something about Sutpen, but because it throws some light on the heredity of Sutpen's children, Henry and Judith. Their Puritan grandfather Coldfield was a being very different from their father. The two men had little in common, but like many strong outcrosses, this one produced unusual progeny. Judith is a beautiful girl of great force, embodying even a vein of iron like that of her father, but she is devoid of his furious impatience. Yet the opposing hereditary forces that meet in Henry tend to tear him apart. Though Henry is more passive than his sister, he is a man of passionate will and with a capacity to suffer intensely and yet endure.

In fact, old Goodhue Coldfield possessed, along with his Puritan squeamishness, his own strong-minded fanaticism. He disapproved of secession, not so much, Mr. Compson believed, because he objected to "the idea of pouring out human blood," but to the "idea of waste: of wearing out and eating up and shooting away material in any cause whatever." At any rate, he refused to "sell any goods for any price to the military" or to any person who supported the Secessionist movement. Finally, he mounted to the attic of his house, nailed the door shut, and threw the hammer out of the window. Thus, he repudiated the Confederacy. But Mr. Compson gives him his due: "He was not a coward. . . . He was a man of uncompromising moral strength."

Rosa was the dutiful daughter. She did not let him starve. She sent food up to her father through his attic window secretly by night for some three years, until he did die, still nailed up in the attic. Meanwhile, Rosa wrote countless odes to the soldiers of the South, for her heart was wholly committed to the cause her father hated.

Ellen, the mother of Judith and Henry, was by all accounts a vain and shallow woman. But otherwise, there seems to have been plenty of rugged strength in both the Coldfield and Sutpen families. The Sutpen children would need it: they would have much to test their powers of endurance.

In the course of his account of the Sutpens, Mr. Compson gave Quentin his theory as to why Henry Sutpen killed his best friend. When Henry was sent to the newly founded

University of Mississippi, he met there a handsome young man, considerably older than himself, a New Orleanian, who had also enrolled in the University. This man, Charles Bon by name, became Henry's companion and his idol. Whereas Henry felt himself to be an awkward provincial, Charles to him seemed to be the elegant cosmopolite. He was attractively foreign, for New Orleans was at this time still culturally a French city. So Henry brought Bon home with him for a brief visit at Christmas, 1859. The friendship deepened: Bon came for a week's visit the next summer, and by this time Judith was in love with the handsome young man. At Christmas time in 1860, Bon once more accompanied Henry home, but there was a quarrel between father and son, and Henry left his father's house for New Orleans with his friend Charles. Henry vowed not to return home.

Mr. Compson's theory was this: Thomas Sutpen, in the summer of 1860, went to New Orleans to check on his prospective son-in-law, and found, as he had suspected, that Bon had a mistress, of color, who had already borne him a child. Bon had established them in a sumptuous apartment. In this period, young gentlemen of wealth in New Orleans were accustomed to meet attractive, carefully nurtured young women at the Quadroon Ballroom, become their "protectors," and live with them, often for many years, in a stable relationship, even after the man had married a woman of his own race and kind.

Mr. Compson knew that Sutpen, for some reason, in the summer of 1860, had made a visit to New Orleans. Charles Bon did indeed, as we shall later find out, have such a mistress and an infant son. At any rate, Mr. Compson thinks that this was what Sutpen had found out on his visit to New Orleans. Thus, when Henry and Bon came home together that Christmas, Sutpen called Henry aside and told him that Judith could not marry Charles because he regarded him as in effect a married man. Henry must have refused to believe his father, for he repudiated his patrimony and rode off that same night with his friend. But, Mr. Compson believed,

Henry eventually found out that his father's story was but too true, and though Henry postponed the act until the last moment, at the last he shot Charles, because Charles insisted on taking Judith to wife.

It is an interesting theory, but there is not a great deal to support it. Even if we make full allowance for Henry's puritanical squeamishness, would he be willing to kill his devoted friend simply because the friend had taken a mistress and begotten a child out of wedlock? After all, Charles Bon was not legally married to anyone, and consequently, in marrying Judith, would not be committing bigamy. Mr. Compson himself is aware that his theory is implausible. Almost as soon as he has outlined it, he confesses to Quentin: " 'It's just incredible. It just does not explain.' " But it is the best he can do to account for Henry's murder of Charles Bon.

Mr. Compson's conjectures as to how Judith felt are more nearly convincing. The way in which she endured these and later calamities proved her to be a woman of courage and of iron endurance. Mr. Compson has some basis, therefore, for describing Judith's state of mind after her father had forbidden her marriage to Bon. He imagines her saying: "I love, I will accept no substitute; something has happened between him and my father; if my father was right, I will never see him again, if wrong he will come or send for me; if happy I can be I will, if suffer I must I can." At any rate, Judith waited for Bon's return from the War and clearly was ready to marry him. Bon had written a letter to Judith toward the end of the War, a curious and almost fatalistic letter, in which he had said among other things: "I now believe that you and I are strangely enough included among those who are doomed to live." Bon did indeed survive the dangers of the War, but was doomed to die just four or five minutes away from taking Judith in his arms.

Mr. Compson, sitting on his porch in the gathering dusk, ends his story with an imagined account of Henry's last words to Bon: "Do you renounce?" That is, "do you renounce Judith as your intended wife?" and he imagines Bon's reply:

"For four years now I have given chance the opportunity to renounce for me, but it seems that . . . she and I both are doomed to live." Mr. Compson imagines that Henry is still not ready to shoot, and that he says to Bon as they approach the gate of Sutpen's Hundred: *"Dont you pass the shadow of this post,* [then, in a moment, the shadow of] *this branch, Charles;"* and Charles's reply *"I am going to pass it, Henry."* He does pass it and Henry pulls the trigger. Mr. Compson ends his account with the way in which the news reached Miss Rosa: the poor-white Wash Jones, on a saddleless mule, outside her cottage, bellowing "'Air you Rosie Coldfield? Then you better come on out yon. Henry has done shot that durn French feller. Kilt him dead as a beef.'" So Mr. Compson's story concludes.

Presumably it has now become dark enough for Quentin to call for Miss Rosa and prepare to drive her out to Sutpen's Hundred. Since the next chapter, chapter 5, save for the last page, consists of one unbroken harangue by Miss Rosa, at least one unwary commentator has assumed that in chapter 5 we are to imagine Quentin and Miss Rosa now seated in the buggy and on the way out to Sutpen's mansion. As a matter of fact, Miss Rosa's long monologue is not delivered as she sits in the buggy riding toward Sutpen's Hundred, and the point is clinched when she asks Quentin: *"Do you mark how the wistaria, sun-impacted on this wall here, distills and penetrates this room?"*

What Faulkner has done in this chapter is to make use of one of his favorite devices: the flashback. Why, with chapter 5, does he take us back in time, back again into Miss Rosa's house, and drench us once more with her passionate tirade against her demonic brother-in-law? Presumably because he wants to develop further Miss Rosa's character and to present through her eyes the haunted quality of the house which she and Quentin are soon to enter, though uninvited.

Whatever Faulkner's reasons for displacing this chapter from its proper place in the narrative just after chapter 1, the maneuver seems to me entirely successful. Chapter 5, though it may be no more than an afterimage left in Quentin's mind by his several hours of listening to Miss Rosa earlier that afternoon, does pick up with the scene with which the previous chapter ends, Jones bellowing in front of her house, "Air you Rosie Coldfield?" and moves on through an account of her ride with Jones out to Sutpen's Hundred, of what she found there, of Judith's conduct, of the burial of Charles Bon, of Rosa's subsequent life with Judith and Clytie, and finally, of the return of the master of the house, Thomas Sutpen.

We learn in this chapter also of the infamous proposal that Sutpen eventually made to Miss Rosa. Having lost a male heir through Henry's departure, and apparently desperate to have a son to carry on the dynasty that he thought he had already established, Sutpen proposed to Miss Rosa that they should cohabit, and if she bore him a son, they would get married. Time was running out; he could not afford to find himself married to a barren wife or one who did not quickly produce male offspring. This proposal is what caused "the old outraged and aghast unbelieving which," as she tells Quentin, has now "lasted forty-three years." After Sutpen's proposal—proposition would be a more accurate term—Miss Rosa returned in furious indignation to her father's house in Jefferson and has lived there ever since, now for some forty-three years.

All of this material in chapter 5—or nearly all of it—is either new or a much fuller development of items merely mentioned in the first chapter. But even more important for the reader is the aura of madness and horror that surrounds these events and actually seems to shroud the plantation house on which Sutpen spent so much heroic effort. Miss Rosa is clearly an obsessed woman, but she has the gift of words. She was not the self-appointed poetess laureate of Yoknapatawpha County for nothing. Perhaps her hundreds of odes to the Confederate soldiers were written in the bad nineteenth-century style that one would expect, but the rhapsodic prose-poetry in which she describes her aspirations, her loneliness, her anguish, and her outrage, carries conviction. Thomas Sutpen was not a demon, but through Miss Rosa's tirade we are convinced that for her he was. In the context provided, what might otherwise be merely involved and overblown rhetoric glows and at times blazes.

Finally in this chapter, at the very end, the author reveals to us why Miss Rosa has sought out a young man of good family to drive her out to Sutpen's Hundred. Miss Rosa says to Quentin: "There's something living in that house," and when Quentin interposes that of course Clytie lives out there, Miss Rosa goes on to explain what she has in mind. She means something is "Hidden in it. It has been out there for four years, living hidden in that house."

Chapter 6 does not tell us what Quentin and Miss Rosa found hidden at Sutpen's Hundred on that September evening, or whether they found anything at all. Instead, with the opening of chapter 6, we are some four or five months further along. It is now mid-January of 1910, and Quentin is sitting in his dormitory room at Harvard. His Canadian roommate has brought in a letter from Quentin's father. The letter reports that Miss Rosa Coldfield has died and describes her burial. So the continuity with the preceding chapter is in a sense sustained. That chapter ends with a reference to Miss Rosa's conviction that something or somebody is living hidden at Sutpen's Hundred. With the reference to her death, Quentin's mind is carried back at once to that hot September evening when he was seated in the buggy beside Miss Rosa as she clutched her cotton umbrella.

Quentin, however, is not left to his reverie. His roommate Shreve at once wants to know all about Miss Rosa, whom he persists in calling "Aunt Rosa." Shreve has obviously been teasing Quentin for some time, and has at some earlier period learned the outline of Sutpen's story and of his infamous proposal to Miss Rosa. Shreve obviously cannot take the South seriously, or really believe in the fantastic creatures who seem to inhabit it; nevertheless, he is also fascinated by the South. He is not going to let Quentin off tonight. He wants to talk, and to talk about the demon Sutpen. In order to warm Quentin to the subject, he even recapitulates the Sutpen story as it has obviously been told to him by Quentin on some earlier occasion.

Listening to Shreve's recital, so calm, so detached from any real involvement in the story, Quentin recalls the smell of his father's cigar and the smell of the wistaria and the "fireflies blowing and winking in the September dusk," as he and his father sat on the porch five months before and waited for dusk. With all this in mind, he says to himself that Shreve "sounds just like father." But then Quentin adds a proviso: Shreve sounds "exactly like father if father had known as much about it the night before I went out there as he did the day after I came back."

What Quentin implies is important: Quentin evidently did find something out at Sutpen's Hundred that September evening, something that had a bearing on the story of Sutpen, a piece of information that he reported to his father the next day. But the reader is not allowed at this point to know what Quentin discovered. Moreover, it is plain that Quentin had not yet passed this information on to Shreve. Otherwise, Shreve would not be pressing Quentin a little later to tell him what he found that night at Sutpen's Hundred.

Shreve does remember something that Quentin must have told him on a prior occasion, about a visit to the Sutpen graves, a visit that Quentin had made some years before when he and his father were out hunting quail. Shreve says: "You told me; how was it? you and your father shooting quail, the gray day after it had rained all night. . . ." And Shreve's bringing it up allows the author to describe the scene to us as it rises once more into Quentin's consciousness. It is a rich and moving passage which supplies further information about Sutpen and, most of all, about Judith.

On the hunt, Quentin and his father had come near the graves, and Quentin goes up and reads what is inscribed on the gravestones. Mr. Compson fills in their history. Sutpen had ordered a marble headstone for himself and one for his wife—had ordered them from Italy and had somehow got them through the Union blockade during the War. Unable to get them to Mississippi, he had carried them with him in a heavy cart everywhere he went: the two tombstones had actually been present at the Battle of Gettysburg. This anecdote speaks volumes about Sutpen's ambition to establish a name and a dynasty.

Quentin now asks his father about the other gravestones, those marking the graves of Charles Bon; his son, Charles Etienne Saint-Velery Bon; and Judith. Not only had Judith placed Charles Bon's body in the family burying-ground. Later she had sent for the octoroon woman to come up from New Orleans to visit Charles's grave. The octoroon had brought with her her little boy, Charles's son. General Compson, who had been helping Judith with business matters, was present and had communicated to Mr. Compson (and so through him to Quentin) a vivid description of the scene: "the magnolia-faced woman . . . whom [Aubrey] Beardsley might have dressed, in a soft flowing gown," kneeling on a silken cushion by the grave to weep, and "the little boy whom Beardsley might not only have dressed but drawn," blinking in the, for him, unaccustomed sunlight. Later, Judith, having heard or perhaps merely sensing that the woman was dying, had sent Clytie to New Orleans to bring back the little orphaned boy, whom she and Clytie would attempt to rear.

Judith was now dirt-poor. She actually had to walk behind the plow, now that Wash Jones, the plantation handyman, was also dead. There were no more silken clothes for little Charles Etienne, but instead patched overalls. Presumably Judith did the best she could to nurture Charles Etienne, but his case was curiously like that of Joe Christmas. He sensed that he was different from Judith, he suspected that he had Negro blood, and though he easily passed for white, he deliberately married a woman who might have been "carved of ebony."

Before Charles Etienne's marriage, General Compson urged the unhappy young man to leave Sutpen's Hundred and go somewhere far away: "Whatever you are, once you are among strangers . . . you can be whatever you will." General Compson even offered him the money he would need for the journey.

Quentin imagines that Judith, later on, after Charles Etienne's marriage, urged the same course: he should go into the North, into faraway cities, where no one would question his parentage or blood. If he wants her to, she will declare that he is Henry's son. As for his child, Judith will rear it. He need have no worries about it—only go. But to this imagined entreaty, Quentin "hears" Charles Etienne answering: "No, Miss Sutpen," until Judith finally begs him to call her "Aunt Judith." But the young man maintains his unrelenting formality.

This scene, I repeat, is not one that necessarily happened. It is a scene imagined by Quentin. Yet I find that it fits Judith's character. For what follows soon afterward is something not merely imagined but vouched for by General Compson. Charles Etienne fell victim to an epidemic of yellow fever. Judith nursed him until his death, and shortly afterward, died herself. Thus the last of the five tombstones is accounted for.

Quentin says that Charles Etienne's son, Jim, is still alive, though he is not called Jim Bon, but Jim Bond. (The change is obviously the result of folk etymology, since in English "Bon" would be a meaningless and unfamiliar word.) A number of years earlier, Quentin and some of his companions had caught a glimpse of Jim Bond, now a hulking, perhaps feeble-minded grown man, and of Clytie, now an old woman. They live in a cabin behind the great empty house.

As the chapter ends, Shreve summarizes as follows: You did drive Miss Rosa out there and—did you find someone? Quentin answers yes. But Shreve does not ask who it was. Instead, he practically shouts: "Wait then. For God's sake wait."

The story of Sutpen is beginning to get to Shreve. He is eager to know, all right, but not immediately. It is as if he wanted to postpone hearing the solution to a murder mystery—to relish the last fifty pages of the book and to defer the answer until the climactic moment. Shreve is enjoying the suspense. He does want to know, but not yet, not quite yet.

No wonder that, as chapter 7 opens, we find Shreve exclaiming: "Jesus, the South is fine, isn't it. It's better than the theatre, isn't it. It's better than Ben Hur, isn't it. No wonder you have to come away now and then. . . ." But for Quentin, the South is not a fascinating but unreal place. It is his homeland; it is reality. And the history of Thomas Sutpen is not simply a piece of exciting fiction which can be dismissed from consciousness when one has closed the covers of the book. It is Shreve who enjoys talking about Sutpen. Clearly, Quentin finds parts of the story painful, and we shall come to see that the story of Henry and Judith Sutpen had a special and excruciatingly personal meaning for him.

In chapter 7, what Quentin tells Shreve about Sutpen has to do largely with Sutpen's boyhood and youth. Sutpen had confided a good deal about his early life to General Compson. He had been born in a log cabin in the mountains of Virginia—or rather, in what would become in 1863 the state of West Virginia. He grew up in a rough frontier society, but his shiftless father took it into his head to move out of the mountains and down into the Virginia Tidewater country. Thomas was at this time a boy of ten. At the end of the Sutpen family's long journey, Thomas found himself in a completely unfamiliar world. There were great houses, carriages drawn by well-groomed horses, immense planted fields, and black people—all of this to him, strange and new. Among the marvels was a white man on whom Thomas liked to spy. On a summer's day, this man would lie in a hammock, with his shoes off, and a black man, wearing far better clothes than Thomas or his father ever expected to own, would fan the man in the hammock and bring him drinks to sip. When Thomas was thirteen or fourteen, however, he had an experience that was not merely curious or amusing. The experience shocked him and indeed changed his whole life.

Thomas's father asked him to deliver a message to one of the planters. The boy in his innocence went up to the front door, naively expecting to be shown in. A black man dressed in broadcloth and linen and wearing silk stockings told him peremptorily never to come to the front door again, but always to go to the back door. The boy was too much upset to do more than hurry away. He went off to be by himself to recover from his shock and to sort things out.

He pondered possible courses of action. He could shoot the black butler, but he realized immediately that this would solve nothing. The black man was only doing someone else's will. How could he get back at that ultimate power? He needed to, for what had happened was so unfair. "He never give me a chance to say it," he tells himself. Only later did he find an answer. To combat these rich and arrogant people, "You got to have land and niggers and a fine house.· . . ." So the boy immediately resolved to acquire them.

He had heard that men made money in the West Indies; so he made his way there and eventually came into a job of some consequence on a Haitian sugar plantation. There was a slave revolt, with savage fighting. In the end, the slaves were subdued. In this action Sutpen had proved brave, resolute, and confident. In short, he had distinguished himself, and part of his reward was his being offered the daughter of the house in marriage, and along with a wife, riches. But the marriage did not last, and it was Sutpen, not his wife, who forced the separation. Years later, he put the matter in this way to General Compson: "I found that she was not and could never be, through no fault of her own, adjunctive or incremental to the design which I had in mind, so I provided for her and put her aside." But Sutpen did not confide to General Compson what the fatal flaw in the woman was.

In the sentence that I just quoted from Sutpen, the reader will note how formal and even stilted Sutpen's vocabulary was. Yet it makes sense that Sutpen should speak in this way. His speech is that of a self-educated man, and a man who has taken that self-education very seriously. Sutpen has drawn his vocabulary from books, not from any actual tradition of spoken English. In a talk with someone like General Compson, the language learned in the one-room log cabin would never do, and Sutpen, knowing that it would never do, has given it up. So he speaks a rather artificial English, a book-learned English, one might call it. And his spoken language is one of the most significant instances of the fact that he is truly a self-made man. He has not only made his money himself; he has deliberately made up everything else about himself. But what a will! What driving power! What determination he shows!

In the same sentence I quoted from him a moment ago, note his use of the word "design." He has found that his wife cannot be adjunctive "to the design which I had in mind." Sutpen has indeed drawn up a blueprint for his career, a carefully plotted and articulated design which he means to follow rigidly. General Compson believed that Sutpen was convinced that in order to achieve anything whatsoever "all that was necessary was courage and shrewdness" and that Sutpen knew he had the one and believed that he could learn the other if it could be taught.

Then something came up to stop the conversation between Sutpen and General Compson, and the narrative was broken off. In fact, it was not resumed for some thirty years—not until 1864. Sutpen, now a colonel in the Confederate army, had returned to Virginia for a brief visit home and had called on General Compson to get some advice. Something in the working out of his special design had gone wrong, and Sutpen needed to talk it over with a man in whose integrity and wisdom he had confidence. Yet Sutpen cannot bring himself to expose the problem fully. He persists in putting the case in general and even hypothetical terms. Again, he refers to his first wife whom he had repudiated, along with her child. True, his conscience had "bothered him somewhat at first," he tells Colonel Compson, but "he had argued calmly and logically with his conscience until it was settled." He had dealt with her justly. He had made a very generous property settlement upon her and her son. Besides, he had from the first dealt frankly with her family, telling them all about himself and his humble origins, withholding nothing, yet they had not dealt fairly with him. They had concealed what they must have known would have kept him from marrying their daughter.

Sutpen, however, still does not volunteer the information as to what that impediment was, nor does General Compson require an explanation. Instead, he gags on that word *conscience*. Sutpen uses it once more in saying "after my conscience had finally assured me that if I had done an injustice, I had done what I could to rectify it." At this point, General Compson interrupts him by exclaiming: "Conscience? Conscience? Good God, man, what else did you expect? Didn't the very affinity and instinct for misfortune of a man who had spent [thirty years] in a monastery even, let alone as many years as you lived them . . . teach you better? What kind of abysmal and purblind innocence could that have been which someone told you to call virginity? what conscience to trade with would have warranted you in the belief that you could have bought immunity from her for no other coin but justice?"

Human beings cannot be dealt with in terms of mere justice—certainly one cannot deal with one's wife in such terms. General Compson is genuinely shocked, and not merely by Sutpen's cold-blooded putting away of his wife and child. He is at least equally shocked that Sutpen could have been so innocent as to believe that his wife would have agreed to be bought off in this fashion.

For Sutpen, love and compassion are evidently nothing. His precious design is everything. General Compson sums up Sutpen's character in a homely but telling simile. Sutpen's innocence was such that he really believed "that the ingredients of morality were like the ingredients of pie or cake and once you had measured them . . . and mixed them and put them into the oven it was all finished and nothing but pie or cake could come out." General Compson himself is presumably no saint, nor does he set himself up as a moralist, but he is appalled to be confronted with the workings of Sutpen's mind. Note that the issue thus far is not why Sutpen repudiated his wife—that is to say, what fault he found—but with his inhumanly innocent mentality.

Then Shreve says something very interesting. He tells Quentin: "All right. So that Christmas Henry brought [Charles Bon] home, into the house, and the demon looked up and saw the face he believed he had paid off and discharged twenty-eight years ago." That is, Shreve is saying that Charles Bon was the son that Sutpen had repudiated. Quentin answers yes and adds that, according to Mr. Compson, Sutpen had probably named Bon himself. Sutpen had not actually told this to General Compson, but General Compson believed that Sutpen would have done so.

This sudden turn of events in the novel calls for comment. Did Shreve suddenly intuit that Charles Bon, the handsome young man from New Orleans, was really the long repudiated son of Thomas Sutpen? Or had Quentin at some earlier point told Shreve that this was so? Quentin had certainly had the opportunity to tell him. There is abundant evidence throughout the novel that since his arrival at Harvard in September, Quentin had told Shreve a good deal about the South and specifically about Sutpen. But what Shreve says at this point indicates that Quentin had not told him earlier that Charles Bon was Sutpen's son. Note, for example, Shreve's reaction to Quentin's rattling on about the likelihood that Sutpen had chosen the names for all his children, not just for Henry and Judith, but for Clytemnestra, whose mother was one of Sutpen's slaves, and for Charles Bon too. Shreve interrupts this account by observing that "Your father . . . seems to have got an awful lot of delayed information awful quick, after having waited forty-five years." For what Quentin had just said makes plain that Charles Bon, Judith's fiancé, is Thomas Sutpen's son. And Shreve goes on to ask: "If he knew all this, what was his reason for telling you that the trouble between Henry and Bon was the octoroon woman?" Why indeed? If Mr. Compson had known all along that Henry and Charles were half brothers, he would have known why Thomas Sutpen forbade the marriage of Judith and Charles, and why Henry too felt that the marriage was intolerable—and if all else failed, would shoot Charles Bon to prevent it.

Quentin's answer to Shreve's question is equally interesting. Quentin declares that his father had not known for the good reason that Sutpen had not divulged this circumstance to General Compson, which was passed on in due course to Mr. Compson. Apparently, in putting his problem to General Compson, Sutpen had spoken so much in circumlocutions and evasive generalities that General Compson never learned that Sutpen's repudiated child was named Charles Bon. Had this information been told to General Compson and then passed down to his son, there would have been no mystery about Sutpen's violent reaction when Henry brought home Charles Bon of New Orleans. New Orleans is not Haiti, but a name so uncommon as Charles Bon would have put Mr. Compson on the alert.

What Quentin goes on to say must have been even more surprising to his roommate. To Shreve's query as to who gave his father this new information, Quentin replies, "I did. The day after we [that is, Miss Rosa and I]—after that night when we—" To which Shreve replies: "After you and the old Aunt. I see, Go on." (Shreve persists in referring to Miss Rosa as Aunt Rosa.)

The attentive reader will find that in the last half of *Absalom, Absalom!* it is Shreve who puts the questions, sets forth the hypotheses, demands that Quentin agree with this or that theory as to what must have happened. Yet Quentin, who after all is the pipeline through which all the information about Sutpen has to be funneled, remains strangely reticent, even sullen and withdrawn. Evidently much of the Sutpen story is very painful for him to recall. Why?

I believe that *The Sound and the Fury* furnishes the answer. The Quentin presented in that novel is guiltily aware of the fact that he proved unable to protect his sister from the man who got her with child, or from her other casual lovers. Quentin took it hard that he could not, and felt that his own honor—even his own masculinity—had been called in question whereas Henry Sutpen had risen to the occasion, had dared all, had killed his best friend, and abandoned his home and his patrimony in order to defend what he felt to be his sister's honor and his own.

To say this is not to say that Quentin condoned Henry's desperate act, but he did sympathize deeply with Henry as he confronted the agonizing choice set before him. Moreover, his own conduct must, in the light of Henry's horrifyingly heroic action, have seemed all the more weak and pusillanimous.

In *Absalom, Absalom!*, to be sure, Quentin never states matters in this fashion. But he is disturbed to have to recall certain aspects of the Sutpen story. In this connection, note that he is not unwilling to talk about *Thomas* Sutpen. It is with reference to retelling Henry's story that he tends to freeze up, and with reference to one scene in particular, that in which, having just shot Charles, Henry bursts in upon Judith and almost screams: *"Now you cant marry him."* And when Judith asks why not, shouts *"Because he's dead."* As Quentin imagines the scene, the young man and the young woman possess a terrific, an almost unbearable, similarity, as they speak "to one another in short brief staccato sentences like slaps, as if they stood breast to breast, striking one another in turn."

One notices too that though Quentin had been Shreve's roommate for four months and had recounted to Shreve much of the Sutpen story, he had never told him what he and Miss Rosa found when they rode out to Sutpen's Hundred, or whom they saw there, or what Quentin discovered that enabled him next morning to set his father straight about the real reason for Thomas Sutpen's forbidding Judith's marriage to Bon. Quentin's reluctance to bring back to mind a painful scene is later ironically reinforced by Shreve's own reluctance to terminate a story which he is thoroughly enjoying.

Shreve's motive is clearly that of a reader completely engrossed in a highly interesting mystery story who hushes the person who wants to tell him prematurely how it all came out. Shreve wants to try to solve it himself, or at least to savor it to the full before getting to the resolution.

For example, at the end of chapter 6, Shreve gives the following recapitulation of the story as it has thus far been unfolded:

> . . . and so you went out there, drove the twelve miles at night in a buggy and you found Clytie and Jim Bond both in [the house] and you said "You see? and she (the Aunt Rosa) still said No and so you went on: and there was?"
>
> "Yes," [Quentin replies and obviously is about to tell what else he found there when Shreve exclaims]
>
> "Wait then. For God's sake wait." (P. 216)

The reader will have to wait even longer than Shreve waited to find out who it was that Quentin found in the ruinous house and what passed between this person and Quentin. Faulkner, in short, has found a means for holding back the climactic scene until almost the last page of the novel. Before we enter that house with Quentin and Miss Rosa, we as readers must be properly prepared with further information and further conjecture if we are to receive the closing scenes in their maximum impact.

Since Shreve was full of theories and hypotheses, ways of accounting for the motivation of Thomas Sutpen and his two sons, Faulkner has found a plausible way of orchestrating them for the reader. Recall that earlier that evening Shreve had brought in a letter to Quentin from his father, a letter reporting the death and burial of Miss Rosa Coldfield. The letter had revived Shreve's interest in the Sutpen story, and so the two roommates rehearse until past midnight what happened and why it had to happen just as it did.

There are a whole series of questions that they find need to be answered. What was the reason that Thomas Sutpen repudiated his first wife and their child? Quentin's grandfather did not know and never guessed what it was. Quentin's father did not know until Quentin, after his night visit to Sutpen's Hundred, told him: namely, that Henry and Bon were half brothers. That point is made absolutely clear by what Quentin tells Shreve in chapter 7. But I think it very unlikely that Mr. Compson and Quentin in their subsequent discussion of the Sutpen story inferred that the reason why Sutpen repudiated his first wife and his infant son was the fact that she had mixed blood. Because throughout their interminable attempts to reconstruct the Sutpen story, Quentin and Shreve never hint that Bon has a trace of Negro blood until almost the end of chapter 8. More than once in the previous pages, the Bon of their speculations is obviously unaware of any such admixture nor do they attribute any such admixture to him.

Assuming that Quentin's and Shreve's guess as to the real nature of the impediment was correct—and I believe that Faulkner means for us to regard their guess as correct—the infusion of Negro blood must have been minute. Charles was regarded as a white man by all and sundry. But even the most minute quantity was enough to settle matters in Thomas Sutpen's mind, though not because he had more racial prejudice than his neighbors did; he seems in fact to have had less. For example, he brought up his mulatto daughter, Clytie, in his own household, and Henry and Judith were quite aware that she was their half sister. After the War, when the Ku Klux Klan was organized, Sutpen refused to join.

Why, then, did he repudiate his son? Because he was rigidly fixated upon his design, and though he had been brought up in the mountains where there were no black people and had been bred to a different way of life, the design that had come to possess his imagination demanded that he ape the Virginia Tidewater planter in every particular. Heirs of mixed blood, however slight the admixture, simply would not do. Here the rigidity that characterized the whole pattern of Sutpen's life exercised its full force.

Sutpen need not have feared what people might have said,

for other people would not have known or even suspected. As Sutpen had told General Compson when he came to him with his problem: "[I can] let matters take the course which I know they will take and see my design complete itself quite normally and successfully to the public eye, yet to my own in such fashion as to be a mockery and betrayal of that little boy who approached that door fifty years ago and was turned away." The General did not know what Sutpen was talking about, but if he is here remembering at all correctly what Sutpen said in this instance, then the tragedy was brought on not merely by the Southern racial code, but by an intense egomania.

General Compson, we have said, was unaware that Charles Bon possessed any Negro blood. Was Charles Bon himself aware that he did? As we have seen, Shreve's earlier conjectures imply that Bon was utterly unaware that he was of mixed blood. But Shreve evidently came to believe at the end that Bon learned that he was part Negro from Henry himself, who had just been told it by his father. Maybe so. But this, too, is a guess, and though plausible, not necessarily true. Quentin at one point declares that "nobody ever did know if Bon ever knew Sutpen was his father or not." If it is uncertain whether Bon ever knew that he was Thomas Sutpen's son, then it follows that nobody could have known whether Bon ever knew that Sutpen had repudiated him and his mother, let alone knew that the reason for the repudiation was that his mother was of mixed blood.

We need, then, to remind ourselves all through the last third of *Absalom, Absalom!* that we are dealing with conjectures, not facts, or rather, what are not necessarily facts. Some of the conjectures may, of course, accurately describe what actually occurred. The point is that we do not *know*. A powerful secondary theme in this novel is the extreme difficulty—if not impossibility—of understanding the past.

There are other matters in the Sutpen story that cry out for explanation. What was the first Mrs. Sutpen doing in New Orleans? Why was it that Charles Bon decided to attend the newly founded University of Mississippi? How was it that he so patly and promptly met his half brother Henry Sutpen in Oxford? Was Mrs. Sutpen intent on revenge? Did she tell Charles why his father had repudiated them? Did she choose the University of Mississippi for her son because she had word that her husband's second son was to enroll there? Or did someone else influence the choice? And if so, why? The odds are too great to believe that the meeting of these half brothers in a little north Mississippi town was a complete accident.

These are only a few of the problems with which Shreve and Quentin concern themselves. There are others, more interesting and even more difficult. Was Bon really in love with Judith? What was Bon's attitude toward his father, assuming that he knew that Sutpen was his father? What went on in Henry's mind when he found that Bon would not be dissuaded from marrying Judith?

We are not to conclude that Quentin's and Shreve's final account of the story is a fiction merely. Some readers may feel that it describes what very probably did happen.

Faulkner, as author, broadly hints that the imaginings of these two young men may have hit upon the truth. Thus, he refers to a New Orleans "drawing room of baroque and fusty magnificence which Shreve had invented," but goes on to add that it "was probably true enough." He refers to Bon's mother as "this slightly dowdy woman . . . whom Shreve and Quentin had likewise invented and [who] was likewise probably true enough." This is a way of saying that the imagination may on occasion deliver itself of truth. The narrative that Quentin and Shreve between them invent is a plausible story, and it is certainly moving, poignant, and tragic. Some of the scenes are gripping. For example, there is the one in which Bon declares his resolution to marry Judith after all. Henry and Bon are serving in General Joseph E. Johnson's army. Johnson, hotly pursued by Sherman, is trying desperately to link up with Lee's army, and so is steadily retreating north to Virginia. Sutpen has paid a visit to

Henry and, as Quentin and Shreve believe, divulges to him for the first time that Bon's mother was of mixed blood. Shreve, and perhaps Quentin too, think that this bit of information would have proved the last straw to a young man who was already tortured by the thought of his sister's being involved in an incestuous marriage. They imagine Henry's returning to Bon, and Bon, having perhaps guessed what Sutpen must have told him, saying to Henry that he would have abandoned the idea of marrying Judith if Sutpen had requested it. For he "didn't need to tell you I am a nigger to stop me. He could have stopped me without that, Henry."

Whether or not this conversation ever took place, it does constitute powerful drama. One has at the least to give Quentin and Shreve high marks as writers of fiction. (They are excellent writers of fiction, for they are, of course, mouthpieces for Faulkner himself.) Shreve and Quentin go on to imagine the next episode in the drama. Bon hands Henry his pistol and says ". . . do it now." But Henry cannot. He pleads: "You are my brother." But Bon replies: "No I'm not. I'm the nigger that's going to sleep with your sister. Unless you stop me, Henry." But Henry cannot fire the pistol. They travel together all the way from North Carolina to Mississippi. At last the pair have reached the gates of Sutpen's Hundred, and Henry can postpone his decision no longer. He pulls the trigger.

So Quentin and Shreve, in their chilly Harvard dormitory room, have, to their own satisfaction, solved the puzzle and so put out the light and prepare for sleep. But in a moment Shreve is calling out from his bed: "Listen. I'm not trying to be funny, smart. I just want to understand [the South] if I can. . . . Because [what it has is] something my people haven't got. Or if we have got it, it all happened long ago across the water." That something is a sense of history, and with it, a sense of the tragic, the experience of human defeat. But Quentin cannot help Shreve here. He simply tells him: "You can't understand it. You would have to be born there."

Quentin shakes in his bed, not with cold, but with a

convulsive trembling. The attempt to reconstruct the story of Henry and Bon has been almost too much for him. He cannot subside into sleep. Instead, he begins to relive the ride out to Sutpen's Hundred with Miss Rosa. In spite of the "snow-breathed New England air on his face," he can again "taste and feel the dust of that breathless . . . Mississippi September night."

So we are back again to the matter of the visit to Sutpen's Hundred, where Quentin has told us he found out the secret concerning Charles Bon's life and death. Before the room-mates put out the light and prepare themselves for sleep, Quentin must, at some time in the evening, have told Shreve what he found out and how he came by the secret. One cannot imagine Shreve's having let Quentin ready himself for sleep without first divulging the key to the mystery. But the reader of *Absalom, Absalom!* has not yet had the secret revealed to *him*. So Faulkner now, after so many postponements, is ready to provide the account. The postponements have made the reader more eager to know just what happened. Moreover, the reader now senses how devastating to Quentin the experience must have been, and how painfully it has affected him.

The night visit is now narrated for the reader's benefit as Quentin relives it in his memory: the arrival at the great ruined house, Quentin's having to force an entrance, Clytie's attempt to prevent Rosa from going up the stairs, Rosa's brushing her aside, and a little later, Rosa's descent of the stairs, "her eyes wide and unseeing like a sleepwalker's."

Quentin had then told himself: "I must see too now. I will have to. Maybe I shall be sorry tomorrow, but I must see." But at this point we are not told what he saw. There ensues yet another postponement of the climactic scene. We are told of Quentin's coming down the stairs and hurrying out of the house after Miss Rosa who, once she had come downstairs, had walked on out into the darkness.

Evidently the memory of the culminating scene is so painful that Quentin's mind once more rejects it, four months later, in New England. Instead, his memory takes him forward to his coming up beside Miss Rosa, his climbing back into the buggy, and their silent ride home. Having deposited Miss Rosa at her own cottage and having quickly stripped the harness from the mare and put her into the stable, Quentin hurries to his room. He remembers that he was wet with perspiration and that he realized that he ought to bathe, but instead tumbled into his bed. But the horrifying scene will no longer be repressed.

What he had seen in the upstairs room could not be blotted out—could not then, on that hot September night in Mississippi and cannot now as he lies in the wintry New England darkness. He sees again "the yellowed sheets and pillow, the wasted yellow face [of Henry Sutpen lying] with closed, almost transparent eyelids on the pillow, the wasted hands crossed on the breast as if he were already a corpse."

The past is not dead. Quentin confronts what is actually a flesh-and-blood ghost. Only a few questions and answers between himself and the figure on the bed repeat themselves in his mind as the terrible vision grips him. Yet the conversation between Quentin and Henry must have told Quentin what the secret was. It need have consisted of no more than, "Yes. Charles was my brother." But Faulkner leaves the precise words to his reader's imagination.

Shreve has spoken again from his bed because he is still mulling over the letter that Quentin had received from his father announcing Miss Rosa's death. Shreve wants to rehash all the circumstances. Some three months or so after Quentin and Miss Rosa had discovered that Henry was indeed hidden in the old Sutpen mansion, she had gone out to Sutpen's Hundred in an ambulance to bring Henry to town. But Clytie, fearful that Rosa meant to have Henry jailed for murder, set fire to the house, and she and Henry perished together as the tinder-dry wooden structure went up in smoke and flame. Such was the end of Sutpen's great design. Quentin had not seen the burning, but he imagines now in vivid detail what it must have been like. This too constitutes one of the great scenes of the novel.

Shreve has been deeply moved by this terrible story of human courage, agony, self-sacrifice, and tragic waste. But for him it is finally just an interesting melodrama, and, at the end of the novel, he is rapidly detaching himself from any emotional involvement. In another moment he is again up to his accustomed banter, teasing Quentin about the strange part of the world from which he comes. Shreve is not, I think, deliberately trying to be cruel, but he cuts deeper than he had intended when he says to Quentin: "Now I want you to tell me just one thing more. Why do you hate the South?" To which Quentin replies "quickly, at once, immediately; *'I dont hate it'* he said, *'I dont hate it'* he thought, panting in the cold air, the iron New England dark; *I dont, I dont! I dont hate it! I dont hate it.*"

What in fact is Quentin's attitude toward the South? If hatred is too simple a term, what is the right term? Faulkner does not try to supply it. With Quentin's *"I dont hate it,"* the novel comes to an end. But if we have read the novel with sufficient care, we know that no single adjective can serve to describe Quentin's attitude toward his native land. It is a complex of emotions, many of them contradictory. If there are features of Southern culture that terrify Quentin and fill him with grief, there are others that he admires and even loves. If what happened to Bon and Henry and Judith is a fearful and tragic waste, their story also has its elements of heroic endurance and austere dignity. Some good has come out of evil; in Judith, at least, virtue has striven with evil and in some sense redeemed it.

The Sutpen children have suffered under the heavy burden of history. Quentin has felt that burden too. Shreve feels no such burden, as we have said, but once at least seems a little envious of what Quentin has that he says he and his people do not have. If Quentin staggers under the burden of history and is almost crushed by his past, Shreve is inclined to dismiss the past too glibly, too easily.

In any case, Faulkner has not stacked his deck in favor of the past. Shreve finds the Southern past fascinating as a melodrama may be fascinating, but finally absurd, and even

Quentin is scarcely a champion of the Southern past: he holds it in awe, but is also more than a little frightened by it. The Old South with its elaborate codes of honor, not to mention its caste system, was difficult to live with or live up to.

Quentin and Shreve are cast as observers and commentators on the Sutpen story. Of the characters active in the novel itself, who is the man who most scorns the past? It is Thomas Sutpen himself. He has no pride in ancestry and no concern for his place of origin. He glories—and with just reason—in the fact that he is truly a self-made man. He is completely oriented toward the future. He lives for the great design he has devised. He is a man of blueprints and schedules. Nothing must be allowed to get in the way of the completion of his plans, not even his children, whom finally he regards principally as instruments for fulfilling the design. Love, compassion, human sympathy, do not concern him. His virtues are courage and justice, at least as he defines justice. But salient above all in his mentality is a terrible rigidity. The design must be completed precisely as planned; no exceptions, no modifications, no alterations are to be allowed. His downfall occurs because of his rigidity. I think Shreve and Quentin are right in supposing that had he accepted Charles Bon as his son—not necessarily as his heir—or if he had just asked him to act as a brother in protecting his sister Judith, the tragedy could have been averted. But his pride in his design, and his overweening confidence in himself precluded a more human, less monstrously mechanical, behavior. Thomas Sutpen was an awesome figure and he had his virtues, but his very virtues were dangerous.

Faulkner said that the great theme was the human heart in conflict with itself. One can find the theme illustrated in Henry's killing the brother he loved in order to save the sister he loved. One might find it in the conduct of Sutpen's other children, and especially, in the conduct of Judith and Clytie. But one cannot illustrate this theme from the conduct of Thomas Sutpen. Brave he is, and steadfast, but there is no conflict in his heart, for his heart is undividedly set upon one object.

The point is worth insisting upon, for to grasp it is to see that *Absalom, Absalom!* is no Southern costume drama about bygone times. It has an all-American theme and a present-day relevance. Sutpen's virtues are those of a typical twentieth-century man. So are his vices—his dismissal of the past, his commitment to the future, and his confidence that, with courage and know-how, he can accomplish literally anything.

BIBLIOGRAPHY

Blotner, Joseph. *William Faulkner: A Biography*. 2 vols. New York: Random House, 1976. A shorter version is in preparation.

————. *Selected Letters of William Faulkner*. New York: Random House, 1977.

Brown, Calvin S. *A Glossary of Faulkner's South*. New Haven: Yale University Press, 1976. Special terms, idioms, flora, fauna, and so forth.

Brooks, Cleanth. *William Faulkner: The Yoknapatawpha Country*. New Haven: Yale University Press, 1963. Much of the material of the present book is drawn from here.

————. *William Faulkner: Toward Yoknapatawpha and Beyond*. New Haven: Yale University Press, 1978. Faulkner's development, his earlier career, and his later career.

Cowley, Malcolm. *The Faulkner-Cowley File*. New York: Viking Press, 1966. Important letters.

Gwynn, F. L., and Joseph Blotner. *Faulkner in the University*. Charlottesville: University of Virginia Press, 1959. Interviews.

Kirk, R. W., and Marvin Klotz. *Faulkner's People: A Complete Guide to Characters in the Fiction of William Faulkner*. Berkeley and Los Angeles: University of California Press, 1963.

Meriwether, James B. *The Literary Career of William Faulkner: A Bibliographical Study*. Columbia: University of South Carolina Press, 1971.

Meriwether, James B., and Michael Millgate, eds. *Lion in the Garden: Interviews with William Faulkner, 1926–1962*. New York: Random House, 1968.

Millgate, Michael. *The Achievement of William Faulkner*. New York: Random House, 1966. A general study containing an excellent short biography.

Volpe, E. L. *A Reader's Guide to William Faulkner*. New York: Farrar, Strauss, and Giroux, 1964.

Warren, R. P. *William Faulkner: A Collection of Critical Essays*. Englewood Cliffs, New Jersey: Prentice-Hall, 1966.

INDEX

Allen, Bobbie, 171–72, 175
American Literature, 47
Ames, Dalton, 53, 55–57
Antigone, 94
Aphrodite, 98
Arcadia: the countryside in *The Hamlet* compared to, 100
Armstid, Henry, 123–24, 126–27, 160
Armstid, Martha, 123–24, 126, 160
Arnold, Matthew, 92
As I Lay Dying: references to, 4, 78–79, 88, 91, 93, 94–95
As You Like It, 90
Aunt Rachel, 31–32

Backus, Joseph M., 47
"Barn Burning," 16, 18–19, 96, 101
Barron, Homer, 10–13
Bascomb, Maury ("Uncle Maury"), 46, 49, 57, 68
Basket, Herman, 25, 27, 29
Beauchamp, Hubert, 131–32
Beauchamp, Molly, 129, 135, 136, 156, 158
Beauchamp, Nat, 133–34
Beauchamp, Samuel Worsham, 158–59
Beauchamp, Sophonsiba, 131–33
Beauchamp, Tennie, 133
Benbow, Judge ———, 198
Benbow, Narcissa, 14–15
Bland, Gerald, 52–53
Bland, Mrs., 52
Bon, Charles, 193–95, 200–03, 206, 212–14, 216–23
Bon, Charles Etienne Saint-Velery, 206–07
Bond, Jim, 207, 215
Bookwright, Odum, 126–27
Brown, Joe, 160–61, 163, 165–66, 171, 182–83, 186, 190
Bunch, Byron, 160–61, 163–65, 168, 181–83, 186–87, 190–91
Bundren, Addie, 78, 80–84, 86, 88–91, 94

Bundren, Anse, 79–85, 89, 92–94
Bundren, Cash, 80, 84–85, 88–89, 92, 94
Bundren, Darl, 80, 85–91, 93–94
Bundren, Dewey Dell, 79–81, 84, 86, 88, 91–92
Bundren, Jewel, 80–90, 94
Bundren, Vardaman, 81, 84, 86, 88, 91
Bundren family, 78–80, 89–90, 93–94, 96
Burden, Joanna, 164–66, 168, 171, 175–80, 181–82, 186, 189, 191

Cable, George Washington, 1–2
Camus, Albert, 175
Christianity, 44, 74, 185; of the Compsons, 69–70; of Addie Bundren, 83; of Isaac McCaslin, 153–54; of the McEacherns, 170
Christmas, Joe, 161, 163, 165–86, 188–91, 194, 206
Clytie. *See* Sutpen, Clytemnestra
Coldfield, Goodhue, 193–94, 198–99
Coldfield, Rosa, 194–99, 202–07, 213–15, 220–21
Community, 3, 36–37, 41; as represented in "A Rose for Emily," 8, 14, 42; as represented in *Light in August*, 161–64, 183–84
Compson, Benjy, 43–50, 57, 60–62, 68–71, 73–77, 81, 98–99
Compson, Candace ("Caddy"), 5, 30, 43–44, 46–59, 61–62, 66–67, 69, 72, 74, 81
Compson, Caroline Bascomb (wife of Jason III), 30–31, 43, 49–53, 62–63, 70–71, 74, 76, 80
Compson, Gen. Jason Lycurgus II, 142, 193, 197, 206–13, 217
Compson, Jason III (father of Quentin, Caddy, and Jason), 30–32, 47, 49–50, 57–58, 66, 68, 70, 76, 80, 196–202, 205–06, 212–13, 216

Compson, Jason IV (son of Jason III), 30–31, 43, 49, 53, 60–76, 80

Compson, Quentin (son of Jason III), 30, 32, 43–44, 49–62, 68–69, 71, 76, 80, 89, 192, 194–99, 201–08, 212–23

Compson, Quentin (daughter of Caddy), 61–63, 66, 69–75

Compson family, 43, 45, 52, 69, 96

Craw-ford, 25–27

"Deacon," 55

Dedalus, Stephen, 91

"Delta Autumn," 137, 151, 154, 157

De Quincey, Thomas, 181

De Spain, Major ———, 17–18, 139, 142, 150, 152–53

Detective Gazette, 20, 22

Devil, the, 110–11

Dilsey ———, 4, 22, 30, 32, 62–63, 66–71, 73–77

Don Quixote, 54

"Doom," 25–27

Du Pre, Virginia Sartoris ("Aunt Jenny"), 14–16, 36, 39, 41

Earl ——— (Jason Compson's employer), 64–65

Edmonds, McCaslin ("Cass"), 130–32, 138, 142–47, 149, 153, 155

Edmonds, Roth, 133–36, 155–59

Eliot, T. S., 92

Empson, William, 88

Eunice (slave, mother of Thomasina), 146, 155

Eurydice, 34

Falstaff, 19, 90

Fathers, Sam, 25, 27, 137–44, 146, 149–50, 153–54

Faulkner, William, 7–8, 16–17, 19, 22–23, 25, 29–32, 35, 44, 48, 51, 58–59, 62, 67–68, 70, 78, 83, 88, 91–94, 103–08, 112, 117–18, 120, 128–30, 133, 137–39, 141–44, 150, 158, 160, 166, 219, 221–22; his differences from the local colorists, 1–2; his concern with universal issues, 2–3; his relation to a community in being, 3; his relation to the South, 4; his character types,

4; his early romanticism and his later development, 5; his women characters and the masculine code of honor, 39; his attitude toward the past, 41–42; his fondness for Housman's poetry, 57; his concern for the crisis in culture, 77; and the detachment of the artist, 87; his ability to develop mythical characters and landscapes, 97–98; as a nature poet, 99–100, 121, 151–52; on the concept of honor, 105, 119; his use of the flashback, 113, 135, 168, 202–03; on the humanity of his famous idiots, 115–16; his use of the tall tales of the Old Southwest, 122; on the community, 162–64; his techniques for building to a climax, 215–16; on the relation of fiction to historic truth, 218; on the great theme of all literary art, 223

Faulkner in the University, 32

Faustus (Marlowe), 109

"The Fire and the Hearth," 129, 133, 137, 155

The Forum, 7

Frenchman's Bend, 96, 99, 101, 104–05, 112, 118–20, 124

Frony ——— (daughter of Dilsey), 73, 75

Go Down, Moses: references to, 4, 6, 32, 128–29, 133, 148, 153–54, 157

Greek influences, and *The Hamlet*, 99–100, 114

Grierson, Emily, 7–14, 16, 41–42

Grimm, Percy, 188–89

Grove, Lena, 5, 160–63, 168, 182–84, 187, 190–91

Grumby, "Major," 37, 41

The Hamlet: references to, 4–5, 18, 96–97, 99–103, 108, 111–12, 118, 121–22, 127–28

Hardy, Thomas, 4

Hathor, 114

Hawk, Drusilla, 37–40

Hawthorne, Nathaniel, 3

Hera (Juno), 114

Hightower, Mrs. Gail, 162, 187
Hightower, Rev. Gail, 161–65, 168, 182–83, 186–91
Hines, Eupheus ("Doc"), 173, 186
Hines, Milly, 186
Hines, Mrs. Eupheus, 186–87
Hipps, Buck, 120, 122–24
Hogganbeck, Boon, 141–43, 150–53
Honor, 19, 22, 41, 56, 89, 90, 157
Housman, A. E., 57
Houston, Jack, 115–19, 128

Indians, 25–30, 36, 145
Intruder in the Dust, 137
Issetibbeha, 27

Jesus (Nancy's husband), 30–32
Job (co-worker of Jason Compson's), 63–65, 72
Jones, Wash, 202–03, 206
Joyce, James, 68, 91, 175
"A Justice," 25

Kafka, Franz, 175

Labove ———, 99, 103–05, 108, 112, 117, 128
"The Legend of Sleepy Hollow," 105
Light in August: references to, 5, 160, 164, 168, 174–75, 182, 186, 189, 194
"Lion," 139, 141–42, 150
Littlejohn, Mrs. ———, 103, 112
Luster (son of Dilsey), 46, 66, 73, 75–76

Macbeth (Shakespeare), 44, 181
McCallum, Lafe, 85
McCannon, Shrevlin, 196, 204–05, 207–08, 212–13. *See also* MacKenzie, Shreve
McCarron, Hoake, 105–07
McCaslin, Amodeus ("Uncle Buddy"), 130–33, 144, 146–47
McCaslin, Isaac ("Ike"), 129–30, 133, 137–57, 159
McCaslin, Old Carothers, 144, 146–47, 155, 159
McCaslin, Theophilus ("Uncle Buck"), 130–33, 144, 146–47
McCaslin family, 96, 129, 133

McEachern, Simon, 169–71, 186
McEachern, Mrs. Simon, 170
McGowan, Skeet, 92
McHaney, Thomas, 20
MacKenzie, Shreve, 58. *See also* McCannon, Shrevlin
Mannie (wife of Rider), 32–34, 129
Mannigoe, Nancy, 32
The Mansion, 6
Marlowe, Christopher, 109
Medea, 84
Moby-Dick, or the Whale (Melville), 3
Moketubbe, 27

Nancy, 30–32

"Ode on a Grecian Urn," 87
"An Odor of Verbena," 4, 14, 16, 36, 42
"Old Ben," 138–41, 143, 150–53, 155
Old Creole Days (Cable), 1
"Old Man," 19, 22–23
"The Old People," 137
Orpheus, 34

"Pantaloon in Black," 32, 129, 137
Parchman (Mississippi Penal Farm), 20
Pastoral, 88
Peabody, Dr. Lucius Quintus, 92
Poe, Edgar Allan, 7
Pound, Ezra, 61
Prince of Hell, 109–11

Ratliff, V. K., 4, 101–03, 108–13, 115, 118, 120–22, 126–28
A Reader's Guide to William Faulkner, 47
"Red Leaves," 25, 27, 32
Redmond, Ben, 37–41
Requiem for a Nun, 32
"Rider" (hero of "Pantaloon in Black"), 32–35, 129
"Ringo" (boyhood companion of Bayard Sartoris), 37, 41
"A Rose for Emily," 5, 7

Sartoris, Bayard ("Old Bayard"), 14–15, 36–42
Sartoris, Col. John, 9, 11, 36–38, 177–78

ALBERTSON COLLEGE OF IDAHO

3 5556 0019 5741 4